Reducing Your Taxes

by Eric Tyson

A Wiley Brand

Reducing Your Taxes For Dummies®

Published by: **John Wiley & Sons, Inc.**, 111 River Street, Hoboken, NJ 07030-5774, www.wiley.com

Copyright © 2024 by Eric Tyson and John Wiley & Sons, Inc., Hoboken, New Jersey

Media and software compilation copyright © 2024 by Eric Tyson and John Wiley & Sons, Inc. All rights reserved.

Published simultaneously in Canada

For general information on our other products and services, please contact our Customer Care Department within the U.S. at 877-762-2974, outside the U.S. at 317-572-3993, or fax 317-572-4002. For technical support, please visit https://hub.wiley.com/community/support/dummies.

Wiley publishes in a variety of print and electronic formats and by print-on-demand. Some material included with standard print versions of this book may not be included in e-books or in print-on-demand. If this book refers to media such as a CD or DVD that is not included in the version you purchased, you may download this material at http://booksupport.wiley.com. For more information about Wiley products, visit www.wiley.com.

Library of Congress Control Number is available from the publisher.

ISBN 978-1-394-24572-7 (pbk); ISBN 978-1-394-24574-1 (ePDF); ISBN 978-1-394-24573-4 (epub)

SKY10070174_032124

Contents at a Glance

Table of Contents

Introduction

Welcome to *Reducing Your Taxes For Dummies*. These pages answer both your tax-planning questions in plain English and with a touch of humor.

About This Book

In this book, I introduce the tax planning essentials that can help you legally reduce your income tax bill. I also help you keep your mind on your taxes — and strategies to reduce what you owe — while you plan your finances for the upcoming year and the years ahead.

As you probably know, Congress and political candidates engage in never-ending discussions about ways to tinker with the nation's tax laws. Where appropriate throughout the book, I highlight how any resulting changes may affect important decisions you'll need to make in the years ahead.

In some chapters of this book, I mention particular tax forms. If you need to look up a tax form or print one out, simply go to www.irs.gov and type the form name in the Search box.

For instructions on filling out tax forms, please see the most recent edition of my co-authored book *Taxes For Dummies* (Wiley). Depending on your situation, you may choose to hire a tax professional.

Foolish Assumptions

I've made some assumptions on how you may want to use this book. Here are the various practical ways that I figure you will use *Reducing Your Taxes For Dummies* to legally reduce your taxes:

>> **As a reference:** For example, perhaps you're interested in saving in a retirement account or purchasing investment real estate but don't know where to begin or the tax issues to consider. Simply use the table of contents or index to find the right spot in the book with the answers to your questions. On the other hand, if you lack investments — in part because you pay so much in taxes — this book also explains legal strategies for slashing your taxes and boosting your savings. Use this book year-round.

>> **As a trusted advisor:** Maybe you're self-employed and you know that you need to be salting money away so that you can someday cut back on those long workdays. Turn to Chapter 4, and find out about the different types of retirement accounts, which one may be right for you, how it can slash your taxes, and even where to set it up.

>> **As a textbook:** If you have the time, desire, and discipline, by all means go for it and read the whole shebang. And please drop the publisher a note and let me know about your achievement!

Icons Used in This Book

To help you find the information you need to reduce your taxes, I've placed icons throughout the text to highlight important points.

REMEMBER

This icon points out stuff too good (and too important) to forget.

TECHNICAL STUFF

This nerdy guy appears beside discussions that aren't critical if you just want to know the basic concepts and get answers to your tax questions. However, reading these gems can deepen and enhance your tax knowledge. And you never know when you'll be invited to go to a town meeting and talk tax reform with a bunch of politicians!

TIP

This target marks recommendations for making the most of your taxes and money (for example, reduce the income taxes on your investment earnings by spending more on pickleball gear).

WARNING

This alert denotes common, costly mistakes people make with their taxes.

Beyond the Book

To access this book's Cheat Sheet, go to www.dummies.com and enter "Reducing Your Taxes For Dummies Cheat Sheet" in the Search box. There you will find the key themes that I emphasize throughout this book.

Where to Go from Here

Where you go from here is up to you. If you're newly considering your tax planning strategy, I recommend that you read straight through, cover to cover, to maximize your knowledge of "taxable income" and explore the year-round planning that can help you reduce the taxes you owe. But the A-to-Z approach isn't necessary. If you feel confident in your knowledge of certain areas, pick the topics that you're most interested in by skimming the table of contents or by relying on the well-crafted index at the back of the book.

1

Tax Reduction Basics

Make sense of the federal income tax system.

Determine which tax-trimming options apply to your situation.

Chapter **1**

Understanding the Taxes You Pay

Taxes are probably one of your largest — if not *the* largest — expenditures. The goal of this chapter is to help you legally and permanently reduce your total taxes. Understanding the tax system is the key to reducing your tax burden — if you don't, you'll surely pay more taxes than necessary. Your tax ignorance can lead to mistakes, which can be costly if the IRS and state government catch your underpayment errors. With the proliferation of computerized information and data tracking, discovering mistakes has never been easier.

Focusing on Total Taxes

Instead of focusing on whether you're going to get a refund when you complete your annual tax return, concentrate on the *total* taxes you pay.

To find out the *total* income taxes you pay, you need to get out your federal and state income tax returns. On each of those returns is a line that shows the *total tax you owed for the year:* If you add up the totals from your federal and state income tax returns, you'll probably see one of your largest expenses.

Some people feel lucky when they get an income tax refund, but all a refund really indicates is that you overpaid your income taxes during the year. You should have had this money in your own account all along.

If you're consistently getting big income tax refunds, you need to pay less tax throughout the year. Fill out a W-4 to determine how much you should be paying in taxes throughout the year. You can obtain a W-4 through your employer's payroll department or from the IRS.

If you're self-employed, you can obtain Form 1040-ES by calling the IRS at 800-TAX-FORM [800-829-3676] or visiting its website at www.irs.gov. The IRS website also has a helpful withholding calculator at www.irs.gov/individuals/tax-withholding-estimator.

The tax system, like other public policy, is built around incentives to encourage desirable behavior and activity. For example, saving for retirement is considered desirable because it encourages people to prepare for a time in their lives when they may be less able or interested in working so much and when they may have additional healthcare expenses. Therefore, the tax code offers all sorts of tax perks to encourage people to save in retirement accounts.

REMEMBER

It's a free country, and you should make choices that work best for your life and situation. However, keep in mind that the *fewer* desirable activities you engage in, the more you will generally pay in taxes. If you understand the options, you can choose the ones that meet your needs as you approach different stages of your financial life.

Recognizing the Importance of Your Marginal Tax Rate

When it comes to taxes, *not all income is treated equally*. This fact is far from self-evident. If you work for an employer and earn a constant salary during the course of a year, a steady and equal amount of federal and state taxes is deducted from each paycheck. Thus, it appears as though all that earned income is being taxed equally.

In reality, however, you pay less tax on your first dollars of earnings and more tax on your *last* dollars of earnings. For example, if you're single and your taxable income (see the next section) totals $50,000 during 2024, you pay federal tax at the rate of 10 percent on the first $11,600 of taxable income, 12 percent on income between $11,600 and $47,150, and 22 percent on income from $47,150 up to $100,525.

Table 1-1 gives federal tax rates for singles and married households filing jointly.

TABLE 1-1 **2024 Federal Income Tax Brackets and Rates**

Federal Income Tax Rate (bracket)	Individual's Taxable Income	Married Filing Jointly Taxable Income
10%	$0 to $11,600	$0 to $23,200
12%	$11,600 to $47,150	$23,200 to $94,300
22%	$47,150 to $100,525	$94,300 to $201,050
24%	$100,525 to $191,950	$201,050 to $383,900
32%	$191,950 to $243,725	$383,900 to $487,450
35%	$243,725 to $609,350	$487,450 to $731,200
37%	$609,350 or more	$731,200 or more

Your *marginal tax rate* is the rate of tax you pay on your *last*, or so-called *highest*, dollars of income. A single person with taxable income of $50,000 has a federal marginal tax rate of 22 percent. In other words, they effectively pay 22 percent federal tax on their last dollars of income — those dollars in excess of $47,150.

Marginal tax rates are a powerful concept. Your marginal tax rate allows you to quickly calculate the additional taxes you'd have to pay on additional income. Conversely, you can enjoy quantifying the amount of taxes you save by reducing your taxable income, either by decreasing your income or by increasing your deductions.

As you're probably already painfully aware, you pay not only federal income taxes but also state income taxes — that is, unless you live in one of the handful of states (Alaska, Florida, Nevada, South Dakota, Tennessee, Texas, and Wyoming) that have no state income tax. *Note:* Some states don't tax employment income but do tax certain investment income: New Hampshire (dividend and interest income) and Washington (capital gains income).

Your *total marginal rate* includes your federal *and* state income tax rates (not to mention local income tax rates in the municipalities that have them).

You can look up your state income tax rate in your current state income tax preparation booklet or on the website for the state agency that collects income tax for your state.

Defining Taxable Income

This book explains strategies for reducing your taxable income. *Taxable income* is the amount of income on which you actually pay income taxes. The following reasons explain why you don't pay taxes on your total income:

>> **Not all income is taxable.** For example, you pay federal income tax on the interest you earn on a bank savings account but not on the interest you earn from municipal

bonds. Some income, such as from stock dividends and long-term capital gains, is taxed at lower rates.

>> **You get to subtract deductions from your income.** Some deductions are available just for being a living, breathing human being. In 2024, single people get an automatic $14,600 standard deduction, and married couples filing jointly get $29,200. (People over age 65 and those who are blind get a slightly higher deduction.) Other expenses, such as mortgage interest and property taxes, are deductible (subject to limitations) if these so-called itemized deductions exceed the standard deductions. When you contribute to qualified retirement plans, you also effectively get a deduction.

Part 4 discusses ways to reduce small business taxes.

Being Mindful of the Second Tax System: Alternative Minimum Tax

You may find this hard to believe, but a second tax system actually exists (as if the first tax system weren't already complicated enough). This second system may raise your taxes even higher than they would normally be.

Over the years, as the government grew hungry for more revenue, taxpayers who slashed their taxes by claiming lots of deductions or exclusions from taxable income came under greater scrutiny. So the government created a second tax system — the alternative minimum tax (AMT) — to ensure that those with high deductions or exclusions pay at least a certain percentage of taxes on their incomes. In its early years of existence, the AMT affected less than 1 percent of taxpayers, but that number greatly expanded over the decades until it impacted 5 million taxpayers. The Tax Cuts and Jobs Act, which took effect in 2018, reduced the impact back down to its original intent of just a few hundred thousand higher-income taxpayers. However, those newer rules are scheduled to expire after 2025, at which time the AMT could hit upwards of 7 million taxpayers.

If you have a lot of deductions or exclusions from state income taxes, real-estate taxes, certain types of mortgage interest, and passive investments (for example, rental real estate), you may fall prey to AMT. You may also get tripped up by AMT if you exercise certain types of stock options or if you have a high amount of capital gains relative to your other ordinary income.

AMT restricts you from claiming certain deductions and requires you to add back in income that is normally tax-free (like certain municipal-bond interest). So you have to figure your tax under the AMT system and under the other system and then pay whichever amount is higher.

BEYOND APRIL 15: WHAT YOU DON'T KNOW CAN COST YOU

Every spring, more than 100 million tax returns (and several million extension requests) are filed with the IRS. The byproduct of this effort is guaranteed employment for the nation's more than 1 million accountants and auditors and 2 million bookkeeping and accounting clerks (not to mention more than a few tax-book authors and their editors). Accounting firms rake in tens of billions of dollars annually, helping bewildered and desperately confused taxpayers figure out all those tax laws. So that you can feel okay about this situation, keep in mind that at least some of the money you pay in income taxes actually winds up in the government coffers for some useful purposes.

Given all the hours that you work each year just to pay your taxes and the time you spend actually completing the dreaded return, on April 16, you may feel like ignoring the whole tax topic until next year. Such avoidance, however, is a costly mistake. You can end up increasing your tax burden and reducing your ability to trim the taxes you owe, and if you file late, you will be subjected to late filing fees with accruing interest.

During the tax year, you can take steps to ensure not only that you're in compliance with the ever-changing tax laws, but also that you're minimizing your tax burden. If your income — like that of nearly everyone I know — is limited, you need to understand the tax code to make it work for you and help you accomplish your financial goals.

Noting the Forever Changing Tax Laws

Since tax law changes are passed by Congress, they change as the makeup of Congress changes. The most recent major piece of tax legislation was the Tax Cuts and Jobs Act of 2017, which took effect for tax years 2018 and beyond. There have been some smaller pieces of legislation since, addressing retirement accounts and savings and the COVID-19 pandemic. This section provides the highlights for this more recent legislation and associated tax law changes.

The Tax Cuts and Jobs Act of 2017

For most individuals, the biggest change from the Tax Cuts and Jobs Act bill was the lowering of tax rates. The lower tax brackets were lowered by three full percentage points (for example, from 15 percent down to 12 percent, from 25 percent down to 22 percent), and the next income bracket up from that was cut four full percentage points from 28 percent down to 24 percent, which produced substantial tax savings for lower- and moderate-income earners. The highest income earning taxpayers saw smaller reductions in their tax brackets.

According to Brian Riedl, a senior fellow at the Manhattan Institute, a greater share of the individual income tax benefits from this bill went to lower- and moderate-income earners.

Here are some of the other major changes in this tax bill:

>> **Increased standard deduction and eliminated personal exemption:** Proponents of the bill liked to talk about how the standard deduction nearly doubled. This amount is deducted from your income before arriving at your taxable income, so a larger standard deduction reduces your taxable income and tax bill. However, Congress also eliminated personal exemptions, which offset much of this change. Ultimately, though, far more taxpayers can simply claim the standard deduction, which is a time-saver when it comes to completing the annual federal 1040 tax form.

- » **Increased child tax credit:** The child tax credit was doubled by this legislation, and up to 70 percent of that credit was made refundable for taxpayers not otherwise owing federal income tax. Also, the incomes at which this credit starts phasing out was more than tripled for married couples and more than doubled for non-married filers.

- » **State and local taxes deduction capped at $10,000:** This also includes property taxes on your home, and for homeowners in high cost-of-living areas with high state income taxes (for example, metro areas such as San Francisco, Los Angeles, New York, and Washington D.C.), this cap poses a modest or even significant negative change. Because these taxes are itemized deductions, only being able to take up to $10,000 (previously unlimited) caused some taxpayers to no longer be able to itemize. Also, by reducing the tax benefits of home ownership, this change effectively raises the cost of home ownership, especially in high-cost and highly taxed areas.

- » **Mortgage-interest deduction for both primary and second homes capped at $750,000 borrowed:** This represents a modest reduction from the previous $1 million limit on mortgage indebtedness deductibility.

The Tax Cuts and Jobs Act also brought some long overdue corporate tax reform. For too long, the United States had way too high a corporate tax rate, which caused increasing numbers of companies to choose to do less business in the United States.

The SECURE ACTs of 2019 & 2022

Retirement accounts and retirement savings rules were ripe for revisions and improvement. Some of those happened with the SECURE (Setting Every Community Up for Retirement Enhancement) Act of 2019. Of course, Congress couldn't leave well enough alone. So another bill — the SECURE Act 2.0 of 2022 — was passed to make yet more changes to retirement accounts. Here are the highlights of these two bills:

- » **Small-business owners are eligible for up to $5,000 in tax credits when starting a retirement plan.** This credit applies to new 401(k), profit sharing, SEP, and SIMPLE plans for small employers (up to 100 employees).

» **More workers can participate in company 401(k) plans.** Previously, employees had to work at least 1,000 hours per year to take part in a company's 401(k) plan. Now, workers who achieve at least 500 hours over three consecutive years may participate. Effective in 2025, employees must be eligible to participate in their employer's qualified retirement plans after two years of service.

» **You can withdraw up to $5,000 per parent penalty-free from your retirement plan for the birth or adoption of a child.** This new provision waives the normal 10 percent early withdrawal penalty and allows you to repay the withdrawn money as a rollover contribution.

» **529 funds can be used to pay down student loans.** You can pay down up to $10,000 in student loans and pay for qualifying apprenticeship programs.

» **Employer matching of student loan repayments permitted.** Beginning in 2024, employers can elect to match student loan repayments in the form of retirement account contributions.

» **Automatic employee enrollment in company 401(k) and 403(b) plans.** Beginning with new 401(k) and 403(b) plans in 2025, companies must automatically enroll eligible employees.

» **Increase in retirement plan contribution limits for older workers.** As of 2024, workers aged 50 and older are able to contribute $7,500 more per year (increased annually with inflation) than younger workers to most retirement plans. Beginning in 2025, the contribution limits for those aged 60 to 63 increases so that that age group may contribute up to $10,000 more per year (increasing annually with inflation) than younger workers in most retirement plans and $5,000 more annually for SIMPLE plans.

» **Required minimum distributions (RMDs) from retirement accounts begin at age 72, not 70½.** Effective in 2023, the RMD increased to 73, and then goes to age 75 in 2033. This gives you more options and flexibility, but delaying required distributions that are based upon your life expectancy may or may not be in your best long-term interests.

>> **You can make traditional IRA contributions past age 70½ so long as you continue earning employment income.** This brings the contribution rules for these accounts into alignment with those for Roth IRAs and 401(k)s.

>> **Inherited retirement accounts must now be tapped and emptied through distributions generally within a decade.** Before when folks inherited a retirement account, the inheritor could stretch their distributions and associated tax payments out over their life expectancy. For retirement accounts now inherited from original owners who have passed away in 2020 or later years, most beneficiaries must complete withdrawals from the account within ten years of the death of the account holder. There are some exceptions to this ten-year rule for retirement accounts left to a surviving spouse, a minor child, a disabled or chronically ill beneficiary, and beneficiaries who are less than ten years younger than the original retirement account owner.

Possible upcoming changes

Congress continually tinkers with our nation's tax laws. Bigger changes tend to occur when the same party controls both chambers of congress as well as the presidency. As this book goes to press in 2024, Americans have been through a lengthy period where there has been lots of talk of tax increases by the Democrats, the party currently in control of the Senate and the presidency, but that has largely been blocked to date due to their super-slim majority in the Senate and by the Republican controlled House of Representatives.

With the 2024 elections on the horizon, history suggests that the most likely outcome for those elections will be continued divided government, which likely will mean more gridlock and less likelihood for tax increases or tax changes in general.

IN THIS CHAPTER

» Lowering your income taxes

» Claiming deductions

» Reducing taxes on investment income

» Being aware of education tax breaks

» Seeking help from professionals and other tax resources

» Knowing what to do if you receive an audit request letter

Chapter **2**

Trimming Your Taxes

The tax system is built around incentives to encourage desirable behavior and activity. Home ownership, for example, is considered good because it encourages people to take more responsibility for maintaining properties and neighborhoods. Therefore, the government offers numerous tax benefits, referred to as *allowable deductions*, to encourage people to own homes (see Chapter 13). But if you don't understand these tax benefits, you probably don't know how to take full advantage of them, either.

Don't feel dumb when it comes to understanding the tax system. You're not the problem — the complexity of the income tax system is. Making sense of the tax jungle is more daunting than hacking your way out of a triple-canopy rainforest with a dinner knife. That's why, throughout this book, I help you understand the tax system, and I promise not to make you read the actual tax laws.

You should be able to keep much more of your money by applying the tax-reducing strategies I present in this book. This chapter summarizes those strategies, and later parts delve into the nitty-gritty for each.

Reducing Taxes on Work Income

When you earn money from work, you're supposed to pay income tax on that income. Some people avoid taxes by illegal means, such as by not reporting work income (which isn't really possible if you're getting a regular paycheck from an employer), but you can very well end up paying a heap of penalties and extra interest charges on top of the taxes you owe. And you may even get tossed in jail. This section focuses on the legal ways to reduce your income taxes on work-related income.

Self-employed workers and business owners also must pay income tax, but their considerations are subject to some unique rules and can be a bit more complex. Part 4 covers these considerations and more.

Contributing to retirement investment plans

A retirement investment plan is one of the few relatively painless and authorized ways to reduce your taxable employment income. Besides reducing your taxes, retirement plans help you build up a nest egg so you don't have to work for the rest of your life.

You can exclude money from your taxable income by tucking it away in employer-based retirement plans, such as 401(k) or 403(b) accounts, or self-employed retirement plans, such as SEP-IRAs. If your combined federal and state marginal tax rate is, say, 33 percent and you contribute $1,000 to one of these plans, you reduce your federal and state taxes by $330. Do you like the sound of that? How about this: Contribute another

$1,000, and your taxes drop *another* $330 (as long as you're still in the same marginal tax rate). And when your money is inside a retirement account, it can compound and grow without taxation.

WARNING

Many people miss this great opportunity to reduce their taxes because they *spend* all (or too much) of their current employment income and, therefore, have nothing (or little) left to put into a retirement account. If you're in this predicament, you first need to reduce your spending before you can contribute money to a retirement plan.

If your employer doesn't offer the option of saving money through a retirement plan, lobby the benefits and human resources departments. If they resist, you may want to add this to your list of reasons for considering another employer. Many employers offer this valuable benefit, but some don't. Some company decision-makers either don't understand the value of these accounts or feel that they're too costly to set up and administer.

If your employer doesn't offer a retirement savings plan, individual retirement account (IRA) contributions may or may not be tax-deductible, depending on your circumstances. You should first maximize contributions to the previously mentioned tax-deductible accounts. Chapter 4 can help you determine whether you should contribute to an IRA, what type you should contribute to, and whether your IRA contributions are tax-deductible.

TIP

Lower- and moderate-income earners can gain a federal tax credit known as the "Saver's Credit." Married couples filing jointly with adjusted gross incomes (AGIs) of less than $76,500 and single taxpayers with an AGI of less than $38,250 can earn a tax credit (claimed on Form 8880) for retirement account contributions. Unlike a deduction, a *tax credit* directly reduces your tax bill by the amount of the credit. This credit, which is detailed in Table 2-1, is a percentage of the first $2,000 contributed (or $4,000 on a joint return). The credit is not available to those under the age of 18, full-time students, or people who are claimed as dependents on someone else's tax return.

TABLE 2-1 **Special Tax Credit for Retirement Plan Contributions**

Singles Adjusted Gross Income	Married-Filing-Jointly Adjusted Gross Income	Tax Credit for Retirement Account Contributions
$0–$23,000	$0–$46,000	50%
$23,000–$25,000	$46,000–$50,000	20%
$25,000–$38,250	$50,000–$76,500	10%

Using health savings accounts

You can reduce your taxable income and sock away money for future healthcare expenses by taking advantage of a *health savings account* (HSA). In fact, HSAs can offer superior tax savings versus retirement accounts because in addition to providing upfront tax breaks on contributions and tax-free accumulation of investment earnings, you can also withdraw money from HSAs tax-free so long as the money is used for healthcare costs. No other retirement accounts offer this triple tax-free benefit.

Shifting some income

Income shifting, which has nothing to do with money laundering, is a more esoteric tax-reduction technique that's an option only to those who can control *when* they receive their income.

For example, suppose your employer tells you in late December that you're eligible for a bonus. You're offered the option to receive your bonus in either December or January. If you're pretty certain that you'll be in a higher tax bracket next year, you should choose to receive your bonus in December.

Or, suppose you run your own business and you think that you'll be in a lower tax bracket next year. Perhaps you plan to take time off to be with a newborn or take an extended trip. You can send out some invoices later in the year so your customers won't pay you until January, which falls in the next tax year.

Increasing Your Deductions

Deductions are amounts you subtract from your adjusted gross income before calculating the tax you owe. To make things more complicated, the IRS gives you two methods for determining your total deductions. The good news is that you get to pick the method that leads to greater deductions — and hence, lower taxes. This section explains your options.

Choosing standard or itemized deductions

The first method for figuring deductions requires no thinking or calculating. If you have a relatively uncomplicated financial life, taking the so-called *standard deduction* is generally the better option. With the tax reform bill implemented in 2018, more people are better off taking the standard deduction. And that is in fact what has been happening with nearly nine in ten taxpayers now taking the standard deduction (down from about two-thirds previously).

Single folks qualify for a $14,600 standard deduction, and married couples filing jointly get a $29,200 standard deduction in 2024. If you're 65 or older, or blind, you get a slightly higher standard deduction.

Itemizing your deductions on your tax return is the other method for determining your allowable deductions. This method is definitely more of a hassle, but if you can tally up more than the standard amounts noted in the preceding paragraph, itemizing will save you money. Use Schedule A of IRS Form 1040 to tally your itemized deductions.

TIP

Even if you take the standard deduction, take the time to peruse all the line items on Schedule A to familiarize yourself with the many legal itemized deductions. Figure out what's possible to deduct so you can make more-informed financial decisions year-round.

Purchasing real estate

When you buy a home, you can claim two big ongoing expenses of homeownership as deductions on Schedule A: your property taxes and the interest on your mortgage. You're allowed to claim mortgage interest deductions for a primary residence (where you actually live) and on a second home for mortgage debt totaling up to $750,000, which is down from the previous limit of $1 million (and a home equity loan of up to $100,000). You may be grandfathered under the higher $1 million limit if your mortgage was taken out before December 16, 2017, or if you had a home under contract by that date and closed on that purchase by April 1, 2018.

Before 2018, there was no limit on property tax deductions on Form 1040, Schedule A. Now, property taxes (combined with state and local income tax payments) are limited to a maximum $10,000 annual deduction.

To buy real estate, you need to first collect a down payment, which requires maintaining a lid on your spending. Check out Part 5 for more on investing in real estate.

Trading consumer debt for mortgage debt

When you own real estate, you haven't borrowed the maximum, and you've run up high-interest consumer debt, you may be able to trade one debt for another. You may be able to save on interest charges by refinancing your mortgage or taking out a home equity loan and pulling out extra cash to pay off your credit card, auto loan, or other costly credit lines. You can usually borrow at a lower interest rate for a mortgage and get a tax deduction as a bonus, which lowers the effective borrowing cost further. Consumer debt, such as that on auto loans and credit cards, isn't tax-deductible.

WARNING

This strategy involves some danger. Borrowing against the equity in your home can be an addictive habit. I've seen cases where people run up significant consumer debt three or four times and then refinance their home the same number of times over the years to bail themselves out.

An appreciating home creates the illusion that excess spending isn't really costing you. But debt is debt, and all borrowed money ultimately has to be repaid (unless you file bankruptcy). In the long run, you wind up with greater mortgage debt, and paying it off takes a bigger bite out of your monthly income. Refinancing and establishing home equity lines cost you more in terms of loan application fees and other charges (points, appraisals, credit reports, and so on).

At a minimum, the continued expansion of your mortgage debt handicaps your ability to work toward other financial goals. In the worst case, easy access to borrowing encourages bad spending habits that can lead to bankruptcy or foreclosure on your debt-ridden home.

Contributing to charities

You can deduct contributions to charities if you itemize your deductions on Form 1040, Schedule A. Consider the following possibilities:

>> Most people know that when they write a check for $50 to their favorite church or college, they can deduct it. *Note:* Make sure that you get a receipt for contributions of $250 or more.

>> Many taxpayers overlook the fact that you can deduct expenses for work you do with charitable organizations. For example, when you go to a soup kitchen to help prepare and serve meals, you can deduct some of your transportation costs. Keep track of your driving mileage and other commuting expenses.

>> You can deduct the fair market value (which can be determined by looking at the price of similar merchandise in thrift stores) of donations of clothing, household appliances, furniture, and other goods to charities. (Some charities will drive to your home to pick up the stuff.) Find out whether organizations such as the Salvation Army, Goodwill, or others are interested in your donation. Just make sure that you keep some documentation — write up an itemized list and get it signed by the charity. Take pictures of your more valuable donations.

>> You can even donate securities and other investments to charity. In fact, donating an appreciated investment gives you a tax deduction for the full market value of the investment and eliminates your need to pay tax on the (unrealized) profit.

Remembering auto registration fees and state insurance

TIP

If you don't currently itemize, you may be surprised to discover that your state income taxes can be itemized. When you pay a fee to the state to register and license your car, you can itemize a portion of the expenditure as a deduction (on Schedule A, "State and Local Personal Property Taxes"). The IRS allows you to deduct the part of the fee that relates to the value of your car. The state organization that collects the fee should be able to tell you what portion of the fee is deductible. (Some states detail on the invoice what portion of the fee is tax-deductible.) There's a $10,000 annual federal income tax deduction limit on all deductible state and local taxes combined with property tax payments on your home.

Several states have state disability insurance funds. If you pay into these funds (check your W-2), you can deduct your payments as state and local income taxes on Schedule A. You may also claim a deduction on this line for payments you make into your state's unemployment compensation fund.

Deducting self-employment expenses

TIP

When you're self-employed, you can deduct a multitude of expenses from your income before calculating the tax you owe. If you buy a computer or office furniture, you can deduct those expenses. (Sometimes they need to be gradually deducted, or *depreciated*, over time.) Salaries for your employees, office supplies, rent or mortgage interest for your office space, and phone/communications expenses are also generally deductible.

Many self-employed folks don't take all the deductions they're eligible for. In some cases, people simply aren't aware of the wonderful world of deductions. Others are worried that large deductions will increase the risk of an audit. Spend some time finding out more about tax deductions; you'll be convinced that taking full advantage of your eligible deductions makes sense and saves you money.

Part 4 discusses small business deductions and other considerations for small business owners.

Lowering Investment Income Taxes

The distributions and profits on investments that you hold outside of tax-sheltered retirement accounts are exposed to taxation. Interest, dividends, and *capital gains* (profits from the sale of an investment at a price that's higher than the purchase price) are all taxed. The good news: You can take action to reduce the taxes in those accounts.

When you invest, you can invest in a way that fits your tax situation. This strategy can make you happier and wealthier come tax time. For example, you can choose tax-friendly investments (such as tax-free bonds) that reduce your tax bill and increase your after-tax investment returns.

Part 3 explains how investment income is taxed. The chapters in that part help you consider an investment strategy that works for your situation.

Enlisting Education Tax Breaks

The U.S. tax laws include numerous tax breaks for education-related expenditures. Here are the important tax-reduction opportunities you should know about for yourself and your kids if you have them:

>> **Tax deductions for college expenses:** You may take up to a $2,500 tax deduction on IRS Form 1040 for college costs

as long as your modified adjusted gross income (AGI) is less than $80,000 for single taxpayers and less than $165,000 for married couples filing jointly. (*Note:* You may take a partial tax deduction if your AGI is between $80,000 and $95,000 for single taxpayers and between $165,000 and $195,000 for married couples filing jointly.)

>> **Tax-free investment earnings in special accounts:** Money invested in Section 529 plans is sheltered from taxation and is not taxed upon withdrawal as long as the money is used to pay for eligible education expenses. 529 plans allow you to sock away more than $200,000. However, funding such accounts may harm your kid's qualifications for financial aid.

>> **American Opportunity tax credit:** The American Opportunity credit provides tax relief to low- and moderate-income earners facing education costs. The full credit (up to $2,500 per student) is available to individuals whose modified adjusted gross income is $80,000 or less, or $160,000 or less for married couples filing jointly. The credit is phased out for single taxpayers above $90,000 and married couples filing jointly above $180,000. The credit can be claimed for expenses for the first four years of postsecondary education. You may be able to claim an American Opportunity tax credit in the same year in which you receive a distribution from either an ESA or 529, but you can't use expenses paid with a distribution from either an ESA or 529 as the basis for the American Opportunity credit.

>> **Lifetime Learning tax credit:** The Lifetime Learning credit may be up to 20 percent of the first $10,000 of qualified educational expenses — up to $2,000 per taxpayer. For parents filing tax returns, only this credit or the American Opportunity tax credit may be claimed for each child per tax year. Single taxpayers' phaseout for being able to take this credit is at modified adjusted gross incomes (MAGIs) of $80,000 to $90,000. Other taxpayers' phaseout is from $160,000 to $180,000.

Getting Help from Tax Resources

There are all sorts of ways to prepare your tax return. Which approach makes sense for you depends on the complexity of your situation and your knowledge of taxes.

Regardless of which approach you use, you should be taking financial steps during the year to reduce your taxes. By the time you actually file your return in the following year, it's often too late for you to take advantage of many tax-reduction strategies.

Obtaining IRS assistance

If you have a simple, straightforward tax return, filing it on your own using only the IRS instructions is likely fine. This approach is as cheap as you can get. The main costs are time, patience, photocopying expenses (you should always keep a copy for your files), and postage for mailing the completed tax return (unless you're filing electronically).

WARNING

IRS publications don't have Tip or Warning icons. And the IRS has been known to give wrong information from time to time. When you call the IRS with a question, be sure to take notes about your conversation to protect yourself in the event of an audit. Date your notes and include the name and identification number of the tax employee you talked to, the questions you asked, and the employee's responses. File your notes in a folder with a copy of your completed return.

TIP

In addition to the IRS's standard tax-return preparation instructions, the IRS offers some free (actually, paid for with your tax dollars) and sometimes-useful booklets. Publication 17, *Your Federal Income Tax*, is designed for individual tax-return preparation. Publication 334, *Tax Guide for Small Businesses*, is for (you guessed it) small-business tax-return preparation (particularly those small business owners who use Form 1040, Schedule C). These publications are more comprehensive than the basic IRS instructions. Call 800-829-3676 to request these booklets or visit the IRS website at www.irs.gov.

Consulting preparation and advice guides

TIP

Books about tax preparation and tax planning that highlight common problem areas and are written in clear, simple English are invaluable. They supplement the official instructions not only by helping you complete your return correctly but also by showing you how to save as much money as possible.

Check out the latest edition of *Taxes For Dummies*, which I co-authored, and my *Small Business Taxes For Dummies*, both published by Wiley.

Using software and websites

TIP

If you have access to a computer, good tax-preparation software can be helpful. TurboTax, H&R Block Tax Software, and Tax-Slayer are programs that I have reviewed and rated as the best. If you go the software route, I highly recommend having a good tax advice book by your side.

For you web surfers, the Internal Revenue Service website (www. irs.gov) is among the better internet tax sites, believe it or not.

Hiring professional help

Competent tax preparers and advisors can save you money — sometimes more than enough to pay their fees — by identifying tax-reduction strategies you may overlook. They can also help reduce the likelihood of an audit, which can be triggered by blunders. Mediocre and lousy tax preparers, on the other hand, may make mistakes and be unaware of sound ways to reduce your tax bill.

Tax preparers and advisors come with varying backgrounds, training, and credentials. The four main types of tax practitioners are preparers, enrolled agents (EAs), certified public accountants (CPAs), and tax attorneys. The more training and specialization a tax practitioner has (and the more affluent their clients), the higher their hourly fee usually is. Fees and competence vary greatly. If you hire a tax advisor and you're not sure of the quality of the work performed or the soundness of the advice, try getting a second opinion.

Preparers

Preparers generally have the least amount of training of all the tax practitioners, and a greater proportion of them work part-time. As with financial planners, no national regulations apply to preparers, and no licensing is required.

Preparers are appealing because they're relatively inexpensive — they can do most basic returns for around $100 or so. The draw-back of using a preparer is that you may hire someone who doesn't know much more than you do.

TIP

Preparers make the most sense for folks who have relatively simple financial lives, who are budget-minded, and who hate doing their own taxes. If you're not good about hanging on to receipts or you don't want to keep your own files with background details about your taxes, you should definitely shop around for a tax preparer who's committed to the business. You may need all that stuff someday for an audit, and many tax preparers keep and organize their clients' documentation rather than return everything each year. Also, going with a firm that's open year-round may be a safer option (some small shops are open only during tax season) in case tax questions or problems arise.

Enrolled agents (EAs)

A person must pass IRS scrutiny in order to be called an *enrolled agent*. This license allows the agent to represent you before the IRS in the event of an audit. Continuing education is also required; an EA's training is generally longer and more sophisticated than that of a typical preparer.

Enrolled agents' fees tend to fall between those of a preparer and a CPA (see the next section). Returns that require a few of the more common schedules (such as Schedule A for deductions and Schedule D for capital gains and losses) shouldn't cost more than a few hundred dollars to prepare.

EAs are best for people who have moderately complex returns and don't necessarily need complicated tax-planning advice throughout the year (although some EAs provide this service as well). You can get names and telephone numbers of EAs in your area by contacting the National Association of Enrolled Agents (NAEA). You can call the NAEA at 202-822-6232 or visit its website at www.naea.org.

Certified public accountants (CPAs)

Certified public accountants go through significant training and examination before receiving the CPA credential. In order to maintain this designation, a CPA must also complete a fair number of continuing education classes every year.

CPA fees vary tremendously. Most charge $150+ per hour, but CPAs at large companies and in high-cost-of-living areas tend to charge somewhat more.

If you're self-employed and/or you file lots of other schedules, you may want to hire a CPA. But you don't need to do so year after year. If your situation grows complex one year and then stabilizes, consider getting help for the perplexing year and then using preparation guides, software, or a lower-cost preparer or enrolled agent in the future.

Tax attorneys

Tax attorneys deal with complicated tax problems and issues that usually have some legal angle. Unless you're a super-high-income earner with a complex financial life, hiring a tax attorney to prepare your annual return is prohibitively expensive. In fact, many tax attorneys don't prepare returns, but they may offer tax preparation as an ancillary service through others in their office.

Because of their level of specialization and training, tax attorneys tend to have the highest hourly billing rates — $300+ per hour is not unusual.

Dealing with an Audit

On a list of real-life nightmares, most people would rank tax audits right up there with root canals, rectal exams, and court appearances. Many people are traumatized by audits because they feel like they're on trial and being accused of a crime. Take a deep breath and don't panic.

You may be getting audited simply because someone at the IRS or a business that reports tax information on you made an error regarding the data on your return. In the vast majority of cases, the IRS conducts its audit by corresponding with you through the mail.

Audits that require you to schlep to the local IRS office are the most feared type of audit. In these cases, about 20 percent of such audited returns are left unchanged by the audit — in other words, the taxpayer doesn't end up owing more money. In fact, if you're the lucky sort, you may be one of the 5 percent of folks who actually gets a refund because the audit finds a mistake in your favor!

Unfortunately, you'll most likely be one of the roughly 75 percent of audit survivors who end up owing more tax money. The amount of additional tax that you owe in interest and penalties hinges on how your audit goes.

WARNING

Whatever you do, *don't ignore your audit request letter.* The IRS is the ultimate bill-collection agency. And if you end up owing more money (the unhappy result of most audits), the sooner you pay, the less interest and penalties you'll owe.

Certified tax professionals, such as an EA or CPA, can help take some of the sting out of dealing with an audit, but you will still need to do some legwork on your own. For information on preparing for an audit, see the most recent edition of my book, *Taxes For Dummies.*

Personal Finance and Taxes

2

Find out how to make tax-wise personal finance decisions.

Utilize your retirement account to slash your income taxes.

Make the most of your children's tax reduction opportunities.

Plan your estate for minimal hassle and taxes.

Chapter **3**

Making Tax-Wise Personal Finance Decisions

M anaging your personal finances involves much more than simply investing money. It includes making all the pieces of your financial life fit together. And, just like designing a vacation itinerary, managing your personal finances means developing a strategy to make the best use of your limited dollars and being prepared to deal with some adversity and changes to the landscape. This chapter explains how to keep the right perspective as you plan for and make financial decisions, and I also point out some pitfalls so you can steer clear of them when making financial and tax decisions.

Including Taxes in Your Financial Planning

Taxes are a large and vital piece of your financial puzzle. The following list shows some of the ways that tax issues are involved in making sound financial decisions throughout the year:

» **Spending:** The more you spend, the more taxes you'll pay for taxed purchases and for being less able to take advantage of the many benefits in the tax code that require you to have money to invest in the first place. For example, contrary to the hucksters on late-night infomercials, you need money to purchase real estate, which offers many tax benefits (see Part 5). And because taxes are probably your largest or second biggest expenditure, a budget that overlooks tax-reduction strategies is likely doomed to fail. Unless you have wealthy, benevolent relatives, you may be stuck with a lifetime of working if you can't save money.

» **Retirement accounts:** Taking advantage of retirement accounts can mean tens, perhaps even hundreds of thousands more dollars in your pocket come retirement time. Who says there are no free lunches? Check out Chapter 4.

» **Investing:** Merely choosing investments that generate healthy rates of return isn't enough. What matters is not what you make but what you keep — after paying taxes. Understand and capitalize on the many tax breaks available to investors in stocks, bonds, mutual funds, exchange-traded funds, real estate, and your own business (see Part 4 for details on the latter).

» **Protecting your assets:** Some of your insurance decisions also affect the taxes you pay. You'd think that after a lifetime of tax payments, your heirs would be left alone when you pass on to the great beyond — wishful thinking. Estate planning can significantly reduce the taxes to be siphoned off from your estate. Peruse Chapter 6 to find out more about estate planning.

Taxes infiltrate many areas of your personal finances. Some people make important financial decisions without considering taxes (and other important variables). Conversely, in an obsession to minimize or avoid taxes, other people make decisions that are counterproductive to achieving their long-term personal and financial goals. Although this chapter shows you that taxes are an important component to factor into your major financial decisions, taxes should not drive or dictate the decisions you make.

Taxing Mistakes

Even if some parts of the tax system are hopelessly and unreasonably complicated, there's no reason why you can't learn from the mistakes of others to save yourself some money. With this goal in mind, this section details common tax blunders that people make when it comes to managing their money.

Seeking advice after a major decision

Too many people come across information and hire help after making a decision, even though seeking preventive help ahead of time generally is wiser and less costly. Before making any major financial decisions, educate yourself. This book can help answer many of your questions.

TIP

If you're going to hire a tax advisor to give advice, do so before making your decision(s). The wrong move when selling a piece of real estate or taking money from a retirement account can cost you thousands of dollars in taxes!

Failing to withhold enough taxes

WARNING

If you're self-employed or earn significant taxable income from investments outside retirement accounts, you need to be making estimated quarterly tax payments. Likewise, if, during the year, you sell an investment at a profit, you may need to make a (higher) quarterly tax payment.

Not having a human resources department to withhold taxes from their pay as they earn it, some self-employed people dig themselves into a perpetual tax hole by failing to submit estimated quarterly tax payments. They get behind in their tax payments during their first year of self-employment and thereafter are always playing catch-up. People often don't discover that they "should've" paid more taxes during the year until after they complete their returns in the spring — or get penalty notices from the IRS and their states. Then they have to come up with sizable sums all at once. Don't be a "should've" victim.

To make quarterly tax payments, complete IRS Form 1040-ES, Estimated Tax for Individuals. This form and accompanying instructions explain how to calculate quarterly tax payments — which you can do through the IRS website or by mailing payment coupons with your check.

TIP

Although I — and the IRS — want you to keep your taxes current during the year, I don't want you to overpay. Some people have too much tax withheld during the year, and this overpayment can go on year after year. Although it may feel good to get a sizable refund check every spring, why should you loan your money to the government interest-free? When you work for an employer, you can complete a new W-4 to adjust your withholding. Turn the completed W-4 in to your employer. When you're self-employed, complete Form 1040-ES.

If you know that you'd otherwise spend the extra tax money that you're currently sending to the IRS, then this forced-savings strategy may have some value. But you can find other, better ways to make yourself save. You can set up all sorts of investments, such as mutual funds (see Chapter 9), to be funded by automatic contributions from your paychecks (or from a bank or investment account). Of course, if you happen to prefer to loan the IRS money — interest-free — go right ahead!

Overlooking legitimate deductions

Some taxpayers miss out on perfectly legal tax deductions because they just don't know about them. Ignorance is not bliss when it comes to your income taxes . . . it's costly. If you aren't going to take the time to discover the legitimate deductions available to you (you bought this book, so why not read the relevant parts of it?), spring for the cost of a competent tax advisor at least once.

Fearing an audit, some taxpayers (and even some tax preparers) avoid taking deductions that they have every right to take. Unless you have something to hide, such behavior is foolish and costly. Remember that a certain number of returns are randomly audited every year, so even when you don't take every deduction to which you're legally entitled, you may nevertheless get audited. An hour or so with the IRS is not as bad as you may think. It may be worth the risk of claiming all the tax breaks to which you're entitled, especially when you consider the amounts you can save over the years.

Passing up retirement accounts

All the tax deductions and tax deferrals that come with accounts such as 401(k)s, 403(b)s, SEP-IRAs, and IRAs were put in the tax code to encourage you to save for retirement. So why not take advantage of the benefits?

You probably have your reasons or excuses, but most excuses for missing out on this strategy just don't make good financial sense. People often underfund retirement accounts because they spend too much and because retirement seems so far away. Many people also mistakenly believe that retirement account money is totally inaccessible until they're old enough to qualify for senior discounts. See Chapter 4 to find out all about retirement accounts and why you should probably fund them.

Ignoring tax considerations when investing

Suppose that you want to unload some stock so that you can buy a new car. You sell an investment at a significant profit and feel good about your financial genius. But, come tax time, you may feel differently.

REMEMBER

Don't forget to consider the taxes due on profits from the sale of investments (except those in retirement accounts) when making decisions about what you sell and when you sell it. Your tax situation should also factor in what you invest outside retirement accounts. When you're in a relatively high tax bracket, you probably don't want investments that pay much in taxable distributions such as taxable interest, which only add to your tax burden. See Part 3 for details on the tax considerations of investing and which investments are tax-friendly for your situation.

Not buying a home

In the long run, owning a home should cost you less than renting. And because mortgage interest and property taxes may be partially deductible, the government, in effect, subsidizes the cost of home ownership.

Even if the government didn't help you with tax benefits when buying and owning a home, you'd still be better off owning throughout your adult life. If you rent instead, all your housing expenses are exposed to inflation, unless you have a great rent-controlled deal. So owning your own abode makes good financial and tax sense. And don't let the lack of money for a down payment stand in your way — methods exist for buying real estate with little upfront money. See Part 5 to find out about real estate and taxes.

Allowing your political views to distort your decision-making

Some folks have strong political views. I'm sure you have your reasons for why you believe and advocate what you do, and I'm not here to talk you out of that. But I will tell you that I've seen plenty of people make poor financial decisions, especially with investments, because their political concerns get in the way.

Consider some examples. In late 2008, President Barack Obama was elected and his being a pretty liberal guy freaked out some conservatives, especially because the Democrats then controlled the Presidency and the House and Senate. Pundits, especially those of the conservative persuasion, warned that the economy, already in tough shape when he took office, was going to be in tatters for years to come as Obama would raise taxes and investments would do poorly. While economic growth wasn't rapid, the economy performed pretty well in 2009 and the following years, and stock prices bounced back nicely, as they generally do after a major bear market.

In late 2016, President Donald Trump was elected, and his being an outspoken, inexperienced politician who espoused conservative policies freaked out some liberals, especially with Republicans in control of the House, Senate, and Presidency. Prognosticators, especially on the left politically, opined that Trump would cause the economy and stock market to crash and burn as his reckless tax-cutting policies would explode the deficit and cause myriad other problems. That didn't happen as economic growth accelerated, and stock prices did quite well. And while the COVID-19 pandemic and mandated government economic shutdowns upset things for some months in early 2020, the economy and stock prices quickly bounced back.

TIP

There's a simple moral to the stories here. To be a successful investor and make sound financial decisions, try to leave your political beliefs out of it and be unemotional. Extreme changes rarely occur even when one party-rule occurs for a couple of years in Washington, D.C. It's often soon replaced by divided government, which leads to more incremental change and eventually a switch in power back to the current out-of-power party.

Ignoring the financial aid (tax) system

WARNING

The college financial aid system in this country assumes that the money you save outside tax-sheltered retirement accounts is available to pay educational expenses. As a result, families who save money outside instead of inside retirement accounts may qualify for far less "financial aid" than they otherwise would. Financial aid is actually a misnomer because what colleges and universities are doing is charging a different price to different families after analyzing their finances. So, when a college appears to be giving you money, what they're actually doing is reducing their inflated prices to a more reasonable level.

If you're affluent and have done a good job saving and investing money, colleges are generally going to charge you more. So in addition to normal income taxes, an extra financial aid "tax" is effectively exacted. To find out about the best ways to save and invest for educational costs, see Chapter 5.

Neglecting the timing of events you can control

The amount of tax you pay on certain transactions can vary, depending on the timing of events. If you're nearing retirement, for example, you may soon be in a lower tax bracket. To the extent possible, you should consider delaying and avoid claiming investment income until your overall income level drops, and you need to take as many deductions or losses as you can now while your income is still high. Following are two tax-reducing strategies — income shifting and bunching or shifting deductions — that you may be able to put to good use when you can control the timing of either your income or deductions.

Shifting income

Suppose that your employer tells you in late December that you're eligible for a bonus. You find out that you have the option of receiving your bonus in either December or January (ask your payroll and benefits department if this is an option). Looking ahead, if you're pretty certain that you're going to be in a higher tax bracket next year, request to receive your bonus in December. (See Chapter 1 to find out about your tax bracket.)

Or suppose that you run your own business and operate on a cash accounting basis and think that you'll be in a lower tax bracket next year. Perhaps business has slowed of late or you plan to take time off to be with a newborn or take an extended trip. You can send out some invoices later in the year so that your customers won't pay you until January, which falls in the next tax year.

Bunching or shifting deductions

When the total of your itemized deductions on Schedule A is lower than the standard deduction, you need to take the standard deduction. This itemized deduction total is worth checking each year, because you may have more deductions in some years than others, and you may occasionally be able to itemize.

When you can control the timing of payment of particular expenses that are eligible for itemizing, you can shift or bunch more of them into select years when you're more likely to have enough deductions to take advantage of itemizing. Suppose that because you don't have many itemized deductions this year, you use the standard deduction. Late in the year, however, you feel certain that you'll itemize next year, because you plan to buy a home and will therefore be able to claim significant mortgage interest and some property tax deductions. It makes sense, then, to shift and bunch as many deductible expenses as possible into next year. For example, if you're getting ready to make a tax-deductible donation of old clothes and household goods to charity, wait until January to do so.

In any tax year that you're sure you won't have enough deductions to be able to itemize, shift as many itemizable expenses as you can into the next tax year.

WARNING

Be careful when using your credit card to pay expenses. These expenses must be recognized for tax purposes in the year in which the charge was made on the card and not when you actually pay the credit card bill.

Not using tax advisors effectively

If your financial situation is complicated, going it alone and relying only on the IRS instructions to figure your taxes usually is a mistake. Many people find the IRS publications tedious and not geared toward highlighting opportunities for tax reductions.

Instead, you can start by reading the relevant sections of this book. You can figure out taxes for yourself, or you can hire a tax advisor to figure them out for you. Doing nothing isn't an advisable option!

TIP

When you're overwhelmed by the complexity of particular financial decisions, get advice from tax and financial advisors who sell their time and nothing else. Protect yourself by checking references and clarifying what advice, analysis, and recommendations the advisor will provide for the fee charged. If your tax situation is complicated, you'll probably more than recoup a preparer's fee, as long as you take the time to hire a good advisor.

TIP

Remember that using a tax advisor is most beneficial when you face new tax questions or problems. If your tax situation remains complicated, or if you know that you'd do a worse job on your own, by all means keep using a tax preparer. But don't pay a big fee year after year to a tax advisor who simply plugs your numbers into the tax forms. If your situation is unchanging or isn't that complicated, consider hiring and paying someone to figure out your taxes one time. After that, go ahead and try completing your own tax return.

Comprehending the Causes of Bad Tax Decisions

When bad things happen, it's usually for a variety of reasons. And so it is with making financial blunders that cause you to pay more tax dollars. The following sections describe some common culprits that may be keeping you from making tax-wise financial maneuvers and what you can do about them.

"Financial planners" and brokers' advice

Wanting to hire a financial advisor to help you make better financial decisions is a logical inclination, especially if you're a time-starved person. But when you pick a poor planner or someone who isn't a financial planner but rather a salesperson in disguise, watch out!

Unfortunately, many people calling themselves financial planners, financial consultants, or financial advisors actually work on commission, which creates enormous conflicts of interest with providing unbiased and objective financial advice. Brokers and commission-based financial planners (who are also therefore brokers) structure their advice around selling you investment and other financial products that provide them with commissions. As a result, they tend to take a narrow view of your finances and frequently ignore the tax and other consequences of financial moves. Or they may pitch the supposed tax benefits of an investment they're eager to sell you as a reason for you to buy it. It may provide a tax benefit for someone, but not necessarily for you in your specific situation.

The few planners who work on a fee basis primarily provide money-management services and typically charge about 1 percent per year of the money they manage. Fee-based planners have their own conflicts of interest, because all things being equal, they want you to hire them to manage your money. Therefore, they can't objectively help you decide whether you should pay off your mortgage and other debts, invest in real estate or a small business, or invest more in your employer's retirement plan. In short, they have a bias against financial strategies that take your investment money out of their hands.

Be especially leery of planners, brokers, and money-managing planners who lobby you to sell investments that you've held for a while and that show a profit. If you sell these investments, you may have a hefty tax burden. (See Part 3 for more insight on how to make these important investing decisions.)

Advertising

Another reason you may make tax missteps in managing your personal finances is advertising. Although reputable financial firms with terrific products advertise, the firms that spend the most on advertising often are the ones with inferior offerings. Being bombarded with ads whenever you listened to the radio, watched television, or read magazines and newspapers was bad enough, but now email boxes, websites, and social media platforms are stuffed full of spam and promos, too.

WARNING

Responding to ads usually is a bad financial move, regardless of whether the product being pitched is good, bad, or so-so, because the company placing the ad typically is trying to motivate you to buy a specific product. The company doesn't care about your financial alternatives, whether its product fits with your tax situation, and so on. Many ads try to catch your attention with the supposed tax savings that their products generate.

Advice from websites and publications

You read an article that recommends some investments. Tired of not taking charge and making financial decisions, you get on the phone, call an investment company, and — before you know it — you've invested. You feel a sense of relief and accomplishment — you've done something.

Come tax time, you get all these confusing statements detailing dividends and capital gains that you must report on your tax return. Now you see that these investment strategies generate all sorts of taxable distributions that add to your tax burden. And you may be saddled with additional tax forms to complete by April 15. You wish you had known.

WARNING

Articles on websites and in magazines, newspapers, newsletters, and so forth can help you stay informed, but they also can cause you to make ill-advised financial moves that overlook tax consequences. Article writers have limited time and space and often don't consider the big picture or ways their advice can be misunderstood or misused. Even worse is that too many writers don't know the tax consequences of what they're writing about.

Overspending

Far too many tax guides go on and on and on, talking about this tax break and that tax break. The problem is that to take advantage of many of the best tax breaks, you need to have money to invest. When you spend all that you earn, you miss out on many terrific tax benefits that I tell you about in this book. And the more you spend, the more taxes you pay, both on your income and on the purchases you make (through sales taxes).

Just like losing weight, spending less sounds good, but most people have a hard time budgeting their finances and spending less than they earn. Perhaps you already know where the fat is in your spending. If you don't, figuring out where all your monthly income is going is a real eye-opener. The task takes some detective work — looking through your credit card statements and your checkbook register to track your purchases and categorize your spending.

Financial illiteracy

Lack of personal finance education is at the root of most money blunders. You may not understand the tax system and how to manage your finances because you were never taught how to manage them growing up or in high school or college.

Financial illiteracy is a widespread problem not just among the poor and undereducated. Most people don't plan ahead and educate themselves with their financial goals in mind. People react — or, worse, do nothing at all. You may dream, for example, about retiring and never having to work again. Or perhaps you hope that someday you can own a house or even a vacation home in the country or by the shore.

You need to understand how to plan your finances so you can accomplish your financial goals. You also need to understand how the tax system works and how to navigate within it to work toward your objectives.

TIP

If you need more help with important personal financial issues, pick up a copy of the latest edition of my *Personal Finance For Dummies* (Wiley).

Chapter **4**

Maximizing Your Retirement Account

S aving and investing through retirement accounts is one of the simplest yet most powerful methods to reduce your tax burden. Understanding the myriad account options and rules isn't simple, but I do my best at explaining them in this chapter.

Unfortunately, most people can't take advantage of these plans because they spend too much of what they make. So not only do they have less savings, but they also pay higher income taxes — a double whammy. And don't forget, the more you spend, the more sales tax you pay on purchases. To be able to best take advantage of the tax savings that come with retirement savings plans, you should spend less than you earn. Only then can you afford to contribute to these plans.

I walk you through these different retirement accounts and their tax implications in this chapter so you can make well-informed decisions for your retirement savings.

Funding Your Retirement Accounts

Retirement may seem like the distant future to young folks. It's often not until middle age that warning bells start stimulating thoughts about what money they'll live on in their golden years. The single biggest mistake people at all income levels make with retirement accounts is not taking advantage of them. When you're in your 20s and 30s (and for some individuals in their 40s and 50s), spending and living for today and postponing saving for the future seems a whole lot more fun than saving for retirement. But assuming that you don't want to work your entire life, the sooner you start saving, the less painful it is each year, because your contributions have more years to grow.

Each decade that you delay contributing approximately doubles the percentage of your earnings that you need to save to meet your goals. For example, if saving 5 percent per year in your early 20s gets you to your retirement goal, waiting until your 30s may mean socking away 10 percent; waiting until your 40s, 20 percent . . . it gets ugly beyond that!

So, the longer you wait, the more you'll have to save and, therefore, the less that will be left over for spending. As a result, you may not meet your goal, and your golden years may be more restrictive than you hoped.

I use this simple lesson to emphasize the importance of considering now the future benefits you achieve by saving and investing in some type of retirement account.

REMEMBER

Saving money is difficult for most people. Don't make a tough job impossible by forsaking the tax benefits that come from investing through most retirement accounts.

Starting your savings sooner

WARNING

Many investors make a common mistake by neglecting to take advantage of retirement accounts because of their enthusiasm to spend or invest in non-retirement accounts. Not investing in tax-sheltered retirement accounts can cost you hundreds, perhaps thousands, of dollars per year in lost tax savings. Add up that loss over the many years that you work and save, and you find that not taking advantage of these tax-reduction accounts can easily cost you tens of thousands to hundreds of thousands of dollars in the long term. Ouch!

To take advantage of retirement savings plans and the tax savings that accompany them, you must first spend less than you earn. Only then can you afford to contribute to these retirement savings plans (unless you already happen to have a stash of cash from previous savings or inheritance).

REMEMBER

The sooner you start to save, the less painful it is each year to save enough to reach your goals. Why? Because your contributions have more years to compound and sheltered from taxation. As I explain in the preceding section, each decade you delay saving approximately doubles the percentage of your earnings that you need to save to meet your goals. If you enjoy spending money and living for today, you should be more motivated to start saving sooner. The longer that you wait to save, the more you ultimately need to save and, therefore, the less you can spend today!

Choosing retirement account investments

When you establish a retirement account, you may not realize that the retirement account is simply a shell or shield that keeps the federal, state, and local governments from taxing your investment earnings each year. You still must choose which investments you want to hold inside your retirement account shell.

You may invest money for your IRA or self-employed plan retirement account (for example, your SEP-IRA) in stocks, bonds, mutual funds, exchange-traded funds, and even bank accounts. Mutual funds (offered in most employer-based plans) and exchange-traded funds are an ideal choice because they offer diversification and professional management. After you decide which financial institution you want to invest through, simply obtain and complete the appropriate paperwork for establishing the specific type of account you want.

Don't go overboard

Over the years, I've seen some clients "over" contribute to retirement accounts. I don't literally mean that these well-intentioned souls broke the contribution limit rules in a given tax year. I'm talking about unusual situations where people have contributed more to their retirement accounts than what makes good financial and tax sense.

For example, it may not make sense for a taxpayer who is temporarily in a very low tax bracket (or owing no tax at all) to contribute to retirement accounts, especially those offering an upfront tax break. (Roth accounts are an exception because their tax breaks are ongoing and at withdrawal, not upfront.) Ditto the person who has a large estate already and has piles inside retirement accounts that can get walloped by estate and income taxes upon their passing. Few people, of course, have this perhaps enviable "problem."

When in doubt, and if you have reason to believe you should scale back on retirement account contributions, consult with a competent financial/tax advisor who works for an hourly fee and doesn't sell products or manage money. Please see the latest edition of my *Personal Finance For Dummies* (Wiley) for more details.

Gaining Tax Benefits

Retirement accounts should be called "tax-reduction accounts" — if they were, more people would be more motivated to contribute to them. Contributions to these plans are generally deductible for both your federal and state income taxes.

Suppose that you pay about 30 percent between federal and state income taxes on your last dollars of income. With most of the retirement accounts that I describe in this chapter, you can save yourself about $300 in taxes for every $1,000 that you contribute in the year that you make your contribution.

TIP

Check with your employer's benefits department because some organizations match a portion of employee contributions. Be sure to partake of this free matching money by contributing to your retirement accounts.

After your money is in a retirement account, any interest, dividends, and appreciation grow inside the account without taxation. With most retirement accounts, you defer taxes on all the accumulating gains and profits until you withdraw your money down the road, which you can do without penalty after age 59½. In the meantime, more of your money works for you over a long period of time. In some cases, such as with the Roth IRAs described later in this chapter, withdrawals are tax-free, too.

Special tax credit for lower-income earners

In addition to the upfront tax break you get from contributing to many retirement accounts, lower-income earners may receive tax credits worth up to 50 percent on the first $2,000 of retirement account contributions. Like employer-matching contributions, this tax credit amounts to free money (in this case from the government), so you should take advantage!

As you can see in Table 4-1, this retirement account contribution tax credit phases out quickly for higher-income earners, and no such credit is available to single taxpayers with adjusted gross incomes (AGIs) above $38,250, heads of household with AGIs above $57,375, and married couples filing jointly with AGIs above $76,500. (*Note:* This credit isn't available to taxpayers who are claimed as dependents on someone else's tax return or who are under the age of 18 or full-time students.)

TABLE 4-1 **2024 Tax Credit for the First $2,000 in Retirement Plan Contributions**

Single Taxpayers AGI	Head of Household AGI	Married Couples Filing Jointly AGI	Tax Credit
$0 to $23,000	$0 to $34,500	$0 to $46,000	50%
$23,000 to $25,000	$34,500 to $37,500	$46,000 to $50,000	20%
$25,000 to $38,250	$37,500 to $57,375	$50,000 to $76,500	10%

Tax-deferred compounding of investment earnings

After money is placed in a retirement account, any interest, dividends, and appreciation add to the amount in the account without being taxed. You get to defer taxes on all the accumulating gains and profits until you withdraw the money, presumably in retirement. Thus, more money is working for you over a longer period of time.

Your retirement tax rate need not be less than your tax rate during your working years for you to come out ahead by contributing to retirement accounts. In fact, because you defer paying tax and have more money compounding over more years, you can end up with more money in retirement by saving inside a retirement account, even if your retirement tax rate is higher than it is now.

The tax rate on *long-term capital gains* — investments held more than one year — and stock dividends (see Chapter 7) is significantly lower than the rate on ordinary income. Watch out though — the current rates may increase, at least for some higher-income taxpayers. So, keep an eye on Washington and subsequent editions of this book to keep absolutely up-to-date.

You may get an added bonus from deferring taxes on your retirement account assets if you're in a lower tax bracket when you withdraw the money. You may well be in a lower tax bracket in retirement because most people have less income when they're not working.

When you're near retirement and already have money in a tax-sheltered type of retirement account (for example, at your employer), by all means continue to keep it in a tax-favored account if you leave. You can accomplish this goal by rolling the money over into an IRA account. If your employer offers good investment options in a retirement plan and allows you to leave your money in the plan after your departure, consider that option, too.

Naming the Types of Retirement Accounts

When you earn employment income (or receive alimony), you have the option of putting money away in a retirement account that compounds without taxation until you withdraw the money. In most cases, your contributions are tax-deductible. The following sections discuss "IRS-approved" retirement accounts and explain how to determine whether you're eligible for them and some other nitpicky but important rules.

Employer-sponsored plans

You should be thankful that your employer values your future enough to offer these benefits and grateful that your employer has gone to the trouble of doing the legwork of setting up the plan, and in most cases, selecting investment options. If you were self-employed, you'd have to hassle with establishing your own plan and choosing investment options. All you have to do with an employer plan is save enough to invest and allocate your contributions among the (generally few) investments offered.

401(k) plans

For-profit companies generally offer 401(k) plans. The silly name comes from the section of the tax code that establishes and regulates these plans. A 401(k) generally allows you to save up to $23,000 for tax year 2024. Your employer's plan may have lower contribution limits, though, if employees don't save enough in the company's 401(k) plan. Your contributions to a 401(k) generally are excluded from your reported income and thus are free from federal and, in some cases, state income taxes, but not from Social Security and Medicare taxes (and from some other state employment taxes).

Older workers — those at least age 50 — are able to put away even more: up to $7,500 more per year than their younger counterparts. The annual contribution limit on 401(k) plans and the additional amounts allowed for older workers rise, in $500 increments, with inflation.

Some employers don't allow you to start contributing to their 401(k) plan until you've worked for them for a full year. Others allow you to start contributing right away. Some employers also match a portion of your contributions. They may, for example, match half of your first 6 percent of contributions (so in addition to saving a lot of taxes, you get a free bonus from the company). Check with your company's benefits department for your plan's details.

Smaller companies (those with fewer than 100 employees) can consider offering 401(k) plans, too. In the past, it was prohibitively expensive for smaller companies to administer a 401(k) plan. If your company is interested in this option, contact a mutual fund or discount brokerage organization, such as T. Rowe Price, Vanguard, Schwab, or Fidelity. In some cases, your employer may need to work with a separate plan administrator in addition to one of these investment firms.

403(b) plans

Many nonprofit organizations offer 403(b) plans to their employees. (State and local government employees may have 457 plans and federal government workers have the Thrift Savings Plan which are similar.) As with a 401(k), your contributions to these plans generally are federal and state tax-deductible. 403(b) plans often are referred to as tax-sheltered annuities, the name for insurance-company investments that satisfy the requirements for 403(b) plans. For the benefit of 403(b) retirement-plan participants, no-load (commission-free) mutual funds also can be used in 403(b) plans.

Nonprofit employees generally are allowed to contribute up to 20 percent or $23,000 of their salaries, whichever is less. Employees who have 15 or more years of service may be allowed to contribute beyond the $23,000 limit. Ask your company's benefits department or the investment provider for the 403(b) plan (or your tax advisor) about eligibility requirements and details about your personal contribution limit.

As with 401(k) plans, the contribution limit for workers age 50 and older in 2024 is $30,500. The annual contribution limit on 403(b) plans and the additional amounts allowed for older workers rise, in $500 increments, with inflation.

AFTER-TAX 401(K) AND 403(B) CONTRIBUTIONS

Some employer-based retirement plans allow for "Roth" after-tax contributions to both 401(k) and 403(b) plans. Like Roth IRA contributions, Roth 401(k) and Roth 403(b) contributions not only grow tax-deferred but also allow for tax-free withdrawal of investment earnings.

Generally speaking, you still will likely be better off making pre-tax retirement plan contributions before considering after-tax (Roth) contributions. Most people are best served taking the sure tax break than waiting many years for an unspecified tax break. However, you may consider these accounts if you're currently in a very low tax bracket or you're an older worker who already has a large amount saved in traditional pre-tax accounts. Please see my discussion in the section "To Roth or not to Roth?" later in this chapter for further information.

TIP

If you work for a nonprofit or public-sector organization that doesn't offer this benefit, request it. Nonprofit organizations have no excuse not to offer 403(b) plans to their employees. Unlike 401(k) plans, 403(b) plans have virtually no out-of-pocket setup expenses or ongoing accounting fees. The only requirement is that the organization must deduct the appropriate contribution from employees' paychecks and send the money to the investment company handling the 403(b) plan. If your employer doesn't know where to look for good 403(b) investment options, send them to Vanguard (877-859-5756), Fidelity (800-548-2363), or T. Rowe Price (800-492-7670), all of which offer solid mutual funds and 403(b) plans.

SIMPLE plans

Employers in small businesses have yet another retirement plan option, known as the SIMPLE-IRA. SIMPLE stands for Savings Incentive Match Plans for Employees. Relative to 401(k) plans, SIMPLE plans make it somewhat easier for employers to reduce their costs, thanks to easier reporting requirements and fewer administrative hassles. (However, employers may escape the nondiscrimination testing requirements — one of the more tedious aspects of maintaining a 401(k) plan — by adhering to the matching and contribution rules of a SIMPLE plan, as described later in this section.)

The contribution limit for SIMPLE plans is $16,000 for tax year 2024 for younger workers ($19,500 for those age 50 and older). Annual contribution limits increase in increments of $500 with inflation.

Employers must make small contributions on behalf of employees. Employers can either match, dollar for dollar, the first 3 percent the employee contributes or contribute 2 percent of pay for everyone whose wages exceed $5,000. Interestingly, if the employer chooses the first option, the employer has an incentive not to educate employees about the value of contributing to the plan because the more employees contribute, the more it costs the employer. And, unlike a 401(k) plan, greater employee contributions don't enable higher-paid employees to contribute more.

Self-employed plans

Although setting up a self-employed plan means some legwork for you as a business owner, you can select and design a plan that meets your needs. You can actually do a better job than many companies do; often, the people establishing a retirement plan don't do enough homework, or they let some salesperson sweet-talk them into high-expense (for the employees, that is) investments. Your trouble will be rewarded — self-employment retirement plans generally enable you to sock away more money on a tax-deductible basis than most employers' plans do.

WARNING

If you have employees, you're required to make contributions comparable to the company owners' (as a percentage of salary) on their behalf under these plans. Some part-time employees (those working fewer than 500 to 1,000 hours per year) and newer employees (less than a few years of service) may be excluded. Not all small-business owners know about this requirement — or they choose to ignore it, and they set up plans for themselves but fail to cover their employees. The danger is that the IRS and state tax authorities may, in the event of an audit, hit you with big penalties and disqualify your prior contributions if you have neglected to make contributions for eligible employees. Because self-employed people and small businesses get their taxes audited at a relatively high rate, messing up in this area is dangerous. The IRS also has a program to audit small pension plans.

TIP

Don't avoid setting up a retirement savings plan for your business just because you have employees and you don't want to make contributions on their behalf. In the long run, you can build the contributions you make for your employees into their total compensation package — which includes salary and other benefits like health insurance. Making retirement contributions need not increase your personnel costs.

The SECURE (Setting Every Community Up for Retirement Enhancement) ACT of 2019 provides for up to $5,000 in tax credits for eligible small-business owners when starting a retirement plan. This credit applies to new 401(k), profit sharing, SEP, and SIMPLE plans for small employers with up to 100 employees.

To get the most from your contributions as an employer, consider the following:

» Educate your employees about the value of retirement savings plans. You want them to understand how to save for the future and to value and appreciate your investment.

» If you have more than 20 or so employees, consider offering a 401(k) or SIMPLE plan, which allows employees to contribute money from their paychecks.

SEP-IRAs

Simplified Employee Pension Individual Retirement Account (SEP-IRA) plans require little paperwork to set up. Each year, you decide the amount you want to contribute to your SEP-IRA; no minimums exist. Your contributions to a SEP-IRA are deducted from your taxable income, saving you big-time on federal and usually state taxes. As with other retirement plans, your money compounds without taxation until withdrawal.

SEP-IRAs allow you to sock away about 20 percent of your self-employment income (business revenue minus expenses), up to a maximum of $69,000 for tax year 2024.

Self-employed/i401(k) plans

Another alternative is the "Self-employed" or "Individual 401(k)" plan, which offers traditional contribution and Roth (after-tax contribution) features. This plan type is only for sole proprietors (and their working spouses in the business) and partnerships with no eligible employees.

The pre-tax contribution limits are the same as a SEP-IRA. The after-tax limits are the same as the employee 401(k) limits — up to $23,000 except those age 50 or older can make "catch-up" contributions of up to $7,500 more.

Defined-benefit plans

These plans are for people who are able and willing to put away more than the SEP-IRA contribution limit of $69,000 per year. Of course, only a small percentage of people can afford to do so.

Consistently high-income earners who want to save more than $69,000 per year in a retirement account should consider these plans.

If you're interested in defined-benefit plans, you need to hire an actuary to calculate how much you can contribute to such a plan.

Individual Retirement Accounts (IRAs)

A final retirement account option is an Individual Retirement Account (IRA). Because your IRA contributions may not be tax-deductible, contributing to an IRA generally makes sense only after you've exhausted contributing to other retirement accounts, such as the employer- and self-employed-based plans discussed earlier, which allow for tax-deductible contributions. The following sections discuss your IRA options.

"Regular" IRAs

The annual contribution limit for IRAs (both regular and the newer Roth IRAs, see the section later in this chapter, "Nondeductible IRA contributions") is $7,000. People age 50 and older may contribute even more — an extra $1,000 per year for a total of $8,000.

Your contributions to a regular IRA may or may not be tax-deductible if you are covered by a retirement plan at work. For tax year 2024, if you're single and your adjusted gross income (AGI) is $77,000 or less for the year, you can deduct your IRA contribution in full. If you're married and file your taxes jointly, you're entitled to a full IRA deduction if your AGI is $123,000 per year or less. *Note:* These AGI limits will increase in future tax years (more details in a moment).

The only way to know for certain whether you're an active participant in a retirement plan is to look at your W-2 form, that small (4-x-8½-inch) document your employer sends you early in the year to file with your tax returns. An X mark in a little box in section 13 on the W-2 form indicates that you're an active participant in an employer retirement plan.

UNDERSTANDING MANDATORY DISTRIBUTION RULES

If you're self-employed or retired from a company, the year you turn 73 (effective in 2023), you have to make some important decisions about how the money will come out of your regular IRA. (This policy isn't applicable to Roth IRAs.) The first choice: whether you receive yearly distributions based on your life expectancy or based on the joint life expectancies of you and your beneficiary. If your aim is to take out as little as possible, you'll want to use a joint life expectancy. That choice will stretch out the distributions over a longer period.

Next, you have to decide how you want your life expectancy to be calculated.

Sometimes, tax law changes actually make things simpler. You'll be happy to know that changes over the years to IRS regulations make required minimum distribution calculations easier.

Under the prior laws, retirees had several confusing methods for calculating their mandated retirement account withdrawal amounts. With the new regulations, seniors can generally take their retirement account balances and divide that by a number from an IRS life expectancy table. Investment companies typically can provide you with this number as well.

Another benefit of these new rules is that the newer tables generally produce lower required distributions and, therefore, a greater ability to preserve the account tax-free than was possible under the old regulations.

TECHNICAL STUFF

In some cases, you may see that the box is checked on your W-2 form indicating your active participation in a retirement plan when you haven't contributed any of your paycheck into a retirement plan. How can this be? Well, employers offer additional retirement plans outside those you contribute to from your paycheck. You're considered an active participant in a defined benefit plan (such as a traditional pension plan) as long as you're eligible to participate in the plan, even if you didn't make a required contribution, didn't perform the minimum service needed to accrue a benefit for the year, or never actively said you wanted to participate in the plan.

SHOULD YOU CONVERT YOUR REGULAR IRA TO A ROTH IRA?

If the Roth IRA's tax-free withdrawals of accumulated earnings appeal to you, you may be interested in knowing that the tax laws allow taxpayers to transfer money from a regular IRA to a Roth IRA without having to pay any early withdrawal penalties.

Whether you'll come out ahead in the long run by doing this conversion depends largely on your time horizon and retirement tax bracket. The younger you are, the higher the tax bracket you think that you'll be in when you retire, and the smaller the account you're thinking of converting, the more such a conversion makes sense. On the other hand, if you drop into a lower tax bracket in retirement, as many retirees do, you're probably better off keeping the money in a standard IRA account. For assistance with crunching numbers to see whether a conversion makes financial sense, visit `https://www.fidelity.com/calculators-tools/roth-conversion-calculator/`.

Of course, if you can't afford to pay the current income tax you'll owe on the conversion, don't convert. And again, remember that a future Congress may reverse some of the benefits of the Roth IRA. Thus, I generally don't advise many people to convert a regular IRA into a Roth IRA.

For tax year 2024, if you're a single-income earner with an AGI above $77,000 but below $87,000, or married filing jointly with an AGI above $123,000 but below $143.000, you're eligible for a partial IRA deduction, even if you're an active participant. If you're married filing a separate return from your spouse, your ability to deduct your IRA contribution disappears at $10,000 of AGI. The size of the IRA deduction that you may claim depends on where you fall in the income range. For example, a single-income earner at $82,000 is entitled to half of the full IRA deduction because their income falls halfway between $77,000 and $87,000.

Nondeductible IRA contributions

You can contribute to an IRA even if you can't deduct a portion or all of an IRA contribution because you're already covered by another retirement plan and you're a higher-income earner.

An IRA contribution that isn't tax-deductible is called, not surprisingly, a nondeductible IRA contribution. (I've never accused the IRS of being creative.) To make a nondeductible contribution, you have to have employment income during the year equal to at least the amount of your IRA contribution.

The benefit of this type of contribution is that the money can still compound and grow without taxation. For a person who plans to leave contributions in the IRA for a long time (a decade or more), this tax-deferred compounding may make nondeductible contributions worthwhile. However, before you consider making a nondeductible IRA contribution, be sure to read about the newer Roth IRAs (in the next section) that may offer better benefits for your situation.

If you end up making a nondeductible IRA contribution, you may wonder how the IRS will know not to tax you again on those portions of IRA withdrawals (because you've already paid income tax on the nondeductible contribution) in retirement. Surprise, surprise, you must fill out another form, Form 8606, which you file each year with your tax return to track these nondeductible contributions.

Roth IRAs

For years, some taxpayers and tax advisors (and book authors and financial counselors) have complained about the rules and regulations on regular IRAs. The income limits that allowed for taking an IRA deduction were set too low. And many people who can't take a tax deduction on a contribution were unmotivated to make a nondeductible contribution, because earnings on the contribution still would be taxed upon withdrawal. (Granted, the tax-deferred compounding of earnings is worth something — especially to younger people — but that's a more complicated benefit to understand and value.)

So, rather than addressing these concerns by changing regular IRAs, Congress decided to make things even more complicated by introducing another whole IRA known as the Roth IRA, named after the Senate Finance Committee chairman who championed these new accounts. (Perhaps if congressional representatives couldn't name accounts after themselves, we may someday have real tax reform!)

UNDERSTANDING THE ROTH IRA

The Roth IRA allows for up to a $7,000 annual contribution for couples with AGIs under $230,000 and for single taxpayers with AGIs under $146,000. (Those individuals age 50 and older may contribute $8,000.) The contribution limits are reduced for married taxpayers with AGIs above $230,000 ($146,000 if single) and are eliminated for couples with AGIs above $240,000 ($161,000 for singles).

Although this newer IRA doesn't offer a tax deduction on funds contributed to it, it nevertheless offers benefits not provided by regular IRAs and some other retirement accounts. The distinguishing feature of the Roth IRA is that the earnings on your contributions aren't taxed upon withdrawal as long as you're at least age 59½ and have held the account for at least five years.

An exception to the age 59½ rule is made for first-time homebuyers, who can withdraw up to $10,000 income-tax-free from a Roth IRA (in existence for at least five years) to apply to the purchase of a principal residence.

Another attractive feature of the Roth IRA: For those not needing to draw on all their retirement accounts in the earlier years of retirement, the Roth IRA, unlike a standard IRA, doesn't require distributions after the account holder passes age 73.

TO ROTH OR NOT TO ROTH?

Before you race to contribute to a Roth IRA, keep in mind that the lack of taxation on withdrawn earnings is in no way guaranteed for the future — a future Congress can take that benefit away. If the government is running large deficits in future years, taxing Roth IRA withdrawals, especially for the more affluent, would increase tax revenue. (On the other hand, retired voters vote, and members of the Congress that tap the short-term benefit of taxing too many of these accounts may face a voter backlash.)

TIP

Consider contributing to a Roth IRA if you've exhausted your ability to contribute to tax-deductible retirement accounts and you aren't allowed a tax deduction for a regular IRA contribution because your AGI exceeds the regular IRA deductibility thresholds. If you find yourself in the fortunate situation that your high income disallows you from funding a Roth IRA, that would be a good reason to contribute to a nondeductible regular IRA (after having maxed out your contributions to other tax-deductible retirement accounts). In that case, if your nondeductible IRA contribution is the only money you have in IRA accounts, consider converting that money into your Roth IRA. Under current tax law (which can change in the future), you are allowed to do this.

Sorry, but you can't contribute $7,000 in the same tax year to both a regular IRA and a Roth IRA; the sum of your standard and Roth IRA contributions may not exceed $7,000 in a given year ($8,000 if you're over age 50).

Penalty-free IRA withdrawals

TIP

Except for a few situations having mostly to do with emergencies, such as a major illness and unemployment, tapping into an IRA account before age 59½ (called an *early withdrawal*) triggers a hefty 10 percent federal income tax penalty (in addition to whatever penalties your state charges). You're allowed to make a penalty-free early withdrawal from your IRA for some specific expenses. First-time homebuyers — defined as not having owned a home in the past two years — may withdraw up to $10,000. Amounts also may be withdrawn for *qualified higher education costs* (college expenses for a family member such as a child, spouse, the IRA holder, or grandchildren).

You can also withdraw up to $5,000 per parent penalty-free from your retirement plan for a "qualified birth or adoption distribution" for the birth or adoption of a child. This new provision waives the normal 10 percent early withdrawal penalty and allows you to repay the withdrawn money as a rollover contribution.

Early withdrawals from regular IRA accounts still are subject to regular income tax in the year of withdrawal. Withdrawals from a Roth IRA (discussed in the section "Understanding the Roth IRA" earlier in this chapter) can be both penalty-free and federal income tax–free as long as the Roth IRA account is at least five years old.

Roth IRA accounts also are exempt from the normal retirement account requirement to begin taking minimum distributions at age 73 if you aren't working.

Annuities

Annuities, like IRAs, allow your capital to grow and compound without taxation. You defer taxes until withdrawal. Annuities carry the same penalties for withdrawal prior to age 59½ as IRAs do. However, unlike all other retirement accounts except a Roth IRA, you aren't forced to begin withdrawals at age 73; you may leave the money in an annuity to compound tax deferred for as many years as you desire.

And, unlike an IRA that has an annual contribution limit, you can deposit as much as you want in any year into an annuity — even $1 million if you have it! As with a so-called nondeductible IRA, you get no upfront tax deduction for your contributions. Thus, consider an annuity only after fully exhausting your other retirement account options.

What exactly is an annuity? Well, *annuities* are peculiar investment products — contracts, actually — that insurance companies back. If you, the annuity holder (investor), die during the so-called accumulation phase (that is, prior to receiving payments from the annuity), your designated beneficiary is guaranteed to receive the amount of your original investment.

TIP

Annuities carry higher fees than IRAs (which reduce your investment returns) because of the insurance that comes with them, so you should first make the maximum contribution that you can to an IRA, even if it isn't tax-deductible. Generally speaking, you should exhaust contributing to Roth accounts as they are superior because investment earnings aren't taxed upon withdrawal. Also, consider annuities only if you plan to leave the money in the annuity for 15 years or more. The reasons are two-fold. First, it typically takes that long for the tax-deferred compounding of your annuity investment to make up for the annuity's relatively higher expenses. Second, upon withdrawal, the earnings on an annuity are taxed at ordinary income tax rates, which are higher than the more favorable long-term capital gains and stock dividend tax rates. If you don't expect to keep your money invested for 15 to 20-plus years to make up for the annuity's higher ongoing fees and taxes on the back end, you should simply invest your money in tax-friendly investments in nonretirement accounts (see Part 3).

Taxing Retirement Account Decisions

In addition to knowing about the different types of retirement accounts available and the importance of using them, I know from my work with counseling clients that you're going to have other problems and questions. This section presents the sticky issues that you may be struggling with, along with my recommendations.

Transferring existing retirement accounts

With employer-maintained retirement plans, such as 401(k)s, you usually have limited investment options. Unless you are the employer or can convince the employer to change, you're stuck with what is offered. If your employer offers four mutual funds from the Lotsa Fees and Lousy Performance Fund Company, for example, you can't transfer this money to another investment company.

After you leave your employer, however, you generally have the option of leaving your money in the employer's plan or transferring it to an IRA at an investment company of your choice. The process of moving this money from an employer plan to investments of your choice is called a *rollover*. And you thought you weren't going to be reading anything fun today!

When you roll money over from an employer-based retirement plan, don't take personal possession of the money. If your employer gives the money to you, the employer must withhold 20 percent of it for taxes. This situation creates a tax nightmare for you because you must then jump through more hoops when you file your return. You also should know that you need to come up with the extra 20 percent when you do the rollover, because you won't get the 20 percent back that your employer withheld in taxes until you file your tax return. If you can't come up with the 20 percent, you have to pay income tax and maybe even excise taxes on this money as a distribution. Yuck!

I understand that some employers don't want the possible risk of issuing checks to myriad investment firms or advisors, especially smaller ones that they've never heard of. As a result, some employers will always issue a retirement plan check to you, mail it to your address on record, and include the investment company information you provide to them on the check. This is considered a direct rollover and as such, the employer won't withhold the 20 percent federal tax.

After you leave the company, you can move your money held in 401(k)s and many 403(b) plans (also known as tax-sheltered annuities) to nearly any major investment firm you please. Moving the money is pretty simple. If you can fill out a couple of short forms on the investment firm website or call to request forms to be sent to you and send them back in a postage-paid envelope, you can transfer an account. The investment firm to which you're transferring your account does the rest. Here's the lowdown on how to transfer retirement accounts without upsetting Uncle Sam or any other tax collector:

1. **Decide to which investment firm you want to move the account.**

   When investing in stocks and bonds, mutual funds are a great way to go. They offer diversification and professional management, and they're low-cost. (For more information on mutual funds, see *Mutual Funds For Dummies* by Eric Tyson [Wiley].)

2. **Visit the website or call the toll-free number of the firm you're transferring the money to and ask for an account application and asset transfer form for the**

type of account you're transferring — for example, SEP-IRA, Keogh, IRA, or 403(b).

The reason for allowing the new investment company to do the transfer for you is that the tax authorities impose huge penalties if you do a transfer incorrectly. Allowing the company to which you're transferring the money to do the transfer for you is far easier and safer. If the company screws up (good investment firms don't), the company is liable.

3. **Complete and mail back the account application and asset transfer forms to your new investment company.**

Completing this paperwork for your new investment firm opens your new account and authorizes the transfer. If you have questions or problems, the firm(s) to which you're transferring your account has armies of capable employees waiting to help you. Remember, these firms know that you're transferring your money to them, so they normally roll out the red carpet.

Transferring your existing assets typically takes a month to complete. If the transfer isn't completed within a month, get in touch with your new investment firm to determine the problem.

If your old company isn't cooperating, a call to a manager there may help to get the ball rolling. The unfortunate reality is that too many investment firms will cheerfully set up a new account to accept your money on a moment's notice, but they will drag their feet, sometimes for months, when it comes time to relinquish your money. If you need to light a fire under their behinds, tell a manager at the old firm that you're sending letters to the National Association of Securities Dealers (NASD) and the Securities and Exchange Commission (SEC) if they don't complete your transfer within the next week.

Taking money out of retirement accounts

Someday, hopefully not until you retire, you'll need or want to start withdrawing and enjoying the money that you socked away in your retirement accounts. Some people, particularly those who are thrifty and good at saving money (also known by some as cheapskates and tightwads), have a hard time doing this.

You saved and invested money in your retirement accounts to use at a future date. Perhaps you're in a pinch for cash and the retirement account looks as tempting as a catered buffet meal after a day of fasting. Whatever the reason, here's what you need to consider before taking the money out of your retirement accounts.

Some people start withdrawing funds from retirement accounts when they retire. This option may or may not be the best financial decision for you. Generally speaking, you're better off postponing drawing on retirement accounts until you need the money. The longer the money resides inside the retirement account, the longer it can compound and grow, tax-deferred. But don't wait if postponing means that you must scrimp and cut corners — especially if you have the money to use and enjoy.

REMEMBER

Suppose that you retire at age 60 and, in addition to money inside your retirement accounts, you have a bunch available outside. If you can, you're better off living off the money outside retirement accounts before you start tapping the retirement account money.

If you aren't wealthy and have saved most of the money earmarked for your retirement inside retirement accounts, odds are you'll need and want to start drawing on your retirement account soon after you retire. By all means, do so. But have you figured out how long your nest egg will last and how much you can afford to withdraw? Most folks haven't. Take the time to figure how much of your money you can afford to draw on per year, even if you think that you have enough.

Few people are wealthy enough to consider simply living off the investment income and never touching the principal, although more than a few people live like paupers so that they can do just that. Many good savers have a hard time spending and enjoying their money in retirement. If you know how much you can safely use, you may be able to loosen the purse strings.

One danger of leaving your money to compound inside your retirement accounts for a long time after you're retired is that the IRS will require you to start making withdrawals the year you reach age 73. It's possible that because of your delay in taking the money out — and the fact that it will have more time to compound and grow — you may need to withdraw a hefty chunk per year. This procedure can push you into higher tax brackets in those years that you're forced to make larger withdrawals.

This forced distribution no longer applies to people who are working for a company, nor does it apply to money held in the newer Roth IRAs (see "Roth IRAs" earlier in this chapter). Self-employed individuals still have to take the distribution.

If you want to plan how to withdraw money from your retirement accounts so that you meet your needs and minimize your taxes, consider hiring a tax advisor to help. If you have a great deal of money in retirement accounts and have the luxury of not needing the money until you're well into retirement, tax planning will likely be worth your time and money.

If you've reached the magic age of 73 and are required to take an IRA distribution but you don't need that additional income and you really don't want to pay any additional tax, you can now direct that your minimum distribution amount (or more if you're feeling generous) be paid directly to a qualified charity of your choice. The distribution qualifies as your annual required distribution, but the payment to charity excludes it from your adjusted gross income or your taxable income.

Understanding early withdrawal penalties

One objection that some people have to contributing to retirement accounts is the early withdrawal penalties. Specifically, if you withdraw funds from retirement accounts before age 59½, you not only have to pay income taxes on withdrawals, but you also pay early withdrawal penalties — 10 percent in federal plus applicable state charges. (There's a 25 percent penalty for withdrawing from a SIMPLE plan within the first two years, which decreases to 10 percent thereafter.)

The penalties are in place for good reason — to discourage people from raiding retirement accounts. Remember, retirement accounts exist for just that reason — saving toward retirement. If you could easily tap these accounts without penalties, the money would be less likely to be there when you need it during retirement.

If you have an emergency, such as catastrophic medical expenses or a disability, you may be able to take early withdrawals from retirement accounts without penalty. You may withdraw funds from particular retirement accounts free of penalties (and, in some cases, even free of current income taxes) for educational expenses or a home purchase. I spell out the specifics in the "Penalty-free IRA withdrawals" section earlier in this chapter.

What if you just run out of money because you lose your job? Although you can't bypass the penalties because of such circumstances, if you're earning so little income that you need to tap your retirement account, you'll surely be in a low tax bracket. So even though you pay some penalties to withdraw retirement account money, the lower income taxes that you pay upon withdrawal — as compared to the taxes that you would have incurred when you earned the money originally — should make up for most or all of the penalty.

Know also that if you get in a financial pinch while you're still employed, some company retirement plans allow you to borrow against a portion of your cash balance. Just be sure that you can repay such a loan — otherwise, your "loan" becomes a withdrawal and triggers income taxes and penalties.

Another strategy to meet a short-term financial emergency is to withdraw money from your IRA and return it within 60 days to avoid paying penalties. I don't generally recommend this maneuver because of the taxes and potential penalties invoked if you don't make the 60-day deadline.

In the event that your only "borrowing" option right now is a credit card with a high interest rate, you should save three to six months' worth of living expenses in an accessible account before funding a retirement account to tide you over in case you lose your income. Money market mutual funds and bank savings accounts are useful vehicles for this purpose.

TIP

You may be interested in knowing that if good fortune comes your way and you accumulate enough funds to retire "early," you have a simple way around the pre-age-59½ early withdrawal penalties. Suppose that at age 55 you retire and want to start living off some of the money you've stashed in retirement accounts. No problem. The U.S. tax laws allow you to start withdrawing money from your retirement accounts free of those nasty early withdrawal penalties. To qualify for this favorable treatment, you must commit to withdrawals for at least five continuous years, and the amount of the withdrawals must be at least the minimum required based on your life expectancy.

Chapter **5**

Children and Taxes

R aising children involves many decisions and trade-offs. New parents are sometimes surprised at the financial and tax consequences of having kids. I include this chapter so that you can spend more time enjoying the first smile, first step, first word, and first high-five, and save on your taxes.

Raising Kids

Although kids can cost a bunch of money, the expenses, or the thousands of diaper changes during the infant years, rarely deter people from wanting a family. And for good reason — kids are wonderful, at least most of the time. They're the future. (If you don't have kids, who do you think is going to fund your Social Security and Medicare benefits during your retirement years?)

Raising a family can be the financial equivalent of doing a triathlon. It can stretch and break the budgets of even those who consider themselves financially well-off and on top of things. Taxes are an important factor in a number of kid-related issues. These sections include my take on some of the important tax issues that you may confront before conception and during the many years you're raising a child.

Getting Junior a Social Security number

In order to claim tax benefits relating to your newborn, you need to get them a Social Security number. You also need a Social Security number for your child whenever you want to establish investment accounts in the child's name (although you may not want to after you understand the drawbacks of doing so, which I discuss later in this chapter).

The IRS requires a Social Security number because people were inventing children — you know, telling the IRS they'd just had twins when the closest they actually came to becoming parents was babysitting their best friend's kid one evening!

If you need Form SS-5, Application for a Social Security Card, simply contact the Social Security Administration (800-772-1213; www.ssa.gov) and ask to have one mailed to you or you can print it out yourself at www.ssa.gov/forms/ss-5.pdf.

Taking advantage of childcare tax goodies

In addition to the extra personal deduction that you can take with each new child and the tax savings that come with that deduction, you also need to be aware of the tax perks (for child-care and related expenditures) that may save you thousands of dollars.

Dependent-care tax credit

TIP

When you hire childcare assistance for your youngster(s), you may be able to claim a tax credit on your annual return (which you claim on Form 2441). To be eligible for this credit, you (and your spouse, if you're married) must work at least part time, unless you're a full-time student or you're disabled. Your kid(s) must be younger than the age of 13 or physically or mentally disabled.

Because a credit is a dollar-for-dollar reduction in the taxes you owe, it can save you hundreds of tax dollars every year. And not only do you count childcare expenses toward calculation of the tax credit, but you may also be able to count the cost of a housekeeper, or even a cook, if the expense benefits your kids. As the name of this credit suggests, expenses can be for taking care of dependents broadly, not just for your children under age 13. Caring for a physically or mentally ill spouse or others, such as an elderly parent, for at least half of the year, counts, too.

The dependent-care tax credit ranges from 20 to 35 percent of qualifying expenses of $3,000 for one qualifying person's expenses with a $6,000 limit for two or more qualifying persons' expenses.

The income threshold at which the credit begins to be reduced increases to $125,000 of adjusted gross income (AGI) and phases out completely at $438,000 of AGI.

As I discuss later in this section, tax and other considerations influence your desire as a parent to work outside the home. Working at least part-time makes you eligible for this tax credit. If you choose to be a full-time mom or dad, unfortunately, you aren't eligible for the dependent-care tax credit.

If your employer offers a dependent-care assistance plan (discussed in the following section), you may be able to reduce your taxes by taking advantage of that benefit rather than the dependent-care tax credit. Your tax credit is reduced or eliminated whenever you use your employer's dependent-care plan spending account.

Dependent-care spending accounts

Increasing numbers of employers offer flexible benefit or spending plans that enable you to choose from among a number of different benefits, such as health, life, and disability insurance; vacation days; and dependent-care expenses.

You can put away money from your paycheck to pay for childcare expenses on a pretax basis. Doing so saves you from paying federal, state, and even Social Security taxes on that money. These flexible benefits plans allow you to put away up to $5,000 or $2,500 if you're married filing separately. However, the exact amount that you can put away depends on the specifics of your employer's plan.

WARNING

Dependent-care spending accounts historically have been a use-it-or-lose-it benefit. If you don't spend the money for childcare expenses during the current tax year, the IRS forces you to forfeit all the unused money at the end of the year. So, be careful not to go overboard by contributing more than you're certain to use.

As I mention in the preceding section, participating in your employer's dependent-care assistance plan reduces your tax credit. You can't do both.

You can also use the dependent-care tax credit and spending accounts that I discuss in this section to pay for the costs of taking care of other dependents, such as an ill or elderly parent. Please see your employer's employee benefits manual for more information.

Child tax credit

In 2024, the maximum Child Tax Credit is $2,000. Also, the refundable portion of the credit is up to $1,700 and will increase over time with inflation.

Adoption tax credit

Recent tax law changes have substantially increased the tax credits to parents who adopt children.

For 2024, the adoption tax credit is for up to $16,810 in qualifying expenses and increases annually with inflation. This credit phases out between the modified adjusted gross income limits of $252,150 to $292,150 in 2024. To claim the credit, you file Form 8839, Qualified Adoption Expenses.

Tabulating the costs and benefits of a second income

One of the most challenging decisions that new parents face is whether to work full time, part time, or not at all. I mean work at a paying job, that is — parenting is the lowest-paid but potentially most rewarding job there is. The need or desire to take paid work is obvious — doing so brings more money home.

In addition to less sleep at night and frequent diaper changes, children mean increased spending. Although you may have less time to shop for yourself, causing your personal spending to decrease, you're likely to spend more on housing, insurance, food, childcare, clothing, and education. And don't forget the host of not-so-incidental incidentals. Toys, art classes, sports, field trips, musical instruments, and the like can rack up big bills, especially if you don't control what you spend on them.

You may rightfully feel that working full time prohibits you from playing as active a role in raising your children as you want. As you consider the additional expenses of raising children, you may also need to factor in a decrease in income.

TIP

Financially speaking, taxes can have a big impact on the value or benefit of working full time, especially for two-income couples. Remember that the tax brackets are set up so that the last dollars of earnings are taxed at a higher rate (refer to Chapter 1).

Deciding whether to work full time by counting the salary that your employer quotes you as the total value of that second income leaves you open to making a potentially big personal and financial mistake. Of course, people enjoy other benefits from working besides income. Be sure, however, to examine taxes and other expenses on that second income to ensure that you're making your financial decision to work based on complete and accurate information.

Navigating Education Tax Breaks and Pitfalls

What, you may ask, do taxes have to do with educational expenses? How you invest to pay for educating your children can have an enormous impact on your family's taxes, your children's ability to qualify for financial aid, and your overall financial well-being.

The (hidden) financial aid tax system

The financial aid system (to which parents apply so that their children are eligible for college scholarships, grants, and loans) treats assets differently when held outside rather than inside retirement accounts. Under the current financial aid system, the value of your retirement plans is *not* considered an asset. Thus, the more of your money you stash in retirement accounts, the greater your chances of qualifying for financial aid and the more money you're generally eligible for.

WARNING

Most new parents don't place their savings in retirement accounts. Many non-wealthy parents make the error of saving and investing money in a separate account for their child (perhaps even in the child's name) or through some other financial product, such as a life insurance policy. Doing so is a mistake because these products are taxed at a much higher level than other savings strategies.

Most important, parents should save and invest in retirement accounts that offer tax benefits. Contributions to a 401(k), 403(b), SEP-IRA, and other retirement accounts (see Chapter 4) usually produce an upfront tax deduction. An additional and substantial benefit is that after the money is placed in these accounts, it grows and compounds without being taxed until you withdraw it.

Therefore, forgoing contributions to your retirement savings plans so you can save money in a taxable account for Junior's college fund doesn't make sense. When you do, you pay higher taxes both on your current income and on the interest and growth of this money. In addition to paying higher taxes, money that you save *outside* retirement accounts, including money in the child's name, is counted as an asset and leads colleges to charge you higher prices (in other words, reduces your child's eligibility for "financial aid"). Thus, you're expected to contribute more (pay higher prices) for your child's educational expenses.

Note: As I discuss later in the chapter, if you're affluent enough that you expect to pay for your kid's entire educational costs, investing through custodial accounts, Education Savings Accounts, and Section 529 college savings plans can save on taxes.

College cost tax deductions

Student loan interest of up to $2,500 annually is deductible on your tax return as an adjustment to income. Thus, anyone who meets the income limitations can claim this deduction as it's not on the list of itemized deductions on Schedule A.

To qualify for this full deduction, your modified adjusted gross income (MAGI) can be up to $80,000 for single taxpayers (and phases out up to $95,000) and for married couples filing jointly, you get a full deduction for up to $165,000 MAGI (it phases out up to $195,000).

The American Opportunity and Lifetime Learning Credits are discussed later in this chapter.

Section 529 plans — state tuition plans

Section 529 plans (named after Internal Revenue Code section 529) come in two basic varieties: prepaid tuition plans and savings plans.

>> In a *prepaid tuition plan,* you buy tuition credits at today's cost, and those credits are used when your qualifying student actually attends college. You forsake all future investment returns on this money in exchange for paying college costs today. Also, you may be quite limited in which schools your child may attend to use the payments.

>> A *529 savings plan* works more like a traditional investment account, investing your education contributions and allowing them to grow, tax-free, until you need that money to pay for qualified post-secondary educational expenses.

A parent or grandparent can put more than $300,000 into one of these plans for each child. You can put up to $90,000 into a child's college savings account immediately, and that counts for the next five years' worth of $18,000 tax-free gifts (actually, a couple can immediately contribute $180,000 per child) allowed under current gifting laws (see Chapter 6). Money contributed to the account isn't considered part of the donor's taxable estate (although if the donor dies before five years are up after gifting

$90,000, a prorated amount of the gift is charged back to the donor's estate).

Section 529 plan investment earnings can be withdrawn tax-free (that's right — completely free of taxation) as long as the withdrawn funds are used to pay for qualifying higher educational costs. In addition to paying college costs (tuition, room and board, or other related expenses), you can use the money in Section 529 plans to pay for graduate school and for the enrollment and attendance expenses of special-needs students.

Some states provide tax benefits on contributions to their state-sanctioned plans, whereas other states induce you to invest at home by taxing profits from out-of-state plans.

Unlike contributing money to a custodial account, with which a child may do as they please when they reach the age of either 18 or 21 (it varies by state), these state tuition plans must be used for higher education expenses. Many plans even allow you to change the beneficiary or take the money back if you change your mind. (If you do withdraw the money, however, you owe tax on the withdrawn earnings, plus a penalty — typically 10 percent.)

A big potential drawback — especially for families hoping for some financial aid — is that college financial aid offices treat assets in these plans as parent's nonretirement assets, which, as discussed earlier in the chapter, can greatly diminish financial aid eligibility.

Another potential drawback is that you have limited choices and control over how the money in state tuition plans is invested. The investment provider(s) for each state plan generally decides how to invest the money over time within given investment options. In most plans, the more years your child is away from college, the more aggressive the investment mix is. As your child approaches college age, the investment mix is tilted more to conservative investments. Most state plans have somewhat high investment management fees, and some plans don't allow transfers to other plans.

Please also be aware that a future Congress can change the tax laws affecting these plans and diminish the tax breaks or increase the penalties for nonqualified withdrawals.

Clearly, there are pros and cons to Section 529 plans. They generally make the most sense for affluent parents (or grandparents) of children who don't expect to qualify for financial aid. Remember, the income accumulated in these plans remains untaxed, provided it's used to pay for qualified educational expenses.

Do a lot of research and homework before investing in any plan. Check out the investment track record, allocations, and fees for each plan, as well as restrictions on transferring to other plans or changing beneficiaries.

TIP

The Secure 2.0 Act, passed into law in late 2022, created a new provision that allows the owner of a 529 account to transfer up to $35,000 in unused education funds to a Roth IRA for the account's beneficiary. Consult a tax professional to ensure all the requirements needed are met.

Education Savings Accounts

You can establish an Education Savings Account (ESA; sometimes referred to as a "Coverdell ESA") for each child and make contributions of up to $2,000 per child per year until the child reaches age 18. Contributions to an ESA, which can be made up until the due date of the income tax return, aren't tax-deductible. However, ESA investment earnings can compound and be withdrawn free of tax as long as the funds are used to pay for college costs. In the year of withdrawal, the American Opportunity and Lifetime Learning Credits may not be claimed for the student, unless you elect to pay income tax on the earnings portion of your withdrawal — see the next section for more about these credits.

Because of their similarities to Section 529 Plan accounts and the fact that they have much lower contribution limits, some financial institutions no longer offer these accounts.

ESA balances can be used for pre-college educational costs (in other words, for schooling costs up through and including grade 12). Eligible educational expenses for primary and secondary students include tuition, fees, books, supplies, computers and other equipment, tutoring, uniforms, extended-day programs, transportation, internet access, and so on, while qualified expenses for college students include only tuition, fees, room, and board, required books and supplies, and special-needs services. (College room and board expenses qualify only if the student carries at least one-half the normal workload.) Contributions to the accounts of special-needs children are permitted past the age of 18, and balances can continue in those accounts past the age of 30.

There are pros and cons to contributing to an ESA, so don't rush out to contribute to these until you've done your homework. Be aware that college financial aid officers treat these accounts as a parent asset, which reduces aid awards. Contributions to or withdrawals from an ESA can also adversely affect your ability to claim other educational tax benefits (American Opportunity and Lifetime Learning credits) and to qualify for the tax benefits on these accounts.

If you're a high-income earner, you may not be eligible to contribute to an ESA. The full $2,000 per child contribution to an ESA may be made only by couples with AGIs less than $190,000 and single taxpayers with AGIs less than $95,000. The $2,000 limit is reduced for married taxpayers with AGIs of more than $190,000 ($95,000 if single) and eliminated if the AGI is more than $220,000 ($110,000 for singles).

If you earn more than these thresholds and want your kids to have ESAs, there's a loophole. Simply have someone else who isn't earning more than the threshold amounts, such as a grandparent, make the ESA contribution on your behalf.

Here are some other ESA rules and regulations that you need to be aware of:

>> The tax-free exclusion of the earnings isn't available on a distribution from the ESA in the same year you claim a American Opportunity or Lifetime Learning Credit.

>> Contributions to the account must be made before the child reaches 18 unless the child is considered special needs, which is defined as "an individual who, because of a physical, mental, or emotional condition (including learning disability), requires additional time to complete his or her education."

>> The money in the account can't be used to invest in a life insurance policy.

>> When the beneficiary reaches age 30, any balance must be distributed to the beneficiary, and that person must include any earnings in their income (unless the account holder is considered special needs). However, prior to reaching 30, the beneficiary may transfer or roll over the balance to another beneficiary who is a member of their family. The distribution must be made within 30 days of the beneficiary's 30th birthday, or within 30 days of their death.

>> Any part of a distribution that must be included in income because it wasn't used to pay college expenses is subject to a 10 percent penalty, unless the distribution is paid as a result of death or disability, or the amount distributed would have been used for educational expenses except for the fact that your student received a scholarship or some other sort of award.

American Opportunity and Lifetime Learning Credits

Tax credits assist some parents with the often-high costs of education. I say "some" because the credits are phased out for higher-income earners. These credits phase out for single tax filers with AGIs between $80,000 and $90,000 and married couples filing jointly with AGIs between $160,000 and $180,000. These phase-out ranges annually increase with inflation.

The first of the two credits — the American Opportunity tax credit — allows up to a $2,500 annual tax credit toward tuition and fees in each of the first four years of higher education. This credit is composed of 100 percent of the first $2,000 of qualified educational expenses you pay for an eligible student and 25 percent of the next $2,000 in qualified educational expenses. Up to 40 percent of this credit ($1,000 per year) is refundable if you don't owe federal income tax.

The second credit — the Lifetime Learning Credit — allows a credit for up to 20 percent of $10,000 in tuition and fee expenses (worth $2,000) per taxpayer. The Lifetime Learning Credit can be used toward undergraduate and graduate education and toward coursework that upgrades job skills.

If you, as a taxpayer, claim either of these credits in a tax year for a particular student, you aren't eligible to withdraw money without taxation from an ESA or a Section 529 plan account for that same student, nor can you take the tuition and fees tax deduction. Also, you can't take the American Opportunity Credit in the same year that you use the Lifetime Learning Credit for the same student; if you have more than one student who qualifies, though, you may be able to take the American Opportunity Credit for one, and the Lifetime Learning Credit for the other(s).

Taxes and paying for college

Socking money away into your tax-sheltered retirement accounts helps you reduce your tax burden and may help your children qualify for more financial aid. However, accessing retirement accounts before age 59½ incurs tax penalties.

TIP

So how do you pay for your children's educational costs? There isn't one correct answer, because the decision depends on your overall financial situation. Here are some ideas that can help you meet expected educational expenses and minimize your taxes:

» **Don't try to do it all yourself.** Unless you're affluent, don't even try to pay for the full cost of a college education for your children. Few people can afford it. You and your children will, in all likelihood, have to borrow some money.

» **Consider the increasing numbers of faster and lower-cost alternatives to college.** College isn't the right choice for everyone. For starters, the high price can make a traditional four-year college education prohibitively expensive for many families. Also, college simply isn't the only pathway to a rewarding career. Not only are there plenty of well-paying jobs that don't require a four-year degree, but lower-cost alternatives to the four-year degree are also growing fast. It pays to investigate the alternatives and consider all of your child's options before making an informed choice. You can potentially save lots of money and find a great fit that's better for your child and your personal finances.

Some of the programs available today have been around for generations while others are new and emerging. These include last-mile programs/"boot camps," apprenticeships, staffing firms, vocational and trade schools, and college cooperative educational experiences.

>> **Apply for aid, regardless of your financial circumstances.** A number of loan programs, such as Unsubsidized Stafford Loans and Parent Loans for Undergraduate Students (PLUS), are available even if your family isn't deemed financially needy. Only Subsidized Stafford Loans, on which the federal government pays the interest that accumulates while the student is still in school, are limited to those students deemed financially needy.

In addition to loans, a number of grant programs are available through schools, the government, and independent sources. Specific colleges and other private organizations (including employers, banks, credit unions, and community groups) also offer grants and scholarships. Some of these have nothing to do with financial need.

>> **Save in your name, not in your children's.** If you've exhausted your retirement account contributions, saving money that you're earmarking to pay for college is okay. Just do it in your name. If your children's grandparents want to make a gift of money to them for college expenses, keep the money in your name; otherwise, have the grandparents keep the money until the kids are ready to enter college.

>> **Get your kids to work.** Your child can work and save money to pay for college costs during junior high, high school, and college. In fact, if your child qualifies for financial aid, they're expected to contribute a certain amount to their educational costs from money earned from jobs held during the school year or summer breaks and from their own savings. Besides giving the student a stake in their own future, this training encourages sound personal financial management down the road.

>> **Borrow against your home equity.** If you're a homeowner, you can borrow against the equity (market value less the outstanding mortgage loan) in your property. Doing so is usually wise because you can borrow against

your home at a reasonable interest rate, and the interest is generally tax-deductible. Be careful to borrow an amount you can afford to repay and that won't cause you to default on your loan and lose your home. *Mortgages For Dummies*, which I co-wrote with Robert Griswold (Wiley), can help you with such borrowing decisions.

>> **Borrow against your company retirement plans.** Many retirement savings plans, such as 401(k)s, allow borrowing. Just make sure that you're able to pay back the money. Otherwise, you'll owe big taxes for a premature distribution.

REMEMBER

The growing "alternatives" trend to costly four-year colleges is good for you, the consumer. Competition for your time and dollars is slowly spurring some positive changes at colleges and universities, as it should. Colleges should earn your business and not get it by default. Traditional colleges and universities are not the only pathways to success. Keep an open mind about the alternatives available to your child because they too can lead to career satisfaction and a bright future. For more information, please see my book, *Paying For College For Dummies* (Wiley).

Being Aware of Taxes on Your Kids' Investments

Parents of all different financial means need to be aware of the financial aid implications of putting money into an account bearing a child's name. Read the section "Navigating Education Tax Breaks and Pitfalls" earlier in this chapter before investing money in your children's names.

Taxes for kids under 18 and dependent college students

For tax year 2024, if a child is under 18 (or 24 if a full-time student), the so-called kiddie tax applies: The first $1,300 of *unearned income* (income from interest and dividends on investments) that a child earns isn't taxed at all. It's tax-free! In contrast, *earned income* is considered income earned from work.

The next $1,300 of unearned income for this age set is taxed at the child's tax rate. Everything higher than $2,600 is taxed at the parents' income tax rate. The system is set up in this fashion to discourage parents from transferring a lot of assets into their children's names, hoping to pay lower taxes.

WARNING

Because the first $2,600 of unearned income for the child is taxed at such a low rate, some parents are tempted to transfer money into the child's name to save on income taxes. Quite a number of financial books and advisors recommend this strategy. Consider this passage referring to transferring money to your children, from a tax book written by a large accounting firm: "Take advantage of these rules. It still makes sense to shift some income-producing assets to younger children."

This is potentially very wrong for plenty of parents! As I discuss in "The (hidden) financial aid tax system" earlier in this chapter, this shortsighted desire to save a little in taxes today can lead to your losing out on significant financial aid later. And what about your limited discretionary income? You don't want to put money in your child's name if it means that you aren't fully taking advantage of your retirement accounts.

Consider putting money into an account bearing your child's name only if

>> You expect to pay for the full cost of a college education and won't apply for or use any financial aid, including loans that aren't based on financial need.

>> You're comfortable with the notion that your child will have legal access to the money at age 18 or 21 (depending on the state in which you live) if the money is in a custodial account in the child's name. At that age, the money is legally your child's, and they can blow it on something other than a college education.

After all the caveats and warnings, if you're still thinking about putting money into an account bearing your child's name, consider buying tax-friendly investments that won't generate more than $2,600 annually in unearned income. (See Chapter 7 for tax-friendly investment ideas.)

You also can buy investments in your name and then transfer them to your child when they are an adult. (Each parent is limited to giving $18,000 to each child per year before they have to start worrying about preparing and filing a gift tax return.) That way, if the investment declines in value, you can take the tax loss; if the investment turns a profit, you can save on your taxes by transferring the investment to your grown child. This strategy won't work to save on income taxes if your kid enjoys early career success and is in a higher tax bracket than you are!

Tax-wise and not-so-wise investments for educational funds

You hear many sales pitches for "tax-wise" investments to use for college savings. Most aren't worthy of your consideration. Here's my take on the best, the mediocre, and the worst.

Invest in mutual funds and exchange-traded funds

Mutual funds, which offer investors of all financial means instant diversification and low-cost access to the nation's best money managers, and their close cousin, exchange-traded funds, are ideal investments when you're saving money for educational expenses. See Chapter 7 for a discussion of the tax-wise ways to invest in funds.

Think twice about Treasury bonds

Many tax and financial books recommend investing college funds in Treasury bonds issued by the federal government. I'm not enthusiastic about some of these. Zero-coupon Treasuries are particular tax headaches. They are sold at a discount of their value at maturity instead of paying you interest each year. Guess what? You still have to report the effective interest you're earning each year on your tax return. And just to give you a headache or pad your tax preparer's bill, you or your preparer have to calculate this implicit interest. Yuck!

Don't bother with cash-value life insurance

WARNING

Life insurance policies that have cash values are some of the most oversold investments to fund college costs. The usual pitch is this: Because you need life insurance to protect your family, why not buy a policy that you can borrow against to pay for college? Makes sense, doesn't it? Insurance agents also emphasize that the cash value in the policy is growing without taxation over time. Although this part of their sales pitch is true, you have better alternatives.

The reason you shouldn't buy a cash-value life insurance policy is that, as I discuss earlier in this chapter, you're better off contributing to retirement accounts. These investments give you an immediate tax deduction that you don't receive when you save through life insurance. Because life insurance that comes with a cash value is more expensive, parents are more likely to make a second mistake — not buying enough life insurance coverage. When you need life insurance, you're better off buying lower-cost term life insurance.

Make sure your money grows

An investment that fails to keep you ahead of inflation, such as a savings or money market account, is another poor investment for college expenses. The interest on these accounts is also taxable, which doesn't make sense for many working parents. You need your money to grow so you can afford educational costs down the road.

IN THIS CHAPTER

» Arriving at the ultimate and final insult — taxes for dying?!?

» Reviewing strategies for reducing estate taxes

» Using trusts, wills, and more trusts

» Finding help if you need it

Chapter **6**

Reducing Estate Taxes

Among the dreariest of tax and financial topics is the issue of what happens to your money when you die. Depending on how your finances are structured and when you pass on, you (actually, your estate) may get stuck paying estate taxes when you die. These taxes may be assessed at the federal level but also by some states. (Other states levy an inheritance tax.)

Unfortunately, you can't predict when the grim reaper will pay a visit. That doesn't mean, however, that we all need to participate in complicated estate planning. On the contrary, if your assets are modest, some simple moves may be all you need.

Estate planning takes time and money, which are precious commodities for most people. Whether spending your time and money on estate planning is worthwhile depends on your personal and financial circumstances, both now and in the near future. In this chapter, I offer the information you need to figure out whether estate planning is for you and how the decisions you make can impact your tax situation.

Figuring Whether You May Owe Estate Taxes

With all the warnings about the enormous estate taxes that you may owe upon your death, you may think that owing estate taxes is a common problem. It isn't, but that hasn't stopped some insurance agents, attorneys, and estate-planning "specialists" from using scare tactics to attract prospective clients, often by luring them to free estate-planning seminars. What better way to find people with money to invest! Very few folks are subject to federal estate taxes, at least given the current rules. Some states, however, have far lower thresholds at which their estate tax or inheritance tax kicks in. And, I must remind you that any and all of these rules can change in the future. Recent decades clearly show that the rules will keep changing and evolving.

Understanding the federal estate tax exemption and rate

In tax year 2024, upon death, an individual can pass $13.61 million to beneficiaries without paying federal estate taxes. On the other hand, a couple, if they have their assets, wills, and trusts properly structured, can pass $27.22 million to beneficiaries without paying federal estate taxes. (See "Establishing a bypass trust" later in this chapter for more info.) Because most people still are trying to accumulate enough money to retire or take a trip around the world someday, most folks typically don't have this problem and have this much money around when they die.

Under current tax law, if your estate totals more than $13.61 million at your death, you may owe federal estate taxes. The top federal estate tax rate for 2024 is a hefty 40 percent.

I can't and don't want to predict future tax laws. Ultimately, what happens with future changes in the estate tax laws will be driven by the composition of Congress and which party holds the presidency and controls Congress. I discuss a variety of estate tax–reduction strategies later in this chapter, but first let's talk about estate and inheritance taxes at the state level and then discuss how the IRS figures your taxable estate.

State estate and inheritance taxes

States also can levy additional *estate* (levied on the estate) and *inheritance* (charged to the recipient) taxes. With the elimination in 2005 of the provision that allowed states to share in federal estate taxes collected, more states imposed their own estate or inheritance tax or chose to calculate the tax due to the state on the basis of the share of federal estate taxes they would have received under prior federal law.

While the federal estate tax threshold impacts very few people currently, far more people get hit at the state level by state estate and inheritance taxes. A dozen states and the District of Columbia levy estate taxes while six impose inheritance taxes. Maryland holds a unique distinction as it is the only state to impose both an estate and inheritance tax. See Figure 6-1 for a map of state estate and inheritance taxes.

FIGURE 6-1: State estate and inheritance taxes.

Tax Foundation / https://taxfoundation.org/data/all/state/state-estate-tax-inheritance-tax-2022/ last accessed March 05, 2024.

As you can see from the map, many of the states with their own estate taxes have those taxes kick in at far lower levels of net worth than does the federal estate tax. For example, Oregon has an exemption level of just $1 million and Massachusetts is just $2 million. And some of the state estate tax rates are quite high — the peak rate of the District of Columbia, Illinois, Minnesota, New York, and Massachusetts is 16 percent, while Hawaii and Washington state have a 20 percent peak rate. Numerous states with inheritance taxes have rates that top out well above 10 percent.

Determining your taxable federal estate

Unless you already possess great wealth or die prematurely, whether your assets face estate taxes depends on the amount of your assets that you use up during your retirement. How much of your assets you use up depends on how your assets grow over time and how rapidly you spend money.

To calculate the value of your estate upon your death, the IRS totals up your assets and subtracts your liabilities. Assets include your personal property, home and other real estate, savings and investments (such as bank accounts, stocks, bonds, and mutual funds held inside and outside of retirement accounts), and life insurance death benefits (unless properly placed in a trust, as I describe later in this chapter). Your liabilities include any out-standing loans (such as a mortgage), bills owed at the time of your death, legal and other expenses to handle your estate, and funeral expenses.

If you're married at the time of your death, all assets that you leave to your spouse are excluded from estate taxes, thanks to the unlimited marital deduction (which I discuss later in this chapter). The IRS also deducts any charitable contributions or bequests that you dictate in your will from your assets before calculating your taxable estate.

Reducing Expected Estate Taxes

WARNING

You have your work cut out for you as you try to educate yourself about estate planning. You can find many attorneys and non-attorneys selling estate-planning services, and you can encounter many insurance agents hawking life insurance. All are pleased to sell you their services.

The good news is that most people don't need to do complicated estate planning with high-cost attorneys. I give you the straight scoop on what, if anything, you need to be concerned with now and at other junctures in your life, and I tell you the conflicts of interest that these "experts" have in rendering advice.

Thanks to all the changes in the tax laws and the thousands of attorneys and tax advisors working to find new ways around paying estate taxes, numerous strategies exist to reduce estate taxes — including taking up residence in a foreign country! I start with the simpler stuff and work toward the more complex.

Giving it away

Upon your passing, your money has to go somewhere. By directing some of your money to people and organizations now, you can pass on far more because you'll be saving the portion that would have gone to estate and inheritance taxes, both at the state and federal levels. Plus, while you're alive, you can experience the satisfaction of seeing the good that your money can do.

Current tax law allows you to give up to $18,000 per individual each year to as many people — such as your children, grandchildren, or best friends — as you desire without any gift tax consequences or tax forms required. If you're married, your spouse can do the same. The benefit of giving is that it removes the money from your estate and therefore reduces your estate taxes. Even better is the fact that all future appreciation and income on the gifted money also is removed from your estate because the money now belongs to the gift recipient. (The current annual tax-free gifting limit of $18,000 per recipient will increase in future years with inflation.)

You can use gifting to remove a substantial portion of your assets from your estate over time. Suppose that you have three children. You and your spouse each can give each of your children $18,000 per year for a total gift of $108,000 per year. If your kids are married, you can make additional $18,000 gifts to their spouses for another $108,000 per year. You also can gift an unlimited amount to pay for current educational tuition costs and medical expenses. Just be sure to make the payment directly to the institution charging the fees.

Yet another tax — the *generation-skipping transfer tax* — can be assessed on a gift above the $18,000 annual limit per recipient. This tax applies if the gift giver is a grandparent making a gift to a grandchild (and the grandparent's son or daughter is still alive) or in the case of a gift made to an unrelated individual who is more than 37½ years younger. Seek the advice of a qualified tax advisor if this tax may apply.

TIP

You have options in terms of what money or assets you give to others. Start with cash or assets that haven't appreciated since you purchased them. If you want to transfer an asset that has lost value, consider selling it first; then you can claim the tax loss on your tax return and transfer the cash.

Rather than giving away assets that have appreciated greatly in value, consider holding onto them. If you hold such assets until your death, your heirs receive what is called a stepped-up basis. That is, the IRS assumes that the effective price your heirs "paid" for an asset is the value on your date of death — which wipes out the capital gains tax that otherwise is owed when selling an asset that has appreciated in value. (Donating appreciated assets to your favorite charity can make sense because you get the tax deduction for the appreciated value and avoid realizing the taxable capital gain.)

A more complicated way to give money to your heirs without giving them absolute control over the money is to set up a Crummey Trust (named after the first man to gain approval to use this type of trust). Although the beneficiary has a short window of time (a month or two) to withdraw money that's contributed to the trust, you can verbally make clear to the beneficiary that, in your opinion, leaving the money in the trust is in their best interest. You also can specify in the trust document itself that the trust money be used for particular purposes, such as tuition. Some of the other trusts I discuss later in the "Setting up trusts" section may meet your needs if you want more control over the money you intend to pass to your heirs.

MAKING GIFTS GREATER THAN $18,000 PER YEAR

You can make gifts of greater than $18,000 per year to an individual; however, you have to prepare and file Form 709, United States Gift (and Generation-Skipping Transfer) Tax Return. Chances are good that you won't have to pay any tax on the transfer, but when giving gifts that large, the IRS does want to have a record.

You're allowed to make gifts larger than $18,000 per year to pay for another person's tuition or medical expenses without filing a Form 709. If you decide you want to pay your beloved niece's tuition to her pricey private college (how nice of you), just make sure that you write the check directly to the school. Please be aware, however, of the impact that such payments will have on the price (and therefore "financial aid") that that college will provide that student. Likewise, in the case of paying someone else's medical expenses, send your check directly to the medical care provider or institution.

If you make a large gift of cash or property to charity, and you otherwise aren't required to file Form 709, you don't need to report this gift, even if its value is in excess of $18,000, provided that you gave up all interest in the property you transferred. Don't forget to include your gift on Schedule A of your Form 1040 — even though the property you're gifting may not be part of this year's income, you're still entitled to an income tax deduction.

Gifts to political organizations aren't really gifts at all. If you're so inclined and make large payments to political organizations, you don't trigger a requirement to file a Form 709, even if your gift is greater than $18,000. What a deal!

Leaving all your assets to your spouse

Tax laws wouldn't be tax laws without exceptions and loopholes. Here's another one: If you're married at the time of your death, any and all assets that you leave to your spouse are exempt from estate taxes normally due upon your death. In fact, you may leave an unlimited amount of money to your spouse, hence the name *unlimited marital deduction*. Assets that count are those willed to your spouse or for which your spouse is named as beneficiary (such as retirement accounts).

WARNING

Although leaving all your assets to your spouse is a tempting estate-planning strategy for married couples, this "short-term" strategy can backfire. The surviving spouse may end up with an estate tax problem, especially at the state level, upon their death because they will have all the couple's assets. (See the following section for a legal way around this issue, appropriately called a bypass trust.) You face three other less likely but potential problems:

>> You and your spouse may die simultaneously.

>> The unlimited marital deduction isn't allowed if your spouse isn't a U.S. citizen.

>> Some states don't allow the unlimited marital deduction, so be sure to find out about the situation in your state.

Establishing a bypass trust

A potential estate tax problem is created upon the death of a spouse if all the deceased's assets pass to the surviving spouse. When the surviving spouse dies, $13.61 million (for tax year 2024) can be passed on free of federal estate taxes.

If you have substantial assets, both you and your spouse can take advantage of the $13.61 million estate tax–free rule and pass to your heirs a total of $27.22 million estate tax–free. Each of you can, through instructions in your will, direct assets to be placed into a *bypass trust* (also known as credit shelter or exemption equivalent). Please keep in mind that even if you don't have this kind of money, you may well live in a state with a much lower estate tax threshold so you may benefit from a similar trust at that level.

Upon the first death, assets belonging to the deceased spouse equal in value to the amount that can be passed tax-free (the exemption amount) go into a trust. The surviving spouse and/or other heirs still can use the income earned from those assets and even some of the principal. Depending on how the trust is written, they may be able to withdraw a small percentage of the value of the trust or up to a particular dollar amount, whichever is greater, each year. They also can draw additional principal if they need it for educational, health, or living expenses. Ultimately, the assets in the bypass trust pass to the designated beneficiaries (usually, but not limited to, children).

TIP

For a bypass trust to work, you likely will need to rework how you hold ownership of your assets (for example, jointly or individually). You may need to individually title your assets so that each spouse holds some portion of the total assets and so that each can take full advantage of the estate tax–free limit for your state and at the federal level if your net worth is substantial enough. My attorney friends tell me that you need to be careful when setting up a bypass trust so that it's funded up to the full amount of the current federal tax–free exemption amount. The reason: The surviving spouse may otherwise end up with less than what would've been desired. Be sure to read the section "Getting advice and help," later in this chapter, for how to obtain good legal and tax advice.

Buying cash-value life insurance

Two major types of life insurance exist. Most people who need life insurance — and who have someone dependent on their income — should buy *term life insurance,* which is pure life insurance: You pay an annual premium for which you receive a predetermined amount of life insurance protection. If the insured person passes away, the beneficiaries collect; otherwise, the premium is gone but the insured is grateful! In this way, term life insurance is similar to auto or homeowner's insurance.

The other kind of life insurance, called *cash-value life insurance*, is probably one of the most oversold financial products in the history of Western civilization. With cash-value policies (whole, universal, variable, and so on), your premiums not only pay for life insurance, but some of your dollars also are credited to an account that grows in value over time, assuming that you keep paying your premiums. On the surface, a cash-value life policy sounds potentially attractive.

When bought and placed in an irrevocable life insurance trust (which I discuss later in this chapter in the section "Setting up trusts"), life insurance, it's true, receives special treatment with regard to estate taxes. Specifically, the death benefit or proceeds paid on the policy upon your death can pass to your designated heirs free of estate taxes. (Some states, however, don't allow this.)

People who sell cash-value insurance — that is, insurance salespeople and other life insurance brokers masquerading as estate-planning specialists and financial planners — too often advocate life insurance as the best, and only, way to reduce estate taxes. But the other methods I discuss in this chapter are superior in most cases.

WARNING

Insurance companies aren't stupid. In fact, they're quite smart. If you purchase a cash-value life insurance policy that provides a death benefit of, say, $1 million, you have to pay substantial insurance premiums, although far less than $1 million. Is that a good deal for you? No, because the insurance company invests your premium dollars and earns a return the same way as you otherwise could have, had you invested the money instead of using it to buy the life insurance.

Through the years, between the premiums you pay on your life policy and the returns the insurance company earns investing your premiums, the insurance company is able to come up with more than $1 million. Otherwise, how can it afford to pay out a death benefit of $1 million on your policy?

TIP

Using life insurance as an estate-planning tool may be beneficial if your estate includes assets that you don't want to subject to a forced sale to pay estate taxes (either at the state or federal level) after you die. For example, small-business owners whose businesses are worth millions may want to consider cash-value life insurance under special circumstances. If your estate will lack the other necessary assets to pay expected estate taxes and you don't want your beneficiaries to be forced to sell the business, you can buy life insurance to pay expected estate taxes.

For advice on whether life insurance is an appropriate estate-planning strategy for you, don't expect to get objective information from anyone who sells life insurance. Please see the section "Getting advice and help" later in this chapter.

Setting up trusts

If estate planning hasn't already given you a headache, understanding the different types of trusts can. A *trust* is a legal device used to pass to someone else the management responsibility and, ultimately, the ownership of some of your assets. I discuss some trusts, such as bypass, Crummey, and life insurance trusts, earlier in this chapter; in this section, I talk about other trusts you may hear about when planning your estate.

Living trusts

A *living trust* effectively transfers assets into a trust. When you use a *revocable living trust,* you control those assets and can revoke the trust whenever you desire. The advantage of a living trust is that upon your death, assets can pass directly to your beneficiaries without going through probate, the legal process for administering and implementing the directions in a will.

Living trusts keep your assets out of probate but, in and of themselves, do nothing to help you deal with estate taxes. Living trusts can contain bypass trusts and other estate tax–saving provisions.

Property and assets that are owned by *joint tenants with a right of survivorship* (owned by two or more individuals, with the deceased owner's share passing upon death to the surviving owner[s]) or inside retirement accounts, such as IRAs or 401(k)s, that have designated beneficiaries generally pass to heirs without going through probate.

ESTATE PLANNING FROM THE GRAVE

It goes without saying that not everyone does the right type of estate planning before passing on. Some people die before their time, and others just can't seem to get around to the planning part, even when they're in failing health.

Although further planning after you're passing is impossible, your heirs may legally take steps that can, in some cases, dramatically reduce estate taxes. Some legal folks call these steps postmortem planning. Here's an example of how it works.

Suppose that Peter Procrastinator never got around to planning for the distribution of his substantial estate. When he died, all of his estate was to go to his wife. No dummy, his wife hired legal help so that she can disclaim, or reject, part of Peter's big estate. Why would she do that? Simple, so that part of the estate can immediately go to their children. If she hadn't disclaimed, Peter would have missed out on his state's estate tax exclusion. By disclaiming, she possibly saved her heirs substantially on estate taxes.

The person doing the disclaiming, in this case, Peter's wife, may not direct to whom the disclaimed assets will go. Peter's will or other legal documents specify who is second in line. Disclaimers are also irrevocable, must be made in writing, and are subject to other IRS rules and regulations. A knowledgeable executor and attorney can help you with disclaiming.

Many states also allow a special type of revocable trust for bank accounts called a *Totten trust*, sometimes also referred to as a payable-on-death or POD account, which also insulates the bank accounts from probate. Such trusts are established for the benefit of another person, and the money in the trust is paid to that beneficiary upon the account holder's death.

Probate can be a lengthy, expensive hassle for your heirs. Attorney probate fees may approach 5 percent to 7 percent of the estate's value. In addition, the details of your assets become public record because of probate. Properly drafted and funded, a living trust can save on probate fees and maintain your financial privacy. This trust is also useful in naming someone to administer your affairs in the event you become incapacitated.

TIP

You can't escape the undertaker or the lawyers. Setting up a trust and transferring property in and out costs money and time. Thus, living trusts are likely to be of greatest value to people who are age 60 and older, are single, and own assets worth more than $100,000 that must pass through probate (including real estate, nonretirement accounts, and businesses). Small estates are often less expensive to probate in some states than the cost and hassle of setting up a living trust. (The key is to maintain an *independent administration*, which is when the probate court trusts the executor to make most of the decisions without the court's supervision.)

Charitable trusts

If you're feeling philanthropic, charitable trusts may be for you. With a *charitable remainder trust,* you or your designated beneficiary receives income from assets that you donate to a charity.

At the time you fund a charitable remainder trust, you'll also be entitled to a current charitable deduction on Schedule A, calculated on a complicated formula that includes reference to life expectancies and the present value of the gift. Although not inexpensive to set up or to administer, a charitable remainder trust makes especially good sense in cases where a person holds an asset that they want to donate that has greatly appreciated in value. By not selling the asset before the donation, a hefty tax on the profit is avoided.

In a *charitable lead trust,* the roles of the charity and beneficiaries are reversed. The charity receives the income from the assets for a set number of years or until you pass away, at which point the assets pass to your beneficiary. You get a current income tax deduction for the value of the expected payments to the charity.

Getting advice and help

The number of people who will happily charge you a fee for or sell you some legal advice or insurance far exceeds the number actually qualified to render objective estate-planning advice. Attorneys, accountants, financial planners, estate-planning specialists, investment companies, insurance agents, and even some nonprofit agencies stand ready to help you figure out how to dispense your wealth.

WARNING

Most of these people and organizations have conflicts of interest and lack the knowledge necessary to do sound estate planning for you. Attorneys are biased toward drafting legal documents and devices that are more complicated than may be needed. Insurance agents and financial planners who work on commission try to sell cash-value life insurance. Investment firms and banks encourage you to establish a trust account that requires them to manage the assets in the future. Although the cost of free estate-planning seminars is tempting, you get what you pay for — or worse.

For professional advice, you need someone who can look objectively at the big picture. Attorneys and tax advisors who specialize in estate planning are a good starting point. Ask the people you're thinking of hiring whether they sell life insurance or manage money. If they do, they can't possibly be objective and likely aren't sufficiently educated about estate planning, given their focus.

If you want to do more reading on estate planning, pick up a copy of *Plan Your Estate* by attorney Denis Clifford (Nolo Press). When you have a large estate that may be subject to estate taxes, consulting an attorney or tax advisor who specializes in estate planning may be worth your time and money. Get smarter first and figure out the lingo before you seek and pay for advice.

3

Your Investments and Taxes

Minimize your income tax bill when investing.

Understand how each investment type is taxed.

Reap the benefits of investing in tax-efficient funds.

IN THIS CHAPTER

» Understanding tax-friendly investment strategies

» Knowing which tax-favored investments are best

» Deciding what investments to sell when and how

» Understanding special tax issues with mutual funds and stock options

» Reducing taxes in non-retirement accounts

Chapter **7**

Minimizing Your Taxes When Investing

W hen you have money to invest, or you're considering selling investments that you hold outside a retirement account, taxes should be an important factor in your decisions. But tax considerations alone should not dictate how and where you invest your money and when you sell. You also need to weigh issues such as your desire (and the necessity) to take risks, your personal likes and dislikes, and the number of years you plan to hold on to the investment.

Other chapters in this part of the book cover tax matters for investing in real estate or small businesses, investing for your children's future, and protecting your assets from estate taxes.

In this chapter, I focus on tax issues relating to investing in mutual funds, exchange-traded funds, stocks, bonds, and other securities.

Taming Your Taxes in Non-Retirement Accounts

When you invest outside of tax-sheltered retirement accounts, the distributions on your money (for example, dividends) and realized gains when you sell are subject to taxation. So the non-retirement account investments that make sense for you depend (at least partly) on your tax situation.

REMEMBER

If you have money to invest, or if you're considering selling current investments that you hold, taxes should factor into your decision. But tax considerations alone shouldn't dictate how and where you invest your money. You should also weigh investment choices, your desire and the necessity to take risk, personal likes and dislikes, and the number of years you plan to hold the investment.

Knowing what's taxed and when to worry

Interest you receive from bank accounts and corporate bonds is generally taxable. U.S. Treasury bonds pay interest that's state-tax-free. Municipal bonds, which state and local governments issue, pay interest that's federal-tax-free and also state-tax-free to residents in the state where the bond is issued. (I discuss bonds in Chapter 8.)

Taxation on your *capital gains*, which is the *profit* (sales minus purchase price) on an investment, works under a unique system. Investments held less than one year generate *short-term capital gains*, which are taxed at your normal marginal rate. Profits from investments that you hold longer than 12 months are *long-term capital gains*. These long-term gains cap at 20 percent, which is the rate that applies for those in the highest federal income tax brackets. This 20 percent long-term capital gains tax rate actually kicks in (for tax year 2024) at $518,900 of taxable income for single taxpayers and at $583,750 for married couples filing jointly. The long-term capital gains tax rate is just 15 percent for everyone else, except for single taxpayers with taxable income up to $47,025 and married couples filing jointly with taxable income up to $94,050. For these folks, the long-term capital gains tax rate is 0 percent.

To help pay for the Affordable Care Act (Obamacare), taxpayers with total taxable income above $200,000 (single return) or $250,000 (joint return) from any source are also subject to a 3.8 percent extra tax on the lesser of the following:

>> Their net investment income, such as interest, dividends, and capital gains; net investment income excludes distributions from qualified retirement plans

>> The amount, if any, by which their modified adjusted gross income (MAGI) exceeds the dollar thresholds; MAGI is adjusted gross income plus any tax-exempt interest income

Devising tax-reduction strategies

Use these strategies to reduce the taxes you pay on investments that are exposed to taxation:

>> **Make use of retirement accounts and health savings accounts.** Most contributions to retirement accounts gain you an immediate tax break, and once they're inside the account, investment returns are sheltered from taxation, generally until withdrawal. Think of these as tax reduction accounts that can help you work toward achieving financial independence. See Chapter 4 for details on using retirement accounts when investing.

Similar to retirement accounts are health savings accounts (HSAs). With HSAs, you get a tax break on your contributions upfront; investment earnings compound without taxation over time; and there's no tax on withdrawal so long as the money is used to pay for health-related expenses (which enjoy a fairly broad list as delineated by the IRS).

>> **Consider tax-free money market funds and tax-free bond funds.** Tax-free investments yield less than comparable investments that produce taxable earnings, but because of the tax differences, the earnings from tax-free investments can end up being greater than what taxable investments leave you with. If you're in a high-enough tax bracket, you may find that you come out ahead with tax-free investments.

For a proper comparison, subtract what you'll pay in federal and state income taxes from the taxable investment income to see which investment nets you more.

>> **Invest in tax-friendly stock funds.** Mutual funds and exchange-traded funds that tend to trade less tend to produce lower capital gains distributions. For funds held outside tax-sheltered retirement accounts, this reduced trading effectively increases an investor's total rate of return. *Index funds* invest in a relatively static portfolio of securities, such as stocks and bonds. They don't attempt to beat the market; rather, they invest in the securities to mirror or match the performance of an underlying index. Although index funds can't beat the market, the typical actively managed fund usually doesn't either, and index funds have several advantages over actively managed funds. See Chapter 9 to find out more about tax-friendly stock mutual funds, including some non-index funds and exchange-traded funds.

>> **Invest in small business and real estate.** The growth in value of business and real estate assets isn't taxed until you sell the asset. Even then, with investment real estate, you often can roll over the gain into another property as long as you comply with tax laws. Increases in value in small businesses can qualify for the more favorable longer-term capital gains tax rate and potentially for other tax breaks. However, the current income that small business and real estate assets produce is taxed as ordinary income.

Short-term capital gains (investments held one year or less) are taxed at your ordinary income tax rate. This fact is another reason why you shouldn't trade your investments quickly (within 12 months).

Tapping into Tax-Reducing Investment Techniques

For investments that you hold inside *tax-sheltered* retirement accounts such as IRAs and 401(k) plans (see Chapter 4), you don't need to worry about taxes. This money isn't generally taxed until you actually withdraw funds from the retirement account. Thus, you should never invest money that's inside retirement accounts in other tax-favored investments, such as tax-free money market funds and tax-free bonds (discussed later in this chapter).

WARNING

You're far more likely to make tax-related mistakes investing *outside* of retirement accounts. Consider the many types of distributions produced by nonretirement account investments that are subject to taxation:

>> **Interest:** Bank accounts, for example, pay you interest that is fully taxable, generally at both the federal and state levels. Bonds (IOUs) issued by corporations also pay interest that is fully taxable. Bonds issued by the federal government, which are known as *Treasury bonds,* pay interest that is federally taxable.

>> **Dividends:** Many companies distribute some of their profits to shareholders of stock (shares of company ownership) as dividends. Lower tax rates apply to stock dividends than ordinary income (see Table 7-1).

>> **Capital gains:** The profit from the sale of an investment at a price higher than the purchase price is known as a *capital gain.* Capital gains generally are federally and state taxable. Lower tax rates apply to capital gains for investments held for the long term (see Table 7-1 and the next section).

Ordinary income tax brackets top out at 37 percent versus the top rate of 20 percent on stock dividends and long-term capital gains. Obamacare added a 3.8 percent additional tax on investment income on top of the percentages shown in Table 7-1 for higher-income earners (single taxpayers with adjusted gross incomes over $200,000 and married couples filing jointly with adjusted gross incomes over $250,000). So the top tax rate on stock dividends and long-term capital gains is actually 23.8 percent.

TABLE 7-1 **Federal Tax Rate (2024) on Stock Dividends and Long-Term Capital Gains**

2024 Tax Rate	Single Taxpayers Taxable Income	Married Couples Filing Jointly Taxable Income
0%	Up to $47,025	Up to $94,050
15%	$47,025 to $518,900	$94,050 to $583,750
20%	$518,900 or more	$583,750 or more

The following sections detail specific strategies for minimizing your taxes and maximizing your after-tax returns — that is, the return you actually get to keep after payment of required taxes.

Buy and hold for "long-term" capital gains

A *long-term* capital gain, which is the *profit* (sales proceeds minus purchase price) on an investment (such as a stock, bond, or mutual fund) that you own for more than 12 months, is taxed on a different tax-rate schedule. *Short-term* capital gains (securities held for one year or less) are taxed at your ordinary income tax rate.

The maximum federal tax rate on long-term capital gains is currently 20 percent for holding periods of more than 12 months. For investors with an adjusted gross income below $47,025 for singles and $94,050 for married couples filing jointly in tax year 2024, the long-term capital gains tax is 0 percent for assets held more than 12 months.

When investing outside retirement accounts, investors who frequently trade their investments (or who invest in mutual funds that do the same) should seriously reconsider these strategies and holdings. With longer-term capital gains being taxed at lower tax rates, trading that produces short-term gains (from investments held 12 months or less), which are taxed at higher ordinary income tax rates, penalizes higher bracket investors the most. The sane strategy of buying and holding not only minimizes your taxes but also reduces trading costs and the likelihood of being whipsawed by fluctuating investment values.

Why, you may wonder, is there a set of capital gains tax rates that are different from (lower than) the regular income tax rates presented in Chapter 1? In addition to the possibility that our government wants to make our tax lives more difficult, some logic lies behind the lower long-term capital gains tax rates. Some argue that this lower tax encourages investment for long-term growth. However, others complain that it's a tax break that primarily benefits the affluent.

When you buy and hold stocks and stock mutual funds outside retirement accounts, you can take advantage of two major tax breaks. As I discuss in this section, appreciation on investments held more than 12 months and then sold is taxed at the low capital gains tax rate. Stock dividends (not on real estate investment trusts) are also taxed at these same low tax rates.

Pay off high-interest debt

Many folks have credit card or other consumer debt, such as auto loans costing 8 percent, 9 percent, 10 percent, or more per year in interest. Paying off this debt with your savings is like putting your money in an investment with a guaranteed tax-free return that's equal to the interest rate you were paying on the debt. For example, if you have credit-card debt outstanding at a 15 percent interest rate, paying off that loan is the same as putting your money to work in an investment with a guaranteed 15 percent annual return. Because the interest on consumer debt isn't tax-deductible, you actually need to earn more than 15 percent on your other investments to net 15 percent after paying taxes.

REMEMBER

Still not convinced that paying off consumer debt is a great "investment"? Consider this: Banks and other lenders charge higher rates of interest for consumer debt than for debt on investments (such as real estate and businesses). Debt for investments is generally available at lower rates of interest and is tax-deductible. Consumer debt is hazardous to your long-term financial health (because you're borrowing against your future earnings), and it's more expensive.

In addition to ridding yourself of consumer debt, paying off your mortgage quicker may make sense, too. This financial move *isn't always* the best one because the interest rate on mortgage debt is lower than that on consumer debt and is usually tax-deductible.

Fund your retirement accounts

TIP

Take advantage of opportunities to direct your employment earnings into retirement accounts. If you work for a company that offers a retirement savings plan such as a 401(k) or 403(b) plan, try to fund it at the highest level that you can manage. When you earn self-employment income, look into SEP-IRAs and self-employed/i401(k)s. See Chapter 4 for all the details on retirement accounts.

You get three possible tax bonuses by investing more of your money in retirement accounts.

>> Your contributions to most of these retirement accounts come out of your pay before taxes are figured, which reduces your current tax burden. The after-tax Roth accounts offer tax-free retirement withdrawals, but you don't get a tax break on the contributions.

>> Some employers provide matching contributions, which is free money to you.

>> The earnings on the investments inside the retirement accounts compound without taxation until withdrawal. Funding retirement accounts makes particular sense if you can allow the money to compound over many years (at least 10 years, preferably 15 to 20 years or more).

If you need to save money outside retirement accounts for short-term purposes such as buying a car or a home, by all means, don't do all your saving inside sometimes-difficult and costly-to-access retirement accounts. But if you accumulate money outside retirement accounts with no particular purpose in mind (other than that you like seeing the burgeoning balances), why not get some tax breaks by contributing to retirement accounts? Because your investments can produce taxable distributions, investing money outside retirement accounts requires greater thought and consideration, which is another reason to shelter more of your money in retirement accounts.

Use tax-free money market and bond funds

A common mistake many people make is not choosing a tax-appropriate investment given their tax bracket. Here are some guidelines for choosing the best type of investment based on your federal tax bracket:

>> **32 percent or higher federal tax bracket:** If you're in one of these high brackets, you should actively seek to avoid investments that produce taxable income. For tax year 2024, the 32 percent federal bracket started at $191,950 for singles and heads of household, and $383,900 for married couples filing jointly.

>> **22 or 24 percent federal tax bracket:** If you invest outside retirement accounts, in most cases, you should be as well or slightly better off in investments that don't produce taxable income. This may not be the case, however, if you're in tax-free money market and bond funds whose yields are depressed because of a combination of low interest rates and too-high operating expenses.

>> **10 or 12 percent federal tax bracket:** Investments that produce taxable income are mostly just fine. You'll generally end up with less if you purchase investments that produce tax-free income, because these investments yield less than comparable taxable ones even after factoring in the taxes you pay on those taxable investments.

When you're investing your money, it isn't the return that your investment earns that matters; what matters is the return you actually get to keep after paying taxes. The following material and sections describe some of the best investment choices you can make to reduce your overall tax burden and maximize your after-tax return.

TIP

If you're in a high enough tax bracket (federal 32 percent or higher), you may come out ahead with tax-free investments. Tax-free investments yield less than comparable investments that produce taxable earnings. But the earnings from tax-free investments can end up being greater than what you're left with from taxable investments after paying required federal and state taxes.

Tax-free money market funds, offered by mutual fund companies, can be a better alternative to bank savings accounts that pay interest (which is subject to taxation) during periods of normal interest rates. The best money market funds pay higher yields and give you check-writing privileges. If you're in a high tax bracket, you can select a tax-free money market fund, which pays dividends that are free from federal and sometimes from state tax. You can't get this feature with bank savings accounts.

Unlike bank savings accounts, the FDIC (Federal Deposit Insurance Corporation) doesn't insure money market mutual funds. For all intents and purposes, though, money market funds and bank accounts have equivalent safety. Don't allow the lack of FDIC insurance to concern you — fund companies haven't failed. And in those rare instances when a money fund's investments have lost value, the parent company has infused capital to ensure no loss of principal on the investor's part.

Just as you can invest in a tax-free money market fund, so too can you invest in tax-free bonds via a tax-free bond mutual fund. These funds are suitable for higher-tax-bracket investors who want an investment that pays a better return than a money market fund without the risk of the stock market. Bond funds are intended as longer-term investments (although they offer daily liquidity, they do fluctuate in value).

TIP

As a starting point, examine the tax-free money market funds and bond funds offered by Vanguard (800-662-7447; www.vanguard.com). Vanguard has low management fees and highly competitive yields. They also offer increasing numbers of exchange-traded funds which may offer you even lower costs and higher yields.

Invest in tax-friendly stock funds

When selecting investments, people often mistakenly focus on past rates of return. Everyone knows that the past is no guarantee for the future. But an even worse mistake is choosing an investment with a reportedly high rate of return without considering tax consequences. Numerous mutual funds and exchange-traded funds (ETFs) effectively reduce their shareholders' returns because of their tendency to produce more taxable distributions (dividends and capital gains).

Historically, however, many mutual fund and ETF investors and publications haven't compared the tax-friendliness of similar mutual funds. Just as you need to avoid investing in funds with high sales commissions, high annual operating expenses, and poor relative performance, you also should avoid tax-unfriendly funds when investing outside of retirement accounts.

When comparing two similar funds, most people prefer a fund that averages returns of 14 percent per year instead of a fund earning 12 percent. But what if the 14 percent-per-year fund causes you to pay a lot more in taxes? What if, after factoring in taxes, the 14-percent-per-year fund nets just 9 percent, while the 12-percent-per-year fund nets an effective 10 percent return? In that case, you'd be unwise to choose a fund solely on the basis of the higher reported rate of return.

Greater fund distributions = more taxes!

All stock fund managers buy and sell stocks during the course of a year. Whenever a fund manager sells securities, any gain from those securities must be distributed, by year's end, to the fund shareholders. Securities sold at a loss can offset those liquidated at a profit. When a fund manager tends to cash in more winners than losers, significant capital gains distributions can result.

TIP

Choosing mutual funds and ETFs that minimize capital gains distributions, especially short-term capital gains distributions that are taxed at the higher ordinary income tax rates rather than the tax-favored long-term capital gains rates I discuss earlier in this chapter, can help investors defer and minimize taxes on their profits. By allowing their capital to continue compounding, as it would in an IRA or other retirement account, fund shareholders receive a higher total return. (You can find the historic capital gains distribution information on a fund by examining its prospectus.)

Long-term investors benefit the most from choosing funds that minimize capital gains distributions. The more years that appreciation can compound in a fund without being taxed, the greater the value to the fund investor. When you invest in stock funds inside retirement accounts, you need not worry about capital gains distributions.

In addition to capital gains distributions, mutual funds and ETFs produce dividends that are subject to normal income tax rates (except in the case of qualified stock dividends, which are taxed at the same low rates applied to long-term capital gains). Again, all things being equal, nonretirement account investors in high tax brackets should avoid funds that tend to pay a lot of dividends (from bonds and money market funds). Hold such funds inside of tax-sheltered retirement accounts.

Timing of fund purchases affects tax bill

TIP

Investors who purchase mutual funds and ETFs outside tax-sheltered retirement accounts also need to consider the time of year they purchase shares in funds, so they can minimize the tax bite. Specifically, investors should try to purchase funds after rather than just before the fund makes the following types of distributions:

>> **Capital gains distributions:** December is the most common month in which funds make capital gains distributions. If making purchases late in the year, investors should find out whether and when the fund may make a significant capital gains distribution. Often, the unaware investor buys a fund just prior to a distribution, only to see the value of the fund decline. But the investor must still pay income tax on the distribution. The December payout is generally larger when a fund has had a particularly good performance year and when the fund manager has done more trading that year.

>> **Dividend distributions:** Some stock funds that pay reasonably high dividends (perhaps because they also hold bonds) tend to pay out dividends quarterly — typically on a March, June, September, and December cycle. Try to avoid buying shares of these funds just before they pay. Make purchases early in each calendar quarter (early in the months of January, April, July, and October). Remember that the share price of the fund is reduced by the amount of the dividend, and the dividend is taxable.

Don't get too concerned about when funds make distributions, because you can miss out on bigger profits by being so focused on avoiding a little bit of tax. If you want to be sure of the dates when a particular fund makes distributions, that information is generally posted on their website, or you can call the specific fund you have in mind.

Understanding the tax virtues of index funds

TIP

Fund managers of actively managed portfolios, in their attempts to increase their shareholders' returns, buy and sell individual securities more frequently. However, this trading increases the chances of a fund needing to make significant capital gains distributions.

Index funds, by contrast, are funds that invest in a relatively fixed portfolio of securities. They don't attempt to beat the market averages or indexes. Rather, they invest in the securities to mirror or match the performance of an underlying index, such as the S&P 500 index of 500 mostly larger company, U.S. stocks.

Although index funds can't beat the market, they have the following advantages over actively managed funds:

>> Because index funds trade much less often than actively managed funds, index fund investors benefit from lower brokerage fees.

>> Because significant ongoing research need not be conducted to identify companies in which to invest, index funds can be run with far lower operating expenses. All factors being equal, lower brokerage and operating costs translate into higher shareholder returns.

>> Because index funds trade less often, they tend to produce lower capital gains distributions. For funds held outside of tax-sheltered retirement accounts, this reduced trading effectively increases an investor's total rate of return. Thus, index mutual funds are tax-friendlier.

The Vanguard Group (800-662-7447; www.vanguard.com), headquartered in Valley Forge, Pennsylvania, is the largest mutual fund provider of index funds. Vanguard also offers some of the best exchange-traded funds, which are index funds that trade during the trading day on the major stock exchanges.

Exchange-traded funds may offer an even lower-cost way for some investors to buy and hold a broad market index for the longer term.

Uncovering Tax-Favored Investments to Avoid

WARNING

Investment and insurance brokers and "financial planners" (many of whom sell products, work on commission, and are therefore salespeople) love to pitch investment products that supposedly save you on your taxes. Salespeople generally don't examine your entire financial situation. Therefore, the salesperson may sell you an inappropriate or lousy investment that pays (the salesperson!) hefty commissions. The following sections discuss the main investments these commission-driven folks try to sell you — along with the reasons why you shouldn't buy them.

Limited partnerships

Avoid limited partnerships (LPs) sold through brokers and financial planners. They are fundamentally inferior investment vehicles. That's not to say that no one has ever made money on one, but they are burdened with high sales commissions and ongoing management fees that deplete your investment. You can do better elsewhere.

Limited partnerships invest in real estate and a variety of businesses. They pitch that you can get in on the ground floor of a new investment opportunity and make big money. They also usually tell you that while your investment is growing at 20 percent or more per year, you get handsome dividends of 8 percent or so each year. Sound too good to be true? It is. (You can read more about LPs in Chapter 11.)

Many of the yields on LPs have turned out to be bogus. In some cases, partnerships have propped up their yields by paying back investors' original investment (principal) — without clearly telling them, of course. The other LP hook is the supposed tax benefit. The few loopholes that did exist in the tax code for LPs have largely been closed. (Amazingly, some investment sales-people hoodwink investors into putting their retirement account money — which is already tax-sheltered — into LPs!) The other problems with LPs overwhelm any small tax advantage, anyway.

The investment salesperson who sells you this type of invest-ment stands to earn a commission of up to 10 percent or more — so only 90 cents, or less, of your dollar actually gets invested. Each year, LPs typically siphon off another few percentage points for management fees and other expenses. Most partner-ships have little or no incentive to control costs. In fact, the pressure is to charge more in fees to enrich the managing partners.

Unlike with a mutual fund or ETF (which you can sell if it isn't performing), with LPs you can't vote with your dollars. If the partnership is poorly run and expensive, you're stuck. LPs are *illiquid*. You can't get your money out until the partnership is liquidated, typically seven to ten years after you buy in.

REMEMBER

The only thing limited about a limited partnership is its ability to make you money. If you want to buy investments that earn profits and have growth potential, stick with stocks (preferably using mutual funds), real estate, or your own business. For income as opposed to longer-term growth potential, invest in bonds.

Cash-value life insurance

WARNING

Life insurance that combines life insurance protection with an account that has a cash value is usually known as *universal, whole,* or *variable life.* Life insurance should not be used as an invest-ment, especially if you haven't reached the maximum allowable limit for contributing money to retirement accounts. Agents love to sell cash-value life insurance for the high commissions.

The cash-value portion of such policies grows without taxation until withdrawn. However, if you want tax-deferred retirement savings, you should first take advantage of retirement savings plans, such as 401(k)s, 403(b)s, SEP-IRAs, and so on, which give you an immediate tax deduction for your current contributions.

These accounts also allow your investments to grow and compound without taxation until withdrawal.

Money paid into a cash-value life insurance policy gives you no upfront tax breaks. When you've exhausted contributing to tax-deductible retirement accounts, you may find that a nondeductible IRA, Roth IRA, and other employer-based Roth accounts can provide tax-deferred compounding of your investment dollars. Roth retirement accounts allow for tax-free compounding and tax-free withdrawal of investment earnings, something that cash-value life policies don't do. See Chapter 4 for the details on retirement accounts.

The only real financial advantage cash-value life insurance offers is that, with proper planning, the proceeds paid to your beneficiaries can be free of federal estate taxes. You need to have a fairly substantial estate at the time of your death to benefit from this feature. And numerous other, more cost-effective methods exist to minimize your estate taxes (see Chapter 6 for more details on estate planning).

Analyzing Annuities

Annuities are a peculiar type of insurance and investment product — sort of a savings-type account with slightly higher yields that are backed by insurance companies.

WARNING

Insurance agents and financial planners working on commission happily sell annuities to many people with money to invest. The problem is annuities are suitable investments for relatively few people. If annuities do make sense for you, you can buy no-load (commission-free) annuities by bypassing salespeople and dealing directly with mutual fund companies.

The major selling hook of annuities is the supposed tax savings. "Why pay taxes each year on your investment earnings?" the agent or financial planner will ask. As in other types of retirement accounts, money that's placed in an annuity compounds without taxation until withdrawal. However, unlike most other types of retirement accounts (discussed in Chapter 4) — 401(k)s, 403(b)s, SEP-IRAs, and so on — your contributions to an annuity give no upfront tax deductions. And, unlike Roth retirement accounts, you get no tax break upon withdrawal of your investment earnings from an annuity. The only annuity income tax benefit, as with cash-value life insurance, is that the earnings compound without taxation until withdrawal. Thus, it makes sense to consider contributing to an annuity only after you fully fund your tax-deductible and Roth retirement accounts.

TIP

Because annuities carry higher annual expenses due to the insurance that comes with them, they generally make sense only if you have many years to allow the money to compound. So annuities are not appropriate if you're already in or near retirement. Also, the lower tax rate on long-term capital gains and stock dividends (which I discuss earlier in this chapter) makes investing money in annuities relatively less attractive than simply investing in tax-friendly nonretirement account holdings. All earnings on an annuity are taxed upon withdrawal at ordinary income tax rates, whereas with a nonretirement account investment, much of your profits can be deferred into lower-taxed long-term capital gains and lower-taxed stock dividends.

Selling Decisions

After you've owned a stock, bond, mutual fund, or ETF for a while, you may want to contemplate selling some or all of it. Taxes should factor into the decision when you consider selling investments that you hold outside tax-sheltered retirement accounts. For investments held inside retirement accounts, taxes aren't an issue because the accounts are sheltered from taxation (unless you're withdrawing funds from the accounts — see Chapter 4 for the details). In most cases, you need not waste your money or precious free time consulting a tax advisor. In the sections that follow, I outline issues for you to consider in your selling decisions.

Selling selected shares

Before I get into the specific types of investment decisions you're likely to confront, I must deal with a rather unpleasant but important issue: accounting methods for security sales. Although this stuff gets a little complicated, with some minimal advance planning, you can acquire sound methods to reduce your tax burden. If you sell all the shares of a security that you own, you can ignore this issue. Only if you sell a portion of your shares of a security should you consider *specifying* which shares you're selling.

Suppose that you own 200 shares of stock in Intergalactic Computer Software, and you plan to sell 100 shares. You bought 100 of these shares ten years ago at $50 per share, and then another 100 shares two years ago for $100 per share. Today, the stock is worth $150 per share. What a savvy investor you are!

So, which 100 shares should you sell? The IRS gives you a choice, from a tax-accounting standpoint. You can identify the specific shares that you sell. In the case of Intergalactic, you can opt to sell the last or most recent 100 shares you bought, which would minimize your tax bill — because these shares were purchased at a higher price. At the time you want to sell the shares through your brokerage account, identify the shares you want to sell by noting the original date of purchase and/or the cost of those shares. So in the case of your Intergalactic stock holdings, simply tell your broker that you want to sell the 100 shares that you bought two years ago (give the date) at $100 per share. (The broker should include this information on the confirmation you receive for the sale.) Please note that if these shares had been bought within the past year and you had a gain, you may not want to sell those shares, because the profit wouldn't be taxed at the lower long-term capital gains tax rate discussed earlier in this chapter.

The other method of determining which shares you're selling is the method the IRS forces you to use if you don't specify before the sale which shares are to be sold — the *first-in-first-out* (FIFO) method. FIFO isn't a dog with a funny name; it's an accounting term that means that the first shares you bought (*first in*) are the first shares that you sold (*first out*). Not surprisingly, because most stocks appreciate over time, the FIFO method leads to paying more tax sooner. In the case of Intergalactic, FIFO means that the first 100 shares that you bought (ten years ago at the bargain-basement price of $50 per share) are the first 100 shares sold.

Although you'll save taxes today if you specify that you're selling the shares you bought most recently (at a higher price), don't forget (and the IRS won't let you) that when you finally sell the other shares (bought long ago at a low price), you'll then owe taxes on the larger profit you realize from those shares. The longer you hold these shares, the greater the likelihood that their value will rise, realizing a larger profit for you (although you end up paying more taxes). Of course, the risk always exists that Congress will raise tax rates in the future or that your particular tax rate will rise. If you sell some of your investments, keep your life simple by considering selling all your shares of a specific security. That way, you don't have to hassle with all this accounting nonsense for tax purposes.

REMEMBER

To be able to choose, or specify, which shares you're selling, you must select them before you sell. If you don't, the IRS says that you must use the FIFO method. You may wonder how the IRS knows whether you specified which shares before you sold them. The IRS doesn't know. But if you're audited, the IRS will ask for proof.

Selling securities with (large) capital gains

Capital gains tax applies when you sell a security at a higher price than you paid for it. As I explain earlier in this chapter, the long-term capital gains rate is lower than the tax rate you pay on ordinary income (such as from employment earnings or interest on bank savings accounts). Odds are, the longer you hold securities such as stocks, the greater the capital gains you'll accrue, because stocks tend to appreciate over time.

Suppose that your parents bought you 1,000 shares of XYZ company stock ten years ago, when it was selling for $10 a share. Today, it's selling for $20 per share; but you also vaguely recall that the stock split two-for-one a few years ago, so now you own 2,000 shares. Thus, if you sell XYZ stock for $40,000 today, you'd have a capital gain of $30,000 on which to pay taxes. So why would anyone want to sell?

The answer depends on your situation. For example, if you need the money for some other purpose — buying a home, starting a small business, taking some time off to travel — and the stock is your only source of funds, go for it. If you can't do what you want to do without selling, don't let the taxes stand in the way. Even if you pay state and federal taxes totaling some 20 to 25 percent of the profit, you'll have lots left over. Before you sell, however, do some rough figuring to make sure that you have enough to accomplish what you want.

What if you hold a number of stocks? To diversify and meet your other financial goals, all you need to do is prioritize. One approach is to give preference to selling your largest holdings (total market value) that have the smallest capital gains. If some of your securities have profits and some have losses, sell some of each to offset the profits with the losses. (Gains and losses on securities held one year or less are taxed at your ordinary income tax rates.)

WARNING

Don't expect to obtain objective, disinterested, tax-wise advice regarding what to do with your current investments from a stockbroker or from most financial planners. If they earn commissions on the products they sell, their bias will be to tell you to sell. Even though some financial planners don't get commissions, they can charge fees on what they manage. When you seek objective help with these "sell versus hold" decisions, turn to a competent tax or financial advisor who works on an hourly basis.

Selling securities at a loss

Perhaps you own some losers in your portfolio. If you want to raise cash for some particular reason, you may consider selling some securities at a loss. Don't hold on to an investment just because its value now is less than what you paid for it. Waiting until its value rises to what you originally paid is a natural, but silly, human desire. Selling a loser now frees up your money for better investments. Losses can also be used to offset gains (investments sold at a profit) — just remember that long-term losses will offset long-term gains first. Only after you've completely exhausted your long-term gains can you use them against short-term gains, which are taxed at a higher rate.

Both short-term and long-term losses can be deducted against ordinary income, subject to limitations. If you want to sell securities at a loss, be advised that you can't claim more than $3,000 ($1,500 if you're married but filing separately) in short-term or long-term losses on your federal tax return in a given tax year. If you sell securities with losses totaling more than $3,000 in a year, the losses must be carried over to future tax years. This situation not only creates more tax paperwork, but also delays realizing the value of deducting a tax loss. So try not to have net losses (losses plus gains) exceeding $3,000 in a year.

Some tax advisors advocate doing *year-end tax-loss selling*. The logic goes that if you hold a security at a loss, you should sell it, take the tax write-off, and then buy it (or something similar) back. Sounds good in theory, but when you eventually sell the shares that you bought again at the lower price, you'll owe tax on the increased price anyway. (When you sell other stocks during the year at a profit, tax-loss selling to offset these taxable gains makes more sense.) But many people who sell an investment that has declined in value don't want to buy the same investment again. This reluctance can cause other investment blunders. For example, suppose you had the misfortune to buy some stocks back in 2007. In the next couple of years, your stocks plummeted about 50 percent or more. It wasn't because of your poor stock-picking ability. You simply got caught in the U.S. stock market downdraft during the financial crisis that hit hard in 2008. You'd make a bad situation worse by panicking and selling at reduced price levels just to take a tax loss. If anything, under such circumstances consider doing the opposite — take advantage of the sale and buy more!

WARNING

If you do decide to sell for tax-loss purposes, be careful of the so-called *wash sale* rules. The IRS doesn't allow the deduction of a loss for a security that you sell if you buy that same security back within 30 days. As long as you wait 31 or more days, you'll have no problem. When you're selling a mutual fund, you can easily sidestep this rule simply by purchasing a fund similar to the one you're selling.

When you own a security that has ceased trading and appears worthless (or even if you've made a loan that hasn't been repaid — even if to a friend), you can probably deduct this loss. For more information on what situations are deductible and how to claim these losses on your annual tax return, see the recent edition of my *Taxes For Dummies* (Wiley).

Selling mutual fund shares and the average cost method

In the United States, you never have a shortage of choices — so why shouldn't it be the same with accounting methods? When you sell shares in a mutual fund, the IRS allows you an additional method — *the average cost method* — for determining your profit or loss for tax purposes. (This information doesn't apply to money market funds, which don't fluctuate in value.)

If you bought fund shares in chunks over time and/or reinvested the fund distributions (such as from dividends) into more shares of the fund, tracking and figuring what shares you're selling can be a real headache. So the IRS allows you to take an average cost for all the shares you bought over time.

REMEMBER

Be aware that after you elect the average cost method, you can't change to another method for accounting for the sale of the remaining shares. If you plan to sell only some of your fund shares, and it would be advantageous for you to specify that you're selling the newer shares first, choose that method (as I describe in the "Selling selected shares" section earlier in this chapter).

Selling stock options and taxes

Some companies grant particular employees *stock options*. If you're the proud holder of this type of option, congratulations! You're either an important employee or work for a company that believes in sharing the success of its growth with its employees.

If you have *statutory stock options*, sometimes known as *incentive stock options*, you face a number of important decisions that can have significant tax consequences. Basically, stock options grant you the right to buy shares of stock from your employer at a predetermined price. For example, suppose that you take a job with a large discount retailer and the company tells you that, after December 31, 2024, you may "exercise the right" to purchase 1,000 shares of its stock at $50 per share.

In the years ahead, you and other store employees help the company to continue growing and expanding. Suppose the company's stock price eventually rises to $75 per share in the next year. Thus, because your options enable you to buy company stock for $50 per share, and it's now at $75 per share, you have a profit on paper of $25,000 (1,000 shares × $25 profit per share)!

To realize this profit, you must first exercise your option (your company benefits department can tell you how). After you are the proud owner of the shares, you can sell them if you want to. However — and this is a big *however* — if you sell the shares within a year of having exercised the options, or within two years after the grant of the option (whichever is later), you will owe ordinary income tax on the profit. If you hold the shares for the required period of time, then you will pay the lowest possible long-term capital gains tax. (You may also be subject to the Alternative Minimum Tax, or AMT — see Chapter 1 to find out more about this tax.)

When you're a high-income earner, holding on to your exercised stock options for more than 12 months so that you qualify for the favorable capital gains tax treatment is normally to your advantage. The risk in waiting to sell is that your profits shrink as and if the stock price drops.

Nonstatutory stock options are a bit different. Unlike incentive stock options, nonstatutory stock options aren't given special tax treatment. With nonstatutory stock options, you must pay tax on the options either when you receive them (if you can determine their fair market value) or when you exercise them. You must also pay income tax on the difference between the fair market value of the stock at the time you exercise the option minus the value of the option on which you pay tax. After you exercise the option, the decision on when to sell (and the tax consequences) is the same as for incentive stock options. If you don't know which type of option your employer offers, ask the benefits department.

WARNING

If you aren't a high-income earner and waiting to sell offers no tax advantage, selling your shares as the shares become exercisable is usually prudent. When the stock market plunged in the early 2000s, and then again in 2007 to 2009, and 2022, a number of employees, especially in high-tech companies, got clobbered with taxes on nonstatutory stock options on stock they'd held onto that then plummeted in value. So the employees ended up being out a lot of dough in taxes and in some cases holding worthless or near worthless stock. I should also note that having too much of your wealth tied up in the stock of your employer is risky. Remember that your job is already on the line if the company's success wanes.

Selling securities whose costs are unknown

When you sell a security or a fund that you've owned for a long time (or that your parents gave you), you may not know the security's original cost (also known as its *cost basis*). If you can only find the original account statement that shows the original purchase price and amount. . . .

If you can't find that original statement, start by calling the firm through which you purchased the investment. Whether it's a brokerage firm or fund company, it should be able to provide you with copies of old account statements. You may have to pay a small fee for this service. Also, investment firms (particularly fund companies) are required now to track and report cost basis information on investments that you sell through them. This requirement took effect for stocks in 2011; for mutual funds in 2012; and for bonds, options, and commodities in 2014.

IN THIS CHAPTER

» **Playing it safe: Bonds**

» **Growing your wealth: Stocks, real estate, and small business**

» **Eyeballing oddball investments: Precious metals, annuities, crypto, and collectibles**

» **Avoiding gambling and "get rich quick" schemes**

Chapter **8**

Understanding Your Investment Choices

aking wise investments need not be complicated. However, many investors get bogged down in the morass of the thousands of investment choices out there and the often-conflicting perspectives on how to invest. This chapter describes the investment choices you can make, and helps you match the types of investments to your tax situation.

Slow and Steady Investment: Bonds

Everyone should have some money in stable, safe investment vehicles, including money that you've earmarked for your near-term expenses, both expected and unexpected. Likewise, if you're saving money for a home purchase within the next few years, you certainly don't want to risk that money on the roller coaster of the stock market. The investment option of bonds is appropriate for money you don't want to put at great risk.

When you invest in a bond, you effectively lend your money to an organization. When a bond is issued, it includes a specified maturity date at which time the principal will be repaid. Bonds are also issued at a particular interest rate, or what's known as a *coupon*. This rate is fixed on most bonds. So, for example, if you buy a five-year, 6-percent bond issued by Home Depot, you're lending your money to Home Depot for five years at an interest rate of 6 percent per year. (Bond interest is usually paid in two equal, semi-annual installments.)

The value of a bond generally moves opposite of the directional change in interest rates. For example, if you're holding a bond issued at 6 percent and rates on similar bonds increase to 8 percent, your 6-percent bond will decrease in value. (Why would anyone want to buy your bond at the price you paid if it yields just 6 percent and 8 percent can be obtained elsewhere?)

Some bonds are tied to variable interest rates. For example, you can buy bonds that are adjustable-rate mortgages, on which the interest rate can fluctuate. As an investor, you're actually lending your money to a mortgage borrower — indirectly, you're the banker making a loan to someone buying a home.

Bonds differ from one another in the following major ways:

>> **The type of institution to which you're lending your money:** With municipal bonds, you lend your money to the state or local government or agency; with Treasuries, you lend your money to the federal government; with GNMAs (Ginnie Maes), you lend your money to a mortgage holder

(and the federal government backs the bond); and with corporate bonds, you lend your money to a corporation.

>> **The credit quality of the borrower to whom you lend your money:** Credit quality refers to the probability that the borrower will pay you the interest and return your principal as agreed.

>> **The length of maturity of the bond:** Short-term bonds mature within a few years, intermediate bonds within 3 to 10 years, and long-term bonds within 10 to 30 years. Longer-term bonds generally pay higher yields but fluctuate more with changes in interest rates.

TECHNICAL STUFF

Bonds are rated by major credit-rating agencies for their safety, usually on a scale where AAA is the highest possible rating. For example, high-grade corporate bonds (AAA or AA) are considered the safest (that is, most likely to pay you back). Next in safety are general bonds (A or BBB), which are still safe but just a little less so. Junk bonds rated BB or B are actually not all that junky; they're just lower in quality and have a slight (1 or 2 percent) probability of default over long periods of time. Junk bonds with even lower ratings — such as C or lower — carry higher default rates.

Some bonds are *callable*, which means that the bond's issuer can decide to pay you back earlier than the previously agreed-upon date. This event usually occurs when interest rates fall and the lender wants to issue new, lower-interest-rate bonds to replace the higher-rate, outstanding bonds. To compensate you for early repayment, the lender typically gives you a small premium over what the bond is currently valued at.

Building Wealth with Ownership Vehicles

The three best legal ways to build wealth are to invest in stocks (both domestic and international), real estate, and small business. I've found this to be true from observing many clients and other investors and from my own personal experiences. Check out the following sections for more details about these three options.

WARNING

The risk with ownership investments is the short-term fluctuations in their value. During the last century, stocks declined, on average, by more than 10 percent once every five years. Drops in stock prices of more than 20 percent occurred, on average, once every ten years. Real-estate prices suffer similar periodic setbacks.

Therefore, in order to earn those generous long-term returns from ownership investments like stocks and real estate, you must be willing to tolerate volatility. You absolutely should not put all your money in the stock or real-estate market. Investing your emergency money or money you expect to use within the next five years in such volatile investments is not a good idea.

The shorter the time period that you have for holding your money in an investment, the less likely growth-oriented investments like stocks are to beat out lending-type investments like bonds.

REMEMBER

Diversification is one of the most powerful investment concepts. It refers to saving your eggs (or investments) in different baskets. Diversification requires you to place your money in different investments with returns that are not completely correlated, which is a fancy way of saying that when some of your investments are down in value, odds are that others are up in value. To learn more about diversification and asset allocation strategies, see my book *Investing For Dummies* (Wiley).

Selecting stocks

Stocks, which represent shares of ownership in a company, are the most common ownership investment vehicle. When companies *go public,* they issue shares of stock that people like you and me can purchase on the major stock exchanges, such as the New York Stock Exchange and NASDAQ (National Association of Securities Dealers Automated Quotations).

As the economy grows and companies grow with it, earning greater profits, stock prices (and dividend payouts on those stocks) generally follow suit. Stock prices and dividends don't move in lockstep with earnings, but over the years, the relationship is pretty close. In fact, the *price-earnings ratio* — which measures the level of stock prices relative to (or divided by) company earnings — of U.S. stocks has averaged approximately 15 (although it has tended to be higher during periods of low inflation and interest rates). A price-earnings ratio of 15 simply means that stock prices per share, on average, are selling at about 15 times those companies' earnings per share.

Companies that issue stock (called *publicly held* companies) include automobile manufacturers, computer software producers, fast-food and other restaurant chains, hotels, publishers, supermarkets, technology companies, wineries, and everything in between! (You can also invest overseas — see the "Investing internationally in stocks" section.) By contrast, some companies are *privately held*, which means that they've elected to have senior management and a small number of affluent investors own their stock. Privately held companies' stocks do not trade on a stock exchange, so folks like you and me can't buy stock in such firms.

TECHNICAL STUFF

Companies differ in what industry or line of business they're in and also in size. In the financial press, you often hear companies referred to by their *market capitalization,* which is the value of their outstanding stock (the number of total shares multiplied by the market price per share). When describing the sizes of companies, Wall Street has done away with such practical adjectives as *big* and *small* and replaced them with expressions like *large cap* and *small cap* (where *cap* is shorthand for *market capitalization*). Such is the language of financial geekiness.

REMEMBER

Investing in the stock market involves occasional setbacks and difficult moments (just like raising children or going mountain climbing), but the overall journey is almost certainly worth the effort. Over the past two centuries, the U.S. stock market has produced an annual average rate of return of about 9 percent. However, the market, as measured by the Dow Jones Industrial Average, fell more than 20 percent during 16 different periods in the 20th century. On average, these periods of decline lasted less than two years. So if you can withstand a temporary setback over a few years, the stock market is a proven place to invest for long-term growth.

You can invest in stocks by making your own selection of individual stocks or by letting mutual (or exchange-traded) funds do it for you.

Discovering the relative advantages of mutual funds and exchange-traded funds (ETFs)

TIP

Efficiently managed mutual funds offer investors low-cost access to high-quality money managers. Mutual funds span the spectrum of risk and potential returns, from nonfluctuating money-market funds (which are similar to savings accounts) to bond funds (which generally pay higher yields than money-market funds but fluctuate with changes in interest rates) to stock funds (which offer the greatest potential for appreciation but also the greatest short-term volatility).

Investing in individual securities should be done only by those who really enjoy doing it and are aware of and willing to accept the risks in doing so. Mutual funds and exchange-traded funds (see the next section), if properly selected, are a low-cost, quality way to hire professional money managers. Over the long haul, you're highly unlikely to beat full-time professional managers who are investing in securities of the same type and at the same risk level. Chapter 9 is devoted to mutual funds and exchange-traded funds.

Understanding exchange-traded funds, hedge funds, and managed accounts

Mutual funds aren't the only game in town when it comes to hiring a professional money manager. Three additional options you may hear about include

» **Exchange-traded funds (ETFs):** These funds are the most similar to mutual funds except that they trade on a major stock exchange and thus can be bought and sold during the trading day. The best ETFs have low fees and, like an index fund (see Chapter 9), invest to track the performance of a particular stock market index.

» **Hedge funds:** These privately managed funds are for wealthier investors and are generally riskier (some even go bankrupt) than a typical mutual fund. The fees can be steep — typically 15 to 20 percent of the hedge fund's annual returns as well as an annual management fee of

1 percent or so. They're also generally illiquid — there are usually lock-up periods, and it can still be difficult to get your money back out later when needed. I generally don't recommend them.

>> **Managed accounts:** The major brokerage firms, which employ brokers on commission, offer access to private money managers. In reality, this option isn't really different from getting access to fund managers via mutual funds, but you'll generally pay a much higher fee, which reduces this option's attractiveness.

Investing in individual stocks

My experience is that plenty of people choose to invest in individual stocks because they think that they're smarter or luckier than the rest. I don't know you personally, but it's safe to say that in the long run, your investment choices are highly unlikely to outperform those of the best full-time investment professionals and index funds.

WARNING

Of course, you may find some people (with a vested interest) who try to convince you that picking your own stocks and managing your own portfolio of stocks is easy and more profitable than investing in, say, a mutual fund or an ETF. Researching individual stocks can be more than a full-time job, and if you choose to take this path, remember that you'll be competing against the professionals who do so on a full-time basis.

TIP

If you derive pleasure from picking and following your own stocks, or you want an independent opinion of some stocks you currently own, useful research reports are available from Value Line (call 800-825-8354 or visit www.valueline.com). I also recommend that you limit your individual stock holdings to no more than 20 percent of your overall investments.

Investing internationally in stocks

Not only can you invest in company stocks that trade on the U.S. stock exchanges, but you can also invest in stocks around the world. If you're in the United States, you may ask, "Why would you want to invest in international stocks?"

Here are two solid reasons:

>> Many investing opportunities exist overseas. If you look at the total value of all stocks outstanding worldwide, the value of foreign stocks typically equals or exceeds the value of U.S. stocks.

>> When you confine your investing to U.S. securities, you miss a world of opportunities, not only because of business growth available in other countries but also because you get the opportunity to diversify your portfolio even further.

International securities markets don't move in tandem with U.S. markets. During various U.S. stock market drops, some international stock markets drop less, whereas others may sometimes rise in value.

So where are the major investing opportunities outside the United States? International investing managers generally look at opportunities in three major geographic regions:

>> **Latin America:** Includes countries such as Argentina, Brazil, Chile, Columbia, Costa Rica, Mexico, Panama, and Peru

>> **Europe:** Includes countries such as Belgium, Denmark, France, Germany, Ireland, Italy, Netherlands, Norway, Spain, Sweden, Switzerland, and the United Kingdom

>> **Asia-Pacific:** Includes countries such as Australia, China, India, Japan, Hong Kong, India, New Zealand, Singapore, South Korea, Taiwan, Thailand, and Vietnam

Companies in Canada are generally a small investment portion held by many international and global stock funds. Canadian holdings may be listed separately or as a part of North America holdings.

Another way in which foreign stocks are categorized is between developed markets and emerging markets.

>> *Developed markets* are characterized by more mature, stable, and secure economies with relatively high standards of living. Examples include countries such as Australia, Canada, France, Germany, Japan, Switzerland, and the United Kingdom.

>> *Emerging markets* tend to be more volatile and typically higher growth economies that are in their early economic stages. Examples include countries such as Brazil, China, Chile, India, Indonesia, Malaysia, Mexico, South Africa, and Thailand.

Generating wealth with real estate

Over the generations, real-estate owners and investors have enjoyed rates of return comparable to those produced by the stock market, thus making real estate another time-tested method for building wealth. However, like stocks, real estate goes through good and bad performance periods. Most people who make money investing in real estate do so because they invest over many years and do their homework when they buy to ensure that they purchase good property in solid locations at an attractive/fair price. Part 5 covers finding tax breaks by investing in real estate.

TIP

Buying your own home is the best place to start investing in real estate. The *equity* (the difference between the market value of the home and the loan owed on it) in your home that builds over the years can become a significant part of your net worth. Among other things, you can tap this equity to help finance other important personal goals, such as retirement, higher-education costs, and starting or buying a business. Moreover, throughout your adult life, owning a home should be less expensive than renting a comparable home.

Investing in small business

TIP

Small business is the leading investment through which folks have built the greatest wealth. You can invest in small business by starting one yourself (and thus finding yourself the best boss you've probably ever had), buying an existing business, or investing in someone else's small business. Part 4 covers the tax reduction and other details for each of these options.

Off the Beaten Path: Investment Odds and Ends

The investments that I discuss in this section sometimes belong on their own planet (because they're not an ownership or lending vehicle). Here are the basics on these other common, but odd, investments.

Precious metals

Gold and silver have been used by many civilizations as currency or a medium of exchange. One advantage of precious metals as a currency is that they can't be debased by the government. With paper currency, such as U.S. dollars, the government can simply print more. This process can lead to the devaluation of a currency and inflation.

Holdings of gold and silver can provide a so-called *hedge* against inflation. In the late 1970s and early 1980s, inflation rose dramatically in the United States. This largely unexpected rise in inflation depressed stocks and bonds. Gold and silver, however, rose tremendously in value — in fact, more than 500 percent (even after adjusting for inflation) from 1972 to 1980. Such periods are unusual. Precious metals produced decent returns in the 2000s, but, after peaking in 2011, precious metals prices fell steeply before recovering in the 2020s.

Over many decades, precious metals tend to be lousy investments. Their rate of return tends to keep up with the rate of inflation but not surpass it.

TIP

When you want to invest in precious metals as an inflation hedge, your best option is to do so through mutual funds or exchange-traded funds (see Chapter 9). Don't purchase precious metals futures. They're not investments; they're short-term gambles on which way gold or silver prices may head over a short period of time. I also recommend staying away from firms and shops that sell coins and *bullion* (not the soup, but bars of gold or silver). Even if you can find a legitimate firm (not an easy task), the cost of storing and insuring gold and silver is quite costly. You won't get good value for your money — markups can be substantial.

Bitcoin, Ethereum, and other cryptocurrencies

Perhaps you have heard of Bitcoin — the online "currency." I find that far more young adults know about it than older folks do, which makes sense because it's a digital currency used for internet transactions.

Increasingly, Bitcoin has been in the news more and more as its price climbs to ever dizzying higher heights. In December 2017 the price of a Bitcoin neared the $20,000 mark. It then plunged to less than $4,000 late in 2018. The roller coaster continued with Bitcoin surging again and zooming past $68,000 in late 2021. By late 2022, it sank below $16,000, and as of the writing of this book in late 2023, it's at about $26,000.

So what exactly is Bitcoin? For starters, it's not actually a coin — calling it a coin is a marketing gimmick to make it sound like a real currency. Bitcoin and other similar cryptocurrencies only exist in the online world. Bitcoin's creators have limited the number of Bitcoins that can be "mined" and put into online circulation to about 21 million (more on mining later in this section).

As its promoters have talked up its usefulness and dizzying rise, many people who have Bitcoins continue to hold onto them in the hopes that the price will keep rising. Like shares of stock in the next Amazon.com or Apple, its owners and promoters are hoping and expecting for further steep price increases. People don't hoard real currencies with similar pie-in-the-sky hopes for large investment returns.

Ethereum is the second most popular cryptocurrency as people discover that it allows for incorporating *smart contracts*, which are computer-based and enforced contracts that delineate specific conditions that must be met in order for the transaction to be completed. Like Bitcoin, Ethereum has had wild boom-bust price swings.

WARNING

Bitcoin looks attractive, but it comes with risks and problems. Here are some major issues:

>> **No repercussions or recourse:** Online Bitcoin transactions can be done anonymously, and they can't be contested,

disputed, or reversed. If you buy something using Bitcoin and have a problem with the item you bought, that's too bad — you have no recourse, unlike, for example, with a purchase made on your credit card. The clandestine nature of cryptocurrencies makes them attractive to folks trying to hide money or engage in illegal activities (for instance criminals, drug dealers, and so on).

>> **No inherent value:** Contrast that with gold. Not only has gold had a long history of being used as a medium of exchange (currency), gold has commercial and industrial uses. Furthermore, gold costs real money to mine out of the ground, which provides a floor of support under the price of gold at about $1,300 per ounce, not far below the recent price of gold at about $2,000 per ounce. (Bitcoin does have a made-up mining process whereby you need special computer equipment and end up using a bunch of electricity to solve complex math problems.)

>> **Not unlimited:** The supply of Bitcoin is currently artificially limited. And Bitcoin is hardly unique — it's one of hundreds of cryptocurrencies. So if another cryptocurrency or two or three is easier to use online and perceived as attractive (in part because it's far less expensive), Bitcoin will eventually tumble in value.

>> **Not universally accepted:** Even though Bitcoin has been the most popular cryptocurrency in recent years, few merchants actually accept it. And, to add insult to injury, Bitcoin users get whacked with unfavorable conversion rates, which add greatly to the effective price of items bought with Bitcoin.

>> **Problematic exchanges:** There are many safe and reputable brokerage firms, protected by regulatory oversight and insurance, through which you can buy stocks and other securities. That is not the case with buying and selling cryptocurrency. Numerous such crypto brokers have blown up (FTX being the largest and most famous) due to incompetence and in some cases outright fraud. There's a lack of regulatory oversight, and many such brokers are located outside the United States. The U.S. Securities and Exchange Commission is playing catch-up and beginning to get its arms around the industry's myriad problems.

In 2024, about $1.8 trillion was tied up in these cryptocurrencies according to CoinMarketCap.com, which now tracks more than 26,000 cryptocurrencies. Over the preceding years, Bitcoin's market share has dropped from nearly 90 percent to about 52 percent. CoinMarketCap.com tracks the 100 largest cryptocurrencies as measured by their market capitalizations — number 100 on the list recently had a market cap of about $650 million.

I can't tell you what will happen to Bitcoin's price next month, next year, or next decade. But I can tell that it has virtually no inherent value as a digital currency, so those paying thousands of dollars for a Bitcoin will eventually be extremely disappointed. With more than 26,000 of these cryptocurrencies, the field keeps growing as creators hope to get in on the ground floor of the next cryptocurrency, which they hope will soar in value.

A recent *Wall Street Journal* investigation found, "Hundreds of technology firms raising money in the fevered market for cryptocurrencies are using deceptive or even fraudulent tactics to lure investors. . . . The *Wall Street Journal* has found 271 with red flags that include plagiarized investor documents, promises of guaranteed returns, and missing or fake executive teams."

Annuities

Annuities are a peculiar type of insurance and investment product. They're a sort of savings-type account with slightly higher yields, and they're backed by insurance companies. *Fixed annuities* pay a preset interest rate determined by the insurance company. This rate is typically set one year ahead at a time. *Variable annuities'* return varies over time depending on the returns provided by the investment that's chosen within the annuity offerings.

As with other types of retirement accounts (covered in Chapter 4), money placed in an annuity compounds without taxation until it's withdrawn. However, unlike most other types of retirement accounts, such as 401(k)s, SEP-IRAs, and 403(b)s, you don't receive up-front tax breaks on contributions you make to an annuity. Ongoing investment expenses also tend to be much higher than in retirement plan accounts. Therefore, consider an annuity generally only after you fully fund tax-deductible retirement accounts.

There's one other possible personal use for annuities: Those nearing or in retirement with limited resources can insure against the risk of outliving their assets by buying an annuity and annuitizing it — again, at a cost, so proceed carefully.

Collectibles (including NFTs)

The collectibles category is a catchall for antiques, art, autographs, baseball cards, clocks, coins, comic books, diamonds, dolls, gems, photographs, rare books, rugs, stamps, vintage wine, and writing utensils — in other words, any material object that, through some kind of human manipulation, has become more valuable to certain humans. Coinciding with the rise of cryptocurrencies, there are now NFTs, which stands for non-fungible tokens, that some have called digital collectibles.

WARNING

Notwithstanding the few people who discover on *Antiques Roadshow* that they own an antique of significant value, collectibles are generally lousy investment vehicles. Dealer markups are enormous, maintenance and protection costs are draining, research is time-consuming, and people's tastes are quite fickle. All this for returns that, after you factor in the huge markups, rarely keep up with inflation. Furthermore, long-term investment gains (of more than one year) you do earn on collectibles are currently taxed at your ordinary federal income tax rate with a cap of 28 percent, which is higher than the long-term capital gains tax rate on stocks, real estate, and small business (20 percent) held for a year or more.

TIP

Buy collectibles for your love of the object, not for financial gain. Treat collecting as a hobby rather than as an investment. When buying a collectible, try to avoid the big markups by cutting out the middlemen. Buy directly from the artist or producer if you can. With regards to NFTs, I would be very, very, very careful and steer clear until this market, which is in its infancy and largely untested, better proves itself.

Shunning Gambling and Get Rich Quick Vehicles

Although investing is often risky, it's not gambling. *Gambling* is putting your money into schemes that are sure to lose you money over time. That's not to say that everyone loses or that you lose every time you gamble. However, the deck is stacked against you. The house wins most of the time.

WARNING

Casinos and lotteries are set up to pay out 50 to 60 cents on the dollar. The rest goes to profits and covering those business's operating costs. Sure, you may win a bet or two, but in the long run, you're almost guaranteed to lose about 40 to 50 percent of what you bet. Would you put your money in an "investment" where your expected return over the long term was negative 40 percent?

Forsaking futures, options, and other derivatives

Futures, options, and commodity futures are *derivatives*, or financial investments whose value is derived from the performance of another security, such as a stock or bond.

Suppose you're solicited by the firm Fleecem, Cheatem, and Leavem to buy heating oil futures because of conflicts in the Middle East and the upcoming rise in heating oil usage due to the cold-weather months. You're impressed by the smooth-talking vice president. Their logic makes sense, and they spend a lot of time with little ol' you, so you send them $10,000.

Buying futures isn't much different from blowing $10,000 at the craps tables in Las Vegas. Futures prices depend on short-term, highly volatile price movements. As with gambling, you occasionally win when the market moves the right way at the right time. But in the long run, you're gonna lose. In fact, you can lose it all.

Options are as risky as futures. With options, you're betting on the short-term movements of a specific security, which is gambling — not investing. This was fashionable to do among some people who used government-distributed COVID-19 stimulus checks to try to hit it big.

Honest brokers who help their clients invest in stocks, bonds, and mutual funds tell them the truth about commodities, futures, and options. A former broker I know who worked for various major brokerage firms for 12 years told me, "I had just one client who made money in options, futures, or commodities, but the only reason he came out ahead was because he was forced to pull money out to close on a home purchase just when he happened to be ahead. The commissions were great for me, but there's no way a customer will make money in them." Remember these words if you're tempted to gamble with futures, options, and the like.

Futures and options are not always used for speculation and gambling. Some sophisticated professional investors use them to hedge, or actually reduce the risk of, their broad investment holdings. When futures and options are used in this fashion, things don't often work out the way that the pros hoped. You, the individual investor, should steer clear of futures and options.

Ditching day trading

WARNING

Day trading — which is the rapid buying and selling of securities online — is an equally foolish vehicle for individual investors. This is speculation and gambling, not investing. And even if you're using a broker who offers "free" trading, every time you buy and sell, you're effectively paying a fee given the inevitable spread between the buy and sell price for a given security.

Frequent trading also increases your tax bill as profits realized over short time periods are taxed at your highest possible tax rate. You can certainly make some profits when day trading. However, over an extended period of time, you'll inevitably underperform the broad market averages. In those rare instances where you may do a little better than the market averages, the profits are rarely worth the time and personal sacrifices that you, your family, and your friendships endure.

Sidestepping "get rich quick" schemes

REMEMBER

If it sounds too good to be true, it probably is. In today's high-tech world, people are bombarded in all directions — mailers, social media ads, radio and podcast commercials, and on and on — on ways to make money, fast. I'm here to tell you that getting rich quick is more of a pipedream than an investment strategy. Investing for the long term is the way to grow your money.

The best wealth-building investments historically have returned an average of about 8 to 9 percent per year. You should keep that number in mind as you evaluate seemingly attractive alternatives with the belief that you will double or triple your investment in a year or less. That's what lured so many inexperienced and naïve investors into cryptocurrencies in recent years. Websites and social media recounted tales of folks becoming rich over short time periods after buying into a particular cryptocurrency like Bitcoin and Ethereum that zoomed skyward.

New cryptocurrencies sprung up like weeds during a hot summer spell and soon there were more than 26,000 of them! Needless to say, nearly all of these ended up being poor investments. As with past get-rich-quick schemes, investors kept buying into new offerings in the hopes of striking it rich.

Chapter 9

Investing in Funds

W hen you invest in a mutual fund or its close sibling — an exchange-traded fund (ETF) that trades on a stock exchange — an investment company pools your money with the money of many other individuals and invests it in stocks, bonds, and other securities. Think of it as a big investment club without the meetings! When you invest through a typical fund, several hundred million to billions of dollars are typically invested along with your money.

If you're thinking of joining the club, read on to discover the benefits of investing in leading mutual funds and ETFs, and the types of funds available.

Understanding the Benefits of Mutual Funds and Exchange-Traded Funds

Mutual funds and exchange-traded funds (ETFs) rank right up there with microwave ovens, sticky notes, and cellphones as one of the best inventions. To understand their success is to grasp how and why these funds can work for you. Here are the benefits you receive when you invest in the best mutual funds and ETFs:

>> **Professional management:** Mutual funds and ETFs are managed by a portfolio manager and research team whose full-time jobs are to screen the universe of investments for those that best meet the fund's stated objectives. These professionals call and visit companies, analyze companies' financial statements, and speak with companies' suppliers and customers. In short, the team does more research and analysis than you could ever hope to do in your free time.

Fund managers are typically graduates of the top business and finance schools in the country, where they learn the principles of portfolio management and securities valuation and selection. The best fund managers typically have a decade or more of experience in analyzing and selecting investments, and many measure their experience in decades rather than years.

>> **Low fees:** The most efficiently managed stock mutual funds and ETFs cost much less than 1 percent per year in fees (bond and money-market funds cost even less). And, when you buy a *no-load fund*, you avoid paying sales commissions (known as *loads*) on your transactions. I discuss these types of funds throughout this chapter. You can buy an ETF for a low transaction fee through the best online brokers.

>> **Diversification:** Fund investing enables you to achieve a level of diversification that's difficult to reach without tens of thousands of dollars and a lot of time to invest. If you go it alone, you should invest money in at least 15 to 20 different securities in different industries to ensure that your portfolio can withstand a downturn in one or more of the investments. Proper diversification allows a fund to receive the highest possible return at the lowest possible risk given its objectives. The most unfortunate investors during major stock market downswings have been individuals who had all their money riding on only a few stocks that plunged in price by 90 percent or more.

>> **Low cost of entry:** Most mutual funds have low minimum-investment requirements, especially for retirement account investors. (ETFs essentially have no minimum, although you

don't want to do transactions involving small amounts if your brokerage firm charges a fee because that brokerage fee takes up a larger percentage of your investment amount.) Even if you have a lot of money to invest, consider funds for the low-cost, high-quality money-management services they provide.

>> **Audited performance records and expenses:** In their prospectuses, all funds are required to disclose historical data on returns, operating expenses, and other fees. The U.S. Securities and Exchange Commission (SEC) and accounting firms check these disclosures for accuracy. Also, several firms (such as Morningstar and Value Line) report hundreds of fund statistics, allowing comparisons of performance, risk, and many other factors.

>> **Flexibility in risk level:** Among the different funds, you can choose a level of risk that you're comfortable with and that meets your personal and financial goals. If you want your money to grow over a long period of time, you may want to select funds that invest more heavily in stocks. If you need current income and don't want investments that fluctuate in value as widely as stocks, you may choose more-conservative bond funds. If you want to be sure that your invested principal doesn't drop in value (perhaps because you may need your money in the short term), you can select a money-market fund.

Exploring Various Fund Types

In this chapter, I discuss the major types of funds: money-market, bond, and stock funds. When fund companies develop and market funds, the names they give their funds aren't always completely accurate or comprehensive. For example, a stock fund may not be *totally* invested in stocks. Twenty percent of it may be invested in bonds. Don't assume that a fund invests exclusively in U.S. companies, either — it may invest in international firms as well.

Note: If you haven't yet read Chapters 7 and 8, which provide an overview of investment concepts and vehicles, doing so can enhance your understanding of the rest of this chapter.

Money-market funds

Money-market funds are generally considered the safest type of mutual funds (although not insured or guaranteed) for people concerned about losing their invested dollars. As with bank savings accounts, the value of your original investment does not fluctuate.

These funds are closely regulated by the SEC. Trillions of dollars of individuals' and institutions' money are invested in money-market funds. General-purpose money-market funds invest in safe, short-term bank certificates of deposit, U.S. Treasuries, and *corporate commercial paper* (short-term debt), which is issued by the largest and most creditworthy companies.

Since their origination in the early 1970s, money-market funds have been extremely safe. The risk difference versus a bank account is nil. Only twice have funds broken the buck (one by 6 percent, the other by 3 percent), and both funds were used only by institutional investors. Hundreds of trillions of dollars have flowed into and out of money funds over the decades without any retail investors losing principal.

Money-market-fund investments can exist only in the most creditworthy securities and must have an average maturity of less than 120 days. In the unlikely event that an investment in a money-market-fund's portfolio goes sour, the mutual-fund company that stands behind the money-market fund will almost certainly cover the loss.

TIP

If the lack of insurance on money-market funds still spooks you, select a money-market fund that invests exclusively in U.S. government securities, which are virtually risk-free because they're backed by the full strength and credit of the federal government (as is the FDIC insurance system). These types of accounts typically pay slightly less interest, although the interest is free of state income tax.

Bond funds

Bonds are IOUs. When you buy a newly issued bond, you typically lend your money to a corporation or government agency. A bond fund is nothing more than a large group of bonds.

Bond funds typically invest in bonds of similar *maturity* (the number of years that elapse before the borrower must pay back the money you lend). The names of most bond funds include a word or two that provides clues about the average length of maturity of their bonds. For example, a *short-term bond fund* typically concentrates its investments in bonds maturing in the next two to three years. An *intermediate-term fund* generally holds bonds that come due within three to ten years. The bonds in a *long-term fund* usually mature in more than ten years.

In contrast to an individual bond that you buy and hold until it matures, a bond fund is always replacing bonds in its portfolio to maintain its average maturity objective. Therefore, if you know that you absolutely, positively must have a certain principal amount back on a particular date, individual bonds may be more appropriate than a bond fund.

Like money-market funds, bond funds can invest in tax-free bonds, which are appropriate for investing money you hold outside retirement accounts if you're in a reasonably high tax bracket.

TIP

Bond funds are useful when you want to live off interest income or you don't want to put all your money in riskier investments such as stocks and real estate (perhaps because you plan to use the money soon). Also, making small incremental investments in a bond fund is easier, as opposed to the cost of buying a single individual bond, which can be many thousands of dollars. Bonds (especially municipal bonds, which are bonds issued by local or state government) are among the most inefficient parts of the U.S. securities markets. Individual investors can't easily determine the bonds' true value and pay steep markups or markdowns, all of which a larger institutional trader (like a mutual fund) can more easily avoid.

Stock funds

Stock funds, as their name implies, invest in stocks. These funds are often referred to as *equity funds*. Equity — not to be confused with equity in real estate — is another word for stocks. Stock funds are often categorized by the type of stocks they primarily invest in.

Stock types are first defined by size of company (small, medium, or large). The total market value *(capitalization)* of a company's outstanding stock determines its size. Small-company stocks, for example, are usually defined as companies with total market capitalization of less than $2 billion. Mid-cap stocks are defined as having a market capitalization of between $2 and $10 billion, and large-cap stocks are those with market caps over $10 billion. Stocks are further categorized as growth or value stocks:

>> **Growth stocks** represent companies that are experiencing rapidly expanding revenues and profits and typically have high stock prices relative to their current earnings or asset (book) values. These companies tend to reinvest most of their earnings in their infrastructure to fuel future expansion. Thus, growth stocks typically pay low dividends. (See the later "Dividends" section for more information.)

>> **Value stocks** are at the other end of the spectrum. Value stock investors look for good buys. They want to invest in stocks that are cheaply priced in relation to the profits per share and book value (assets less liabilities) of the company. Value stocks are usually less volatile than growth stocks.

These categories are combined in various ways to describe how a mutual fund invests its money. One fund may focus on large-company growth stocks, while another fund may limit itself to small-company value stocks. Funds are further classified by the geographical focus of their investments: U.S., international, worldwide, and so on (see the section "U.S., international, and global funds").

Mixing bonds and stocks: Balanced funds

Balanced funds invest in a mixture of different types of securities. Most commonly, they invest in bonds and stocks. These funds are usually less risky and volatile than funds that invest exclusively in stocks. In an economic downturn, bonds usually hold up in value better than stocks do. However, during good economic times when the stock market is booming, the bond portions of these funds tend to drag down their performance a bit.

Balanced mutual funds generally try to maintain a fairly constant percentage of investments in stocks and bonds. A similar class of funds, known as *asset allocation funds*, tends to adjust the mix of different investments according to the portfolio manager's expectations of the market. Of course, exceptions do exist — some balanced funds adjust their allocations, whereas some asset allocation funds maintain a relatively fixed mix.

Most funds that shift money around instead of staying put in good investments rarely beat the market averages over a number of years.

There are also now increasing numbers of target-date or retirement-date funds, which tend to decrease their risk (and stock allocation) over time. Such funds appeal to investors who are approaching a particular future goal, such as retirement or a child's college education, and want their fund to automatically adjust as that date approaches.

Balanced funds are a way to make fund investing simple. They give you extensive diversification across a variety of investing options. They also make it easier for stock-skittish investors to invest in stocks while avoiding the high volatility of pure stock funds.

U.S., international, and global funds

Unless they have words like *international*, *global*, *worldwide*, or *world* in their names, most American-issued funds focus their investments in the United States. But even funds without one of these terms attached may invest some of its money internationally.

TIP

The only way to know for sure where a fund is currently invested (or where the fund may invest in the future) is to investigate. A fund's annual report (which can be found on the fund company's website) details where the fund is investing (the prospectus will also detail where the fund can be invested). You can also call the toll-free number of the fund company you're interested in and ask.

FUNDS OF FUNDS

An increasing number of fund providers are responding to overwhelmed investors by offering a simplified way to construct a portfolio: a fund that diversifies across numerous other funds — or a *fund of funds*. When a fund of funds is done right, it helps focus fund investors on the important big-picture issue of asset allocation — how much of your investment money you put into bonds versus stocks. Although the best funds of funds appear to deliver a high-quality, diversified portfolio of funds in one fell swoop, funds of funds are not all created equal, and few are worthy of your investment dollars.

The fund of funds idea isn't new. In fact, the concept has been around for many years. High fees gave the earlier funds of funds, run in the 1950s by the late Bernie Cornfeld, a bad name. Cornfeld established a fund of funds outside the United States and tacked on many layers of fees. Although the funds were profitable for his enterprise, duped investors suffered a continual drain of high fees. The Cornfeld episode is an important reason why the SEC has been careful in approving new funds of funds.

The newer funds of funds developed by the larger fund companies are investor friendly and ones that I recommend. Vanguard's LifeStrategy & Target Retirement, Fidelity's Freedom, Schwab Target Date, and T. Rowe Price's Spectrum funds of funds add no extra fees for packaging together the individual funds. Long-term performance of many of these is solid. Annual operating fees on the underlying funds at Vanguard are around 0.1 percent.

When a fund has the term *international* or *foreign* in its name, it typically means that the fund invests anywhere in the world *except* the United States. The term *worldwide* or *global* generally implies that a fund invests everywhere in the world, *including* the United States.

Index funds

Index funds are funds that can be (and are, for the most part) managed by a formulaic approach. An index fund's assets are invested to replicate an existing market index such as Standard & Poor's 500, an index of 500 large U.S. company stocks. (Some exchange-traded funds are index funds with the added twist that they trade on a major stock exchange.)

Over long periods (ten years or more), index funds outperform about three-quarters of their peers! How is that possible? How can mindlessly mimicking the holdings of a given index beat an intelligent, creative, MBA-endowed portfolio manager with a crack team of research analysts scouring the market for the best securities? The answer is largely cost. You can run an index fund with a much smaller management team and without spending gobs of money on research. An index fund doesn't need a team of research analysts.

In contrast to passively managed index funds, most active fund managers can't overcome the handicap of high operating expenses that pull down their funds' rates of return. As I discuss later in this chapter, operating expenses include all the fees and profit that a mutual fund extracts from a fund's returns before the returns are paid to you. For example, the average U.S. stock fund has an operating expense ratio of 1.1 percent per year. So a U.S. stock index fund (or its peer exchange-traded fund, which is an index fund that trades on a stock exchange) with an expense ratio of just 0.1 percent per year has an advantage of 1.0 percent per year.

Another not-so-inconsequential advantage of index funds is that they can't underperform the market. Many actively managed funds do just that because of the burden of high fees and/ or poor management. For money invested outside retirement accounts, index funds have an added advantage: Lower taxable capital gains distributions are made to shareholders because less trading of securities is conducted and a more stable portfolio is maintained.

Yes, index funds may seem downright boring. When you invest in them, you give up the opportunity to brag to others about your shrewd investments that beat the market averages. On the other hand, with a low-cost index fund, you have no chance of doing worse than the market (which plenty of active investment managers do).

TIP

Index funds and exchange-traded funds make sense for a portion of your investments, because beating the market is difficult for portfolio managers. The Vanguard Group (phone 800-662-7447; website www.vanguard.com), headquartered in Valley Forge, Pennsylvania, is the largest and lowest-cost provider of such funds.

Specialty (sector) funds

Specialty funds don't fit neatly into the previous categories. These funds are often known as *sector funds* because they generally invest in securities in specific industries.

WARNING

In most cases, you should avoid investing in specialty funds. Investing in stocks of a single industry defeats one of the major purposes of investing in funds — diversification. Another good reason to avoid specialty funds is that they tend to carry higher expenses than other funds.

TIP

Specialty funds that invest in real estate or precious metals may make sense for a small portion (10 percent or less) of your investment portfolio. These types of funds can help diversify your portfolio because they can do better during times of higher inflation.

Selecting the Best Funds

When you go camping in the wilderness, you can do a number of things to maximize your chances for happiness and success. You can take maps, a smartphone, and a GPS to keep you on course;

food for nourishment; proper clothing to stay dry and warm; and some first-aid gear to treat minor injuries. But regardless of how much advance preparation you do, you may have a problematic experience. You may take the wrong trail, trip on a rock and break your ankle, or lose your food to a tenacious bear that comes romping through camp one night.

And so it is with funds. Although most fund investors are rewarded for their efforts, you get no guarantees. You can, however, follow some simple, common-sense guidelines to help keep you on the trail and increase your odds of investment success and happiness. The factors in the following sections are the main ones to consider.

Reading prospectuses and annual reports

Fund companies produce information that can help you make decisions about fund investments. Every fund is required to issue a *prospectus*. This legal document is reviewed and audited by the SEC. The most valuable information — the fund's investment objectives, costs, performance history, and primary risks — is summarized in the first few pages of the prospectus. Make sure that you read this part. Skip the rest, which is comprised mostly of tedious legal details. Funds also produce what's called a *summary prospectus,* which is an abbreviated version of the full length *(statutory)* prospectus, and which hits the important highlights.

Funds also produce *annual reports* that discuss how the fund has been doing and provide details on the specific investments a fund holds. If, for example, you want to know which countries an international fund invests in, you can find this information in the fund's annual report.

Keeping costs low

The charges you pay to buy or sell a fund, as well as the fund's ongoing operating expenses, can have a big impact on the rate of return you earn on your investments. Many novice investors pay too much attention to a fund's prior performance (in the case of stock funds) or to the fund's current yield (in the case of bond funds) and too little attention to fees. Doing so is dangerous because a fund can inflate its return or yield in numerous (risky) ways. And what worked yesterday may flop tomorrow.

Fund costs are an important factor in the return you earn from a fund. Fees are deducted from your investment. All other things being equal, high fees and other charges depress your returns. What are a fund's fees, you ask? Good question — read on to find the answers.

Eliminating loads

Loads are upfront or ongoing annual commissions paid to brokers who sell mutual funds. Loads typically range from 3 percent to as high as 8.5 percent of your investment. Sales loads have two problems:

>> **Sales loads are an extra cost that drags down your investment returns.** Because commissions are paid to the salesperson and not to the fund manager, the manager of a load fund doesn't work any harder and isn't any more qualified than a manager of a no-load fund. Common sense suggests, and studies confirm, that load funds perform *worse*, on average, than no-loads when factoring in the load because the load charge is subtracted from your payment before your payment is invested.

WARNING

>> **The power of self-interest can bias your broker's advice.** Although this issue is rarely discussed, it's even more problematic than the issue of sales loads. Brokers who work for a commission are interested in selling you commission-based investment products; therefore, their best interests often conflict with your best interests.

Although you may be mired in high-interest debt or underfunding your retirement plan, salespeople almost never advise you to pay off your credit cards or put more money into your 401(k). To get you to buy, they tend to exaggerate the potential benefits and obscure the risks and drawbacks of what they sell. They don't take the time to educate investors. I've seen too many people purchase investment products through brokers without understanding what they're buying, how much risk they're taking, and how these investments will affect their overall financial lives.

Invest in no-load (commission-free) funds. The only way to be sure that a fund is truly no-load is to look at the prospectus for the fund. Only there, in black and white and without marketing hype, must the truth be told about sales charges and other fund fees. When you want investing advice, hire a financial advisor on a fee-for-service basis, which should cost less and minimize potential conflicts of interest.

Minimizing operating expenses

All funds charge ongoing fees. The fees pay for the operational costs of running the fund — employees' compensation, marketing, website development and maintenance, servicing the toll-free phone lines, creating, printing and mailing published materials, technology for tracking investments and account balances, accounting fees, and so on. Despite being labeled "expenses," the profit a fund company earns for running the fund is added to the tab as well.

The fund's operating expenses are quoted as an annual percentage of your investment and are essentially invisible to you because they're deducted before you're paid any return. The expenses are charged on a daily basis, so you don't need to worry about trying to get out of a fund before these fees are deducted. You can find a fund's operating expenses in the fund's prospectus. Look in the expenses section and find a line that says something like "Total Fund Operating Expenses." You can also call the fund's toll-free number and ask a representative.

Within a given sector of funds (for example, money-market, short-term bond, or international stock), funds with low annual operating fees can more easily produce higher total returns for you. Although expenses matter on all funds, some types of funds are more sensitive to high expenses than others. Expenses are critical on money-market funds and very important on bond funds. Fund managers already have a hard time beating the averages in these markets; with higher expenses added on, beating the averages is nearly impossible.

With stock funds, expenses are a less important (but still significant) factor in a fund's performance. Don't forget that, over time, stocks average returns of about 9 percent per year. So, if one stock fund charges 1 percent more in operating expenses than another fund, you're already giving up an extra 11 percent of your expected returns.

Some people argue that investing in stock funds that charge high expenses may be justified if those funds generate higher rates of return. However, evidence doesn't show that these stock funds actually generate higher returns. In fact, funds with higher operating expenses tend to produce *lower* rates of return. This fact makes sense because operating expenses are deducted from the returns a fund generates. (One additional cost not included in a fund's expense ratio is trading costs. The SEC requires funds to report these costs in their annual reports.)

TIP

Stick with funds that maintain low total operating expenses and don't charge loads (commissions). Both types of fees come out of your pocket and reduce your rate of return. You have no reason to pay a lot for the best funds.

Evaluating historic performance

A fund's *performance*, or historic rate of return, is another factor to weigh when selecting a fund. As all funds are supposed to tell you, past performance is no guarantee of future results. An analysis of historic fund performance proves that some of yesterday's stars turn into tomorrow's skid-row bums.

Many former high-return funds achieved their results by taking on high risk. Funds that assume higher risk should produce higher rates of return. But high-risk funds usually decline in price faster during major market declines. Thus, in order for a fund to be considered a *best* fund, it must consistently deliver a favorable rate of return given the degree of risk it takes.

TIP

When assessing an individual fund, compare its performance and volatility over an extended period of time (at least five to ten years) to a relevant market index. For example, compare funds that focus on investing in large U.S. companies to the Standard & Poor's 500 Index. Compare funds that invest in U.S. stocks of all sizes to the CRSP U.S. Total Stock Market Index. Indexes also exist for bonds, foreign stock markets, and almost any other type of security you can imagine.

Assessing fund manager and fund family reputations

Much is made of who manages a specific mutual fund. As Peter Lynch, the retired and famous former manager of the Fidelity Magellan fund, said, "The financial press made us Wall Street types into celebrities, a notoriety that was largely undeserved. Stock stars were treated as rock stars . . . ."

Although the individual fund manager is important, no fund manager is an island. The resources and capabilities of the parent company are equally important. Different companies have different capabilities and levels of expertise in relation to the different types of funds.

When you're considering a particular fund — for example, the Barnum & Barney High-Flying Foreign Stock fund — examine the performance history and fees not only of that fund but also of similar foreign stock funds at the Barnum & Barney company. If Barnum's other foreign stock funds have done poorly, or Barnum & Barney offers no other such funds because it's focused on its circus business, those are strikes against its High-Flying fund.

Also, be aware that "star" fund managers tend to be associated with higher-expense funds to help pay their celebrity salaries. (And star managers tend to leave or get hired away after several years of stellar performance, so you may not be getting the manager who created that good past performance in the first place. Index and asset class funds that use a team approach avoid this issue.)

Rating tax friendliness

Investors often overlook tax implications when selecting funds for nonretirement accounts. Numerous funds effectively reduce their shareholders' returns because of their tendency to produce more taxable distributions — that is, capital gains (especially short-term gains, which are taxed at the highest federal income tax rate) and dividends. (See the "Dividends" and "Capital gains" sections later in this chapter.)

Fund capital-gains distributions have an impact on an investor's after-tax rate of return. All fund managers buy and sell stocks over the course of a year. Whenever a fund manager sells securities, any gain or loss from those securities must be distributed to fund shareholders. Securities sold at a loss can offset securities sold at a profit. When a fund manager tends to cash in more winners than losers, investors in the fund receive taxable gains. So, even though some funds can lay claim to producing higher total returns, *after* you factor in taxes, they actually may not produce higher total returns.

Choosing funds that minimize capital-gains distributions helps you defer taxes on your profits. By allowing your capital to continue compounding as it would in a retirement account, you receive a higher total return. When you're a long-term investor, you benefit most from choosing funds that minimize capital-gains distributions. The more years that appreciation can compound without being taxed, the greater the value to you as the investor.

TIP

If you're purchasing shares in funds outside tax-sheltered retirement accounts, consider the time of year when making your purchases. December is the most common month in which funds make capital-gains distributions. When making purchases late in the year, ask whether the fund may make a significant capital-gains distribution. Consider delaying purchases in such funds until after the distribution date.

Determining your needs and goals

Selecting the best funds for you requires an understanding of your investment goals and risk tolerance. What may be a good fund for your next-door neighbor may not necessarily be a good fund for you. You have a unique financial profile.

REMEMBER

If you've already determined your needs and goals — terrific! Understanding yourself is a good part of the battle. But don't shortchange yourself by not being educated about the investment you're considering. If you don't understand what you're investing in and how much risk you're taking, stay out of the game.

Deciphering Your Fund's Performance

As a fund investor, you can't simply calculate your return by comparing the share price of the fund today to the share price you originally paid. Why not? Because funds make distributions of dividends and capital gains, which, when reinvested, give you more shares of the fund.

Even if you don't reinvest distributions, they create an accounting problem, because they reduce the share price of a fund. (Otherwise, you can make a profit from the distribution by buying into a fund just before a distribution is made.) Therefore, over time, following just the share price of your fund doesn't tell you how much money you've made or lost.

TIP

The only way to figure out exactly how much you've made or lost on your investment is to compare the total value of your holdings in the fund today with the total dollar amount you originally invested. If you invested chunks of money at various points in time and you want to factor in the timing of your various investments, this exercise becomes complicated.

The *total return* of a fund is the percentage change of your investment over a specified period. For example, a fund may tell you that in the past year, its total return was 15 percent. Therefore, if you invested $10,000 in the fund on the last day of the prior year, your investment would be worth $11,500 at the end of that year. To find out a fund's total return, you can visit the company's website, call the fund company's toll-free number, or read the fund's annual report.

The following three components make up your total return on a fund:

>> Dividends (includes interest paid by money-market or bond funds)

>> Capital-gains distributions

>> Share price changes

In short, you calculate a fund's total return as follows:

Dividends + Capital Gains Distributions + Share Price Changes = Total Return

The following sections discuss each of these components in more detail.

Dividends

Dividends are income paid by investments. Both bond funds and stocks can pay dividends. Bond fund dividends (the interest paid by the individual bonds in a fund) tend to be higher (as a percentage of the amount you have invested in a fund). When a dividend distribution is made, you can receive it as cash (which is good if you need money to live on) or reinvest it into more shares in the fund. In either case, the share price of the fund drops to offset the payout. So if you're hoping to strike it rich by buying into a bunch of funds just before their dividends are paid, don't bother. You'll just end up paying more in income taxes.

If you hold your mutual fund outside a retirement account, the dividend distributions are taxable income (unless they come from a tax-free municipal-bond fund). Dividends are taxable whether or not you reinvest them as additional shares in the fund. Stock dividends are taxed at a low rate — 0 percent for those in the federal 10- and 12-percent tax brackets, 15 percent for most people in the higher federal tax brackets, and 20 percent for those in the highest federal income tax brackets. From Obamacare, there is also a 3.8 percent surcharge on investment earnings for higher-income taxpayers.

Capital gains

When a fund manager sells a security in the fund, net gains realized from that sale (the difference from the purchase price) must be distributed to you as a *capital gain*. Typically, funds make one annual capital-gains distribution in December, but distributions can be paid multiple times per year.

As with a dividend distribution, you can receive your capital-gains distribution as cash or as more shares in the fund. In either case, the share price of the fund drops to offset the distribution.

For funds held outside retirement accounts, your capital-gains distribution is taxable. As with dividends, capital gains are taxable whether or not you reinvest them in additional shares in the fund. Capital-gains distributions can be partly comprised of short-term and long-term gains. As I discuss in Chapter 7, profits realized on securities sold after more than a one-year holding period are taxed at the lower long-term capital gains rate. Short-term gains are taxed at the ordinary income tax rate.

TIP

If you want to avoid making an investment in a fund that is about to make a capital-gains distribution, check with the fund to determine when capital gains are distributed. Capital-gains distributions increase your current-year tax liability for investments made outside of retirement accounts.

Share price changes

You also make money with a fund when the share price increases. This occurrence is just like investing in a stock or piece of real estate. If the fund is worth more today than it was when you bought it, you've made a profit (on paper, at least). In order to realize or lock in this profit, you need to sell your shares in the fund.

Evaluating and Selling Your Funds

WARNING

How closely you follow your funds is up to you, depending on what makes you happy and comfortable. I don't recommend tracking the share prices of your funds (or other investments, for that matter) on a daily basis; it's time-consuming and nerve-racking, and it can make you lose sight of the (long-term) big picture. When you track your investments too closely, you're more likely to panic when times get tough. And with invest-ments held outside of retirement accounts, every time you sell an investment at a profit, you get hit with taxes.

TIP

A monthly or quarterly review is more than frequent enough for following your funds. Many publications and websites carry total return numbers over varying periods so you can determine the exact rate of return you're earning.

Trying to time and trade the markets so you buy at lows and sell at highs rarely works. Yet an entire industry of investment newsletters, hotlines, online services, and the like purport to be able to tell you when to buy and sell. Don't waste your time and money on such predictive nonsense.

Consider selling a fund only when it no longer meets the criteria mentioned in "Selecting the Best Funds" earlier in this chapter. If a fund underperforms its peers for at least a two-year period, or if a fund jacks up its management fees, it may be a good time to sell. But if you do your homework and buy good funds from good fund companies, you shouldn't have to do much trading.

TIP

Finding and investing in good funds isn't rocket science. Pick up a copy of the latest edition of my book *Mutual Funds For Dummies* (Wiley) and visit my website at www.erictyson.com for more details on the best exchange-traded funds and mutual funds.

4
Small Business Tax Reduction

Understand how taxes work for small businesses.

Choose a business entity that best reduces your taxes and liability.

Claim deductions and applicable tax credits.

Chapter **10**

Small Business Taxes 101

Though some of my other books deal with the drudgery of completing required tax forms, much of this one deals with the more interesting — and dare I say, fun — part of taxes, which is planning ahead and strategizing so as to reduce and minimize your taxes. You see, if you simply view your role with taxes and your small business as jumping through the many hoops that federal, state, and local authorities require, you're missing out on something really big — saving and keeping more of your hard-earned money.

This chapter introduces the basics of small business taxes. Here, I discuss the value of tax planning all year long, and I define some important tax-related terms regarding the taxes you pay or may come across.

Valuing Year-Round Tax Planning

Taxes are a large, vital piece of your small-business and personal-financial puzzle. You're required by law to complete your tax forms each year and pay the taxes you owe. You do this because you have deadlines and don't want contact initiated by local or state authorities or the IRS, to result in fines, penalties or worse, jail time!

Nothing really forces you to plan ahead regarding your tax situation and small business. That's why the vast majority of small business owners don't take steps year-round to plan and reduce their taxes. However, tax planning all year is valuable because it enables you to stay on top of your tax and business financial situation and minimize the taxes you legally owe. In this section, I explain typical ways in which taxes enter small business decisions and some common tax mistakes folks make in this realm.

Factoring taxes into small business decisions

REMEMBER

Taxes infiltrate many areas of your small business and your personal finances. Some people make important financial decisions without considering taxes (and other important variables). Conversely, in an obsession to minimize or avoid taxes, other people make decisions that are counterproductive to achieving their long-term business and personal financial goals. Although taxes are an important component to factor into your major business and financial decisions, taxes shouldn't drive or dictate the decisions you make.

The following list shows some of the ways that tax issues are involved in making sound financial decisions throughout the year.

>> **Type of business and benefits offered:** The type of business entity you select for your business — sole proprietorship, S corporation, limited liability company (LLC), and so on — can

have significant tax and other consequences. The benefits you're able to utilize and offer to your employees, if you have them, also have tax ramifications (see Chapter 12).

>> **Retirement accounts:** Taking advantage of retirement accounts can mean tens, perhaps even hundreds of thousands more dollars in your pocket come retirement time. Offering retirement account access to your employees can also be a valuable employee benefit for recruiting and retaining good employees if they understand what they have.

>> **Spending:** The spending decisions you may face in your small business, such as buying equipment, spending on employee benefits (Chapter 12), and so on, will often affect your taxes both now and in the future.

>> **Protecting your assets:** Some of your insurance decisions also affect the taxes you pay. You'd think that after a lifetime of tax payments, your heirs would be left alone when you pass on to the great beyond — but that's wishful thinking. Estate planning can reduce the taxes that are siphoned off from your estate. See Chapter 6 to find out more about estate planning.

>> **Tracking your business financials:** Throughout the year, you should stay on top of your business's income and expenses so that you can see your business's financial health and record the numbers you need come tax time.

Checking out common tax mistakes

Even if some parts of the tax system are hopelessly and unreasonably complicated, there's no reason why you can't learn from the mistakes of others to save yourself some money, no matter the time of year. With this goal in mind, this section details common tax blunders that people make when it comes to managing their money.

Seeking advice after an important decision

Too many people seek out information and hire help *after* making a decision, even though seeking preventive help ahead of time generally is wiser and more financially beneficial.

TIP

Before making major small business and financial decisions, educate yourself. This book can help answer many of your questions. You may also want to do further research on your own and/or hire a tax advisor for some advice before making your decision(s). For more in-depth information about small business taxes, check out the most recent edition of my book *Small Business Taxes For Dummies* (Wiley).

Failing to withhold or submit enough taxes

If you're self-employed (or earn significant taxable income from investments outside retirement accounts), you need to make estimated quarterly tax payments. You also need to withhold taxes for your employees and send those taxes along to the appropriate tax agencies. Some small business owners don't have a human resources department to withhold taxes and dig themselves into a perpetual tax hole by failing to submit estimated quarterly tax payments.

To make quarterly tax payments, complete IRS Form 1040-ES, "Estimated Tax for Individuals." This form and its accompanying instructions (and payment coupons) explain how to calculate quarterly tax payments. For more information on the requirement for employee tax withholding, please see *Small Business Taxes For Dummies* (Wiley).

Missing legal deductions

REMEMBER

Some taxpayers miss out on legitimate tax write-offs because they just don't know about them. If you aren't going to take the time to discover the legal deductions that are available to you and that I discuss throughout this book, then you should pay for the cost of a competent tax advisor at least once. Fearing an audit, some taxpayers (and even some tax preparers) avoid taking deductions that they have every right to take. Unless you have something to hide, such behavior is foolish and costly. Note that a certain number of returns are randomly audited every year, so even when you don't take every allowable deduction, you may nevertheless get audited!

Forsaking retirement accounts

All the tax deductions and tax deferrals that come with accounts such as 401(k)s, SEP-IRA plans, and individual retirement accounts (IRAs) were put in the tax code to encourage you to save for retirement. That's something that you as a small business owner should be doing for yourself as well as encouraging your employees to do.

Most excuses for missing out on these accounts just don't make good financial sense. Some folks underfund retirement accounts because they spend too much and because retirement seems so far away. Others mistakenly believe that retirement account money is totally inaccessible until they're old enough to qualify for senior discounts.

Not owning real estate

In the long run, owning a home should cost you less than renting. And because mortgage interest (on up to $750,000 of mortgage debt) and property taxes (up to $10,000 when combined with your state income tax payments) are deductible, the government, in effect, subsidizes the cost of homeownership.

If you have a home office, you may be able to take additional expenses on your tax return. If you need a retail or commercial space for your small business, you should compare leasing to buying and be sure to factor in the tax benefits of owning.

Neglecting the timing of events you can control

TIP

As a small business owner, you should pay attention to how your net income for the year is shaping up for the current year and how things are looking for next year. For example, if you're in the early stages of your business and you can see that you'll have more income next year, then it may be in your best interest tax-wise to delay paying some expenses from late in the current year into early next year. (This works when using cash basis accounting.)

Or suppose that you operate on a cash accounting basis and think that you'll be in a lower tax bracket next year. Perhaps business has slowed of late or you plan to take time off to be with a newborn or take an extended trip. You can send out some invoices later in the year so that your customers won't pay you until January, which falls in the next tax year.

Not using tax advisors effectively

REMEMBER

If your financial situation is complicated, going it alone and relying only on the IRS publications to figure your taxes usually is a mistake. Many people find the IRS instructions tedious and not geared toward highlighting opportunities for tax reductions. Instead, you can start by reading the relevant sections of this book. When you're overwhelmed by the complexity of particular small business and tax decisions, get advice from tax and financial advisors who sell their time and nothing else.

As a small business owner, ask yourself how much you're worth running your business versus how much you're worth as a bookkeeper. Then ask yourself which task you enjoy more and consider hiring a bookkeeper.

Note that using a tax advisor is most beneficial when you face new tax questions or problems. If your tax situation remains complicated or if you know that you'd do a worse job on your own, by all means keep using a tax preparer. If your situation is unchanging or isn't that complicated, consider hiring and paying someone to figure out your taxes one time. After that, go ahead and try completing your own tax returns.

Noting How Corporate and Individual Tax Reform Impacts Small Business

Corporate tax reform in the United States was long, long overdue. For too many years, corporations in the United States faced a much higher corporate income tax rate than did companies based in most overseas economies. As a result, increasing numbers of U.S. companies had chosen to expand more overseas rather than in the United States and to be headquartered outside of the United States, which wasn't good for the long-term health of U.S. economy and labor market.

Congress passed the Tax Cuts and Jobs Act in late 2017, which took effect with tax year 2018. It was the most significant tax reform package passed since the Tax Reform Act of 1986. What follows are the highlights of the most significant provisions that affect (and mostly benefit) small business. Chapter 1 also covers these reforms.

Checking out corporate income tax rate reduction and simplification

At 35 percent, the United States had had one of the highest corporate income tax rates in the world before 2018. The Tax Cuts and Jobs Act slashed the corporate income tax rate to 21 percent, which represented a 40 percent reduction.

The corporate tax rules and deductions were simplified, including eliminating the corporate alternative minimum tax and closing some loopholes. The United States also moved to a *territorial* tax structure whereby U.S. companies would no longer pay a penalty to bring their overseas profits back home. The immediate impact of this change was to enable U.S. corporations to bring back to the United States more than $2 trillion being kept overseas to avoid excessive taxation.

The vast majority of small businesses aren't operated as traditional so-called C-corps (more on those in a moment). Most small business owners operate as sole proprietorships (filing Schedule C), LLCs, partnerships, or S corporations. In those cases, the business owner's profits from the business generally flow or pass through to the owner's personal income tax return and that income is taxed at personal income tax rates (see the section "Noting 20 percent deduction for pass-through entities" for more information).

Reducing individual income tax rates

Just as the corporate income tax rate was reduced by the Tax Cuts and Jobs Act legislation, so too were the individual income tax rates. Most of the tax bracket rates were reduced by several percentage points (see Chapter 1). This, of course, is excellent news for the vast majority of U.S. small business owners who operate their businesses as pass-through entities (for example, sole proprietorships, LLCs, partnerships, S-corps).

Note that at higher levels of income, the individual income tax rates begin to exceed the 21 percent corporate tax rate. Seeing this helps you to better understand the next point as to why pass-through entities are being granted a special tax deduction on their profits.

Noting 20 percent deduction for pass-through entities

In redesigning the tax code, Congress rightfully realized that the many small businesses that operate as so-called pass-through entities would be subjected to higher federal income tax rates compared with the new 21 percent corporate income tax rate. *Pass-through entities* are small business entities such as sole proprietorships, LLCs, partnerships, and S corporations and are so named because the profits of the business pass through to the owners and their personal income tax returns.

To address the concern that individual business owners that operated their business as a pass-through entity could end up paying a higher tax rate than the 21 percent rate levied on C-corporations, Congress provided a 20 percent deduction for those businesses.

Another way to look at this is that the business would only pay taxes on 80 percent of its profits and would be in the 22 percent federal income tax bracket. This deduction effectively reduces the 22 percent tax bracket to 17.6 percent.

This is a major change that not surprisingly has made small business owners exceedingly optimistic about being able to grow their businesses. In fact, in a 2018 survey of small business owners conducted by the nonprofit National Federation of Independent Business just after the tax bill was passed and signed into law, a record percentage of those surveyed (covering the survey's 45-year history) expressed optimism about it being a good time to expand their businesses.

This 20 percent pass-through deduction gets phased out for service business owners (such as lawyers, doctors, real estate agents, consultants, and so on) at single taxpayer incomes above $191,950 (up to $241,950) and for married couples filing jointly incomes more than $383,900 (up to $483,900). For other types of businesses above these income thresholds, this deduction may be limited so consult with your tax advisor.

Enjoying better equipment expensing rules

Through so-called section 179 rules, small businesses have historically been able to immediately deduct the cost of equipment, subject to annual limits, they purchase for use and place into service in their business. But the 2017 tax bill expanded these rules.

Now, more businesses can immediately deduct up to one million dollars in such equipment expense annually (up to the limit of their annual business income). And this deduction can also now be used for purchases on used equipment. These provisions, which don't apply to real estate businesses, remained in effect through 2022 but then gradually phase out by 2027 when the prior depreciation schedules are supposed to kick back in.

Increasing maximum depreciation deduction for automobiles

The new tax bill included a major increase in the maximum amount of auto depreciation that can be claimed. The annual amounts of auto depreciation have more than tripled.

The annual limits will increase with inflation for cars placed into service in future years.

Limiting interest deductions

Effective with 2018, companies with annual gross receipts of at least $25 million on average over the prior three years are limited in their deduction of interest from business debt. Net interest costs are capped at 30 percent of the business's earnings before interest, taxes, depreciation, and amortization (EBITDA). Farmers and most real estate companies are exempt.

Since 2022, this provision got more restrictive and thus impacts more businesses. Now, the 30 percent limit applies to earnings before interest and taxes.

Reducing meal and entertainment deductions

The tax reform bill of 2017 eliminated the entertainment expense deduction for businesses. Under prior tax law, 50 percent of those expenses were deductible, for example, when a business entertained customers and even employees at sporting events, fitness clubs, and restaurants.

The new rules do include some exceptions. On-site cafeterias at a company's offices and meals provided to employees as well as business meals associated with travel are 50 percent deductible. Meals provided to prospective customers as part of a seminar presentation are still fully deductible. Holiday parties and company picnics are also fully deductible as long as they are inclusive of everyone.

Eliminating the health insurance mandate

Since the Affordable Care Act (a.k.a. Obamacare) was passed by Congress in 2010, some Republicans in Congress vowed to repeal it. With the election of Republican Donald Trump in 2016, it seemed that the pieces were in place for Obamacare's successful repeal. But Republicans fell one vote short in the Senate when the late Arizona Senator John McCain gave the repeal measure his infamous thumb down vote.

So, the 2017 tax bill included a little known or discussed measure that eliminated Obamacare's mandate effective in 2019, which required people to have or buy health insurance coverage and if they didn't, they'd face a tax penalty. So, the penalty tax also disappeared in 2019.

Revising rules for using net operating losses

Net operating losses (NOLs) can no longer be carried back for two years. However, NOLs may now be carried forward indefinitely until they are used up. Previously the carry forward limit was 20 years.

NOLs are limited each year to 80 percent of taxable income.

Understanding How Businesses Are Taxed

As I explain earlier in this chapter, the vast, vast majority of small business owners pay income taxes on their business earnings at the personal income tax rates described in Chapter 1. That's because most small businesses are organized as sole proprietorships, which have income taxed as personal income. Also, many other small businesses that are organized as partnerships, LLCs, and S corporations pass through their income to the business owners in such a way that it, too, is taxed as personal income.

Thus, only a small percentage of small business owners have their income taxed as regular, so-called C-corporations. The Tax Cuts and Jobs Act, which took effect in 2018, compressed the previous numerous corporate income tax brackets to just one rate — 21 percent. In the next chapter, I discuss how the tax rate a business pays along with other factors plays a role in determining what's the best business entity for your business.

For more detailed information about how total taxes, taxable income, marginal tax rates, and corporate tax rates affect business owners, please see the most recent edition of my book, *Small Business Taxes For Dummies* (Wiley).

IN THIS CHAPTER

» Understanding why many
businesses go "solo"

» Assessing the incorporation decision

» Surveying S corporations,
partnerships, and limited liability
companies

Chapter **11**

Choosing Your Business Entity

M any small business owners don't fully consider (or aren't even aware of) the options they have for the entity under which they conduct their business. Most entrepreneurs default into sole proprietor status for a variety of reasons. But you should be aware of all your choices — such as C corporations, S corporations, partnerships, and LLCs. That's what I discuss in this chapter.

SIDELINE BUSINESSES, TAX WRITE-OFFS, AND THE HOBBY LOSS RULES

Many supposed tax gurus state that you can slash your taxes simply by finding a product or service that you can sell on the side of your regular employment. The problem, they argue, is that as a regular wage earner who receives a paycheck from an employer, you can't write off many of your other (personal) expenses. Open a sideline business, they say, and you can deduct your personal expenses as business expenses.

The pitch is enticing, but the reality is something quite different. You have to spend money to get tax deductions, and the spending must be for legitimate purposes of your business in its efforts to generate income. If you think that taking tax deductions as a hobby is worth the risk because you won't get caught unless you're audited, the odds are stacked against you. The IRS audits an extraordinarily large portion of small businesses that show regular losses.

You need to operate a real business for the purpose of generating income and profits, not tax deductions. The IRS generally considers an activity a hobby (and not a business) if it shows a loss for three or more of the preceding five tax years. (*Exception:* The IRS considers horse racing and breeding a hobby if it shows a loss for at least five of the preceding seven tax years.) Some years, a certain number of businesses lose money, but a real business can't afford to do so year after year and remain in operation. The IRS commonly views these activities as hobbies, particularly when they generate little if any income: antique collecting, crafts, creating art, photography, stamp collecting, training and showing dogs or horses, and writing.

Even if your sideline business passes this hobby test as well as other IRS requirements, deducting any expenses that aren't directly applicable to your business is illegal. Also, the Tax Cuts and Jobs Act passed in late 2017 and that took effect in 2018 eliminated the ability for those engaged in a hobby to deduct their expenses as an itemized deduction up to the limit of the income from their hobby for the calendar year. Now, those engaged in a hobby are supposed to report their revenue for tax purposes but are no longer able to claim an itemized deduction for their hobby expenses.

Sole Proprietorships

If you're interested in running your own business, odds are you'll do so as a so-called *sole proprietor*. About 70 percent of self-employed folks operate their businesses as sole proprietors because setting up a business this way is easier and generally less costly than other options. In this section I discuss the advantages and disadvantages of operating your business as a sole proprietorship.

Understanding the "solo" advantages

The pros of operating as a sole proprietor (going solo) may or may not outweigh the cons for a given small business owner. Each business (and owner) is unique and should weight the pros and cons. Consider the following advantages:

>> **Simplest tax rules and record keeping compared with other business entity options:** You report your business income and expenses on Schedule C of IRS Form 1040, and the net income or loss carries over to your personal income tax return. Though no walk in the park itself, compared with corporate tax forms, Schedule C is easier to complete.

>> **Low cost to establish or discontinue:** Without incorporating, it's a relative snap to get going or shut down.

>> **High flexibility to switch to other entity forms:** You can easily switch to any of the other entities (corporation, LLC, and so on) I discuss later in this chapter.

>> **Good retirement plan options:** You can stash away a large chunk of your business earnings in a tax-advantaged retirement account (discussed in Chapter 4).

So does this mean that running your small business as a sole proprietorship is the way to go for you and your company? Not necessarily — next up are the drawbacks, which you should weigh in your case.

Weighing the disadvantages of operating "solo"

WARNING

Organizing and running your small business as a sole proprietorship has its cons, and these may outweigh the pros, depending on the type of business you're running. Here are the drawbacks you should be aware of:

>> **Liability exposure:** Unlike in a corporation, where you have some shielding from liability thanks to the corporate structure, a sole proprietorship offers no such protection. However, as I discuss in the later section "Investigating liability insurance," you may be able to buy liability insurance, depending on the type of business you operate.

>> **Only one owner is permitted:** If you want to provide some small ownership stakes to key employees, you can't do that in a solo business. One exception: You can share ownership with your spouse so long as your spouse "materially participates" (that is, works) in the business. If both you and your spouse are owners, you each need to file your own Schedule C (more work), and you each need to pay Social Security tax on your share of the earnings (more tax).

>> **Estate issues:** With some business entities, the business structure survives your passing, but not so with a sole proprietorship. This may have negative consequences on the tax front and if you want your survivors to be able to easily continue with the company.

>> **You're taxed on all profits, even if you don't want to take them all out of the business:** If you have a big year or two, don't need all the money your business is generating, and want to leave some of it in the business, you still pay personal income tax on all those earnings as a solo. Not so with some other entities I discuss later in this chapter.

>> **Increased audit risks:** The IRS knows that it finds more tax mistakes and fraud with solo businesses, so on average, it tends to audit such companies at a somewhat higher rate.

Now, in enumerating these possible drawbacks to operating a business as a sole proprietorship, I'm not trying to scare you off from doing so or talk you into, for example, incorporating. You need to consider which pros and cons may or may not apply to your situation and the type of business you're envisioning or operating. And you need to consider the alternative entities, like the ones later in this chapter.

Deciding Whether to Incorporate

A corporation, technically speaking, is a legal entity that's separate from its founders, managers, and employees; it's owned by shareholders. Your personal assets are protected in case the corporation is sued. C corporations (the subject of this section) provide the most financial protection to shareholders, but many small businesses choose to be S corporations because they're cheaper to start and easier to maintain and have just one level of taxation compared with the two levels of taxation for C corporations. (I discuss S corporations in more detail later in this chapter.)

Limited liability companies (LLCs) are an increasingly popular option that offer numerous corporate-like benefits (chief among them liability protection) without some of the costs and downsides. Please be sure to read that important discussion later in this chapter.

Before you call a lawyer or your state government offices to figure out how to incorporate, you need to know that incorporating takes time and costs money. Corporations generally involve the highest costs and most administrative hassles among the range of business entities for you to use. There are fees to incorporate, and each state levies an annual fee that you must pay, even if you have no business income that year. You also have higher legal and accounting costs thanks to the more complex tax rules and filings required of corporations, including the dreaded IRS Form 1120, "U.S. Corporation Income Tax Return" (www.irs.gov/pub/irs-pdf/f1120.pdf).

In some instances, the decision to incorporate is complicated, but in most cases, it need not be a difficult choice. Taxes may be important to the decision but aren't the only consideration. This section presents an overview of the critical issues to consider. I discuss liability considerations, including whether you can obtain liability insurance for your chosen profession, as well as tax and other considerations.

TIP

If you weigh the following considerations of incorporating and you're still on the fence, my advice is to keep it simple: Don't incorporate. After you incorporate, un-incorporating takes time and money. Start as a sole proprietorship and then take it from there. Wait until the benefits of incorporating for your particular case clearly outweigh the costs and drawbacks of incorporating. Likewise, if the only benefits of incorporating can be better accomplished through some other means (such as purchasing insurance), save your money and time and don't incorporate.

Getting a handle on liability protection

The chief reason to consider incorporating your small business is for purposes of liability protection. Attorneys speak of the "protection of the corporate veil." Don't confuse this veil with insurance. You don't get any insurance when you incorporate. You may need or want to buy liability insurance instead of (or in addition to) incorporating (see the next section for details). Liability protection doesn't insulate your company from being sued, either.

When you incorporate, the protection of the corporate veil provides you with the separation of your business assets and liabilities from your personal finances in most situations (gross negligence and bad faith being notable counterexamples). You must follow the ground rules, though, for being a corporation.

Why should you care about the separation of personal and business assets and liabilities? Suppose that your business is doing well, and you take out a bank loan to expand. Over the next few years, however, your business ends up in trouble. Before you know it, your company is losing money, and you're forced to close up shop. If you can't repay the bank loan because of your business failure, the bank shouldn't be able to go after your personal assets if you're incorporated, right?

Unfortunately, many small business owners who need money find that bankers ask for personal guarantees, which negate part of the liability protection that comes with incorporation. Additionally, if you play financial games with your company (such as shifting money out of the company in preparation for defaulting on a loan), a bank may legally be able to go after your personal assets. So you must adhere to a host of ground rules and protocols to prove to the IRS that you're running a bona fide company. For example, you need to keep corporate records and hold an annual meeting — even if it's just with yourself!

REMEMBER

A business can be sued if it mistreats an employee or if its product or service causes harm to a customer. But the owner's personal assets should generally be protected when the company is incorporated and meets the other protocols for being a legitimate business just discussed.

Investigating liability insurance

Before you incorporate, investigate and find out what actions can cause you to be sued. You can do this by asking others in your line of business or advisors who work with companies like yours. Then see whether you can purchase insurance to protect against these potential liabilities. Insurance is superior to incorporation because it pays claims and the annual cost should be tax deductible as a business expense.

TIP

If you belong to a professional group(s), especially if it has a national office, the group may be able to provide information on the percentage of members who are incorporated and on legal and insurance issues. Also, insurance agents may be able to advise on their experience with claims in your specific industry.

Suppose that you perform professional services but make a major mistake that costs someone a lot of money, or worse. Even if you're incorporated, if someone sues you and wins, your company may have to pay a sizeable settlement. This situation not only costs a great deal of money but also can sink your business. Only insurance can cover such financially destructive claims.

You can also be sued if someone slips and breaks a bone or two. To cover these types of claims, you can purchase a property or premises liability policy from an insurer.

TIP

Accountants, doctors, and a number of other professionals can buy liability insurance. A good place to start searching for liability insurance is through the associations that exist for your profession. Even if you aren't a current member, check out the associations anyway. You may be able to access any insurance they provide without membership or you can join the association long enough to get signed up. Incorporating, however, doesn't necessarily preclude insuring yourself. Both incorporating and covering yourself with liability insurance may make sense in your case.

Understanding corporate taxes

Corporations are taxed as entities separate from their individual owners. This situation can be both good and bad. Suppose that your business is doing well and making lots of money. If your business isn't incorporated, all your company's profits are taxed on your personal tax return in the year that you earn those profits.

If you intend to use the profits to reinvest in your business and expand, incorporating can appear to potentially save you some tax dollars. When your business is incorporated (as a regular or so-called *C corporation*), effective 2018, all of your profits are taxed at the 21 percent corporate tax rate, which is lower than most of the individual income tax brackets for moderate- and higher-income earners.

But, there's more to this tax rate comparison story. Unincorporated small businesses that operate as so-called pass-through entities (for example, sole proprietorships, LLCs, partnerships, and S corporations), named so because the profits of the business *pass through* to the owners and their personal income tax returns, have a new advantage. To address the fact that business owners that operated their business as a pass-through entity could face a higher personal federal income tax rate than the

21 percent rate levied on C-corporations, Congress provided a 20 percent deduction for those pass-through businesses. So, for example, if your sole proprietorship, LLC, partnership, or S-corporation netted you $80,000 in 2018 as a single taxpayer, that would push you into the 22 percent federal income tax bracket, a bit above the corporate rate of 21 percent. But, you get to deduct 20 percent of that $80,000 of income ($16,000), so you would only owe federal income tax on the remainder $64,000 ($80,000 – $16,000). Another way to look at this is that the business pass-through owner would only pay federal income taxes on 80 percent of his profits and would be in the 22 percent federal income tax bracket. This deduction effectively reduces the 22 percent federal income tax bracket to 17.6 percent, which is lower than the 21 corporate tax rate.

One caveat to the previous points: The 20 percent pass-through deduction gets phased out for service business owners (such as lawyers, doctors, real estate agents, consultants, and so on) at single taxpayer incomes above $170,050 (up to $220,050) and for married couples filing jointly incomes over $340,100 (up to $440,100). For other types of businesses above these income thresholds, this deduction may be limited so consult with your tax advisor.

WARNING

Resist the temptation to incorporate just so you can leave your money in the corporation, which may be taxed at a lower rate than you'd pay on your personal income. Don't be motivated by this seemingly short-term gain. If you want to pay yourself the profits in the future, you can end up paying more taxes. Why? Because you pay taxes first at the corporate tax rate in the year your company earns the money, and then you pay taxes again on these same profits (this time on your personal income tax return) when you pay yourself from the corporate till in the form of a dividend.

Another possible tax advantage for a corporation is that corporations can pay, on a tax-deductible basis, for employee benefits such as health insurance, long-term care insurance, disability insurance, and up to $50,000 of term life insurance. The owner usually is treated as an employee for benefits purposes. Sole proprietorships and other unincorporated businesses usually can take only tax deductions for these benefit expenses for employees. Benefit expenses for owners who work in the business aren't deductible, except for pension contributions and health insurance, which you can deduct on the front of IRS Form 1040.

Another reason not to incorporate, especially in the early years of a business, is that you can't claim the losses for an incorporated business on your personal tax return. On your business tax return, you have to wait to claim the losses against profits. Because most companies produce little revenue in their early years and have all sorts of start-up expenditures, losses are common.

Examining other incorporation considerations

Because corporations are legal entities distinct from their owners, corporations offer other features and benefits that a sole proprietorship or partnership doesn't. For example, corporations have shareholders who own a piece or percentage of the company. These shares can be sold or transferred to other owners, subject to any restrictions in the shareholders' agreement.

Corporations also offer *continuity of life*, which simply means that corporations can continue to exist despite the death of an owner or the owner's transfer of his or her share (stock) in the company.

REMEMBER

Don't incorporate for ego purposes. If you want to incorporate to impress friends, family, or business contacts, you need to know that few people would be impressed or even know that you're incorporated. Besides, if you operate as a sole proprietor, you can choose to operate under a different business name ("doing business as" or d.b.a.) without the cost — or the headache — of incorporating.

Knowing where to get advice

If you're totally confused about whether to incorporate because your business is undergoing major financial changes, getting competent professional help is worth the money. The hard part is knowing where to turn because finding one advisor who can put all the pieces of the puzzle together can be challenging. And be aware that you may get wrong or biased advice.

TIP

Attorneys who specialize in advising small businesses can help explain the legal issues. Tax advisors who do a lot of work with business owners can help explain the tax considerations. Also, a tax advisor should be able to prepare tax illustrations comparing the same business operated as a sole proprietorship, LLC, S corporation, and C corporation and the tax that the business would owe under different scenarios. If you find that you need two or more advisors to help make the decision, getting them together in one room with you for a meeting may help and ultimately save you time and money.

One Step Further: S Corporations

Subchapter S corporations, so named for that part of the tax code that establishes them, offer some business owners the best of both worlds. You get the liability protection that comes with being incorporated as with a C corporation, and the business profit or loss passes through to the owner's personal tax returns (like in a sole proprietorship). In this section, I discuss the tax specifics of using S corporation status and the requirements for S corporations.

S corporation tax specifics

An S corporation is known as a *pass-through entity* for tax purposes. This simply means that the income that the company earns passes through to the company's owner/shareholders and is taxed at each person's individual level.

So if the business shows a loss in some years, the owners/shareholders may claim those losses in the current year of the loss on their tax returns against other income earned. This is potentially useful in the early years of a new business, a time when most companies lose money. To be able to claim losses, you must "materially participate" in the business, which generally means that you actively work in the company at least 500 hours per year, although 100 hours will suffice if that's the most among all other shareholders.

If, like most businesses, the company becomes profitable, it may actually make sense then to convert back to a regular C corporation to partake of the potential advantages of that status. That includes being able to retain earnings in the company, which you can't do with an S corporation, and being able to use tax-advantaged fringe benefits. (If you plan to take all the profits out of the company, an S corporation may make sense for you.)

Even though the corporation doesn't pay federal income tax, the company must annually complete and file IRS Form 1120S — "U.S. Income Tax Return for an S Corporation" (www.irs.gov/pub/irs-pdf/f1120s.pdf). Also, some states levy a state income tax on S corporations, and many states require paying an annual fee.

TIP

One way an S corporation can save its owner/shareholders tax money is by paying them some of their compensation in the form of dividends. The reason this saves tax money is because dividends aren't subject to payroll or employment taxes. You must be careful, though, to ensure employee salaries are reasonable and not set artificially low and made up for by high dividend payments. Speak with a tax advisor who has experience advising other small business owners in situations similar to yours.

S corporation requirements

All corporations actually begin as so-called *C corporations*, which are the corporations discussed in the section "Deciding Whether to Incorporate" earlier in this chapter. The United States has more than twice as many S corporations today as C corporations. To become an S corporation, your business must go through an additional "tax election" step. See IRS Form 2553, "Election by a Small Business Corporation."

U.S. tax laws allow most, but not all, small businesses to be S corporations. To be an S corporation in the eyes of the almighty IRS, a company must meet all the following requirements:

>> Be a U.S. company

>> Have just one class of stock

>> Have no more than 100 shareholders who are all U.S. residents or citizens and aren't partnerships, other corporations, or, with certain exceptions, trusts

TIP

Be sure to investigate limited liability companies (LLCs), the subject of a later section, before committing to forming an S corporation. LLCs offer the passing through of income that S corporations do and are generally simpler to initiate and operate. As the operator of an LLC, you can still have the future option of converting to an S corporation.

Partnerships

A *partnership* occurs in the eyes of the tax authorities when two or more people — the *general partners* (GPs) — operate a business together and divide the profits (or losses). The division need not be done equally.

The GPs are responsible for the company's debts and liabilities. A partnership may also have *limited partners* (LPs) who generally provide financing to the business and who aren't active in the company itself. Most small business partnerships don't have LPs.

A partnership is similar to a sole proprietorship and other pass-through entities for income tax purposes. Partners pay personal income taxes on their share of the partnership's income distributed to them. This is done on IRS Form 1040 Schedule E, "Supplemental Income and Loss" (www.irs.gov/pub/irs-pdf/f1040se.pdf). As sole proprietors do, partners pay self-employment taxes on income earned.

REMEMBER

Though the partnership itself doesn't pay any federal income tax, it has plenty of federal income tax reporting requirements. In fact, the tax rules and reporting requirements of a partnership are quite extensive and challenging. The partnership must file IRS Form 1065, "U.S. Return of Partnership Income." And the partnership must complete and annually issue IRS Schedule K-1 of Form 1065 to each partner. You'd be well advised to use the services of a tax advisor if you're going to have your business function as a partnership.

Limited Liability
Companies (LLCs)

In recent decades, a new type of corporation has appeared. *Limited liability companies* (LLCs) offer business owners benefits similar to those of S corporations and partnerships but are even better in some cases.

Like an S corporation, an LLC offers liability protection for the owners — hence the name limited liability company. In addition to the veil of overall liability protection for the owner's personal finances, an owner's liability for business debts is limited in an LLC to their percentage ownership share in the business.

LLCs also pass the business's profits through to the owner's personal income tax returns, like a sole proprietorship or partnership. You can pass through losses as well and deduct them against your other income so long as you materially participate in the business.

LLCs are generally much simpler to set up and administer than a corporation. But, to be realistic going into it, don't expect an LLC to be as simple as a sole proprietorship. And LLCs don't give you the ability to tap into some of the tax advantages derived from specific fringe benefits that some corporations offer.

LLCs have fewer restrictions regarding shareholders than S corporations. For example, LLCs have no limits on the number of shareholders, and the shareholders can be foreigners, corporations, or partnerships.

Compared with S corporations, the only additional restriction LLCs carry is that sole proprietors and professionals can't always form LLCs (although some states allow this). All states now permit the formation of LLCs, but most state laws require you to have at least two partners for an LLC to be taxed as a partnership and not be a professional firm.

Single-owner LLCs (which also include married couples in community property states) are treated as sole proprietorships and file Schedule C of Form 1040 for tax purposes, unless the owner elects to file as a corporation on Form 8832, "Entity Classification Election." A domestic entity that has more than one member will default to a partnership. An LLC with multiple owners can either accept its default classification as a partnership, or file Form 8832 to elect to be classified as an association taxable as a corporation. This form is for informational purposes only. Keep in mind that LLCs aren't taxed federally; income is passed through to the company's owners/shareholders. However, numerous states levy a tax on LLCs and require an annual tax filing. Some states like California go even further with fees. California has a fee based on gross receipts, not net income. A California LLC with $500,000 in gross receipts pays $820 tax plus a $2,500 fee for a total of $3,320, even if it reports a net loss for the year after expenses.

IN THIS CHAPTER

» Saving money and headaches with effective record-keeping

» Determining whether to itemize deductions

» Choosing the simplified home office deduction

» Qualifying for health insurance deductions

» Seeking tax breaks for minority-owned and other businesses

Chapter **12**

Trimming Small Business Taxes

This chapter presents some ways to reduce your small business taxes that I want to be sure you don't miss. I discuss the importance of keeping good records, knowing which deductions are worth itemizing, and being ready in the event of an audit. I also include some reasons married couples may choose to file separately and describe the tax breaks that may be available for minority-owned businesses and those businesses located in low-income areas.

Keeping Track of Your Small Business Revenues and Costs

One of the ways that you keep score in your small business is to track your business revenue and expenses; the difference between the two is the profit or loss for your company. I strongly recommend that you utilize a system for accounting for your business inflows and outflows to stay on top of what's going on in your business and to ease the pains of completing the never-ending stream of tax forms required by state and federal government tax authorities quarterly and annually.

REMEMBER

If you're thinking about starting a business or you're already in the thick of one, make sure you keep a proper accounting of your income and expenses. If you don't, you'll have a lot more stress and headaches when it comes time to complete and submit the necessary tax forms for your business.

Besides helping you over the annual tax-filing hurdle and fulfilling quarterly requirements, accurate records allow you to track your company's financial health and performance during the year. How are your profits running compared with last year? Can you afford to hire new employees? Analyzing your monthly or quarterly business financial statements (profit and loss statement, balance sheet, and so on) can help you answer these and other important questions.

WARNING

The IRS targets small businesses for audits because more than a few small business owners break the tax rules, and many areas exist where small business owners can mess up. If your small business is audited, well-prepared and organized financial records will help. Being organized in and of itself helps establish you in the auditor's eyes as a responsible business person.

You can find information about fulfilling the myriad filing requirements of the tax authorities by keeping proper records in my book *Small Business Taxes For Dummies* (Wiley).

The following sections cover the key tax-organizing things that small business owners need to keep in mind and get right.

Separating business from personal finances

One of the IRS's concerns is that, as a small business owner, you'll try to minimize your company's profits (and therefore taxes) by hiding business income and inflating business expenses. Uncle Sam thus looks suspiciously at business owners who use personal checking and personal credit card accounts for company transactions. You may be tempted to use your personal accounts this way because opening separate accounts is a hassle — not because you're dishonest.

TIP

Take the time to open separate accounts (such as bank accounts and credit card accounts) for your business and your personal use. Doing so not only makes the tax authorities happy but also makes your accounting easier. And don't make the mistake of thinking that paying for an expense through your business account proves to the IRS that it was a legitimate business expense. If the IRS finds that the expense was truly for personal purposes, it will likely dig deeper into your company's financial records to see what other shenanigans are going on.

Keeping current on income, employment/payroll, and sales taxes

When you're self-employed, you're responsible for the accurate and timely filing of all your income taxes. Without an employer and a payroll department to handle the paperwork for withholding taxes on a regular schedule, you need to make estimated tax payments on a quarterly basis.

If you have employees, you need to withhold taxes from each paycheck they receive, and you must make timely payments to the IRS and the appropriate state and local authorities. In addition to federal and state income taxes, you must withhold and send in Social Security and any other state or locally mandated employment (payroll) taxes and sales taxes. You also need to issue W-2s annually for each employee and 1099-MISCs for each independent contractor paid $600 or more. Got a headache yet?

For paying taxes on your own self-employment income, you can obtain Form 1040-ES, "Estimated Tax for Individuals." This form comes complete with an estimated tax worksheet and four payment coupons to send in with your quarterly tax payments. It's amazing how user-friendly government people can be when they want your money!

To discover all the amazing rules and regulations of withholding and submitting taxes from employees' paychecks, ask the IRS for Form 941, "Employer's Quarterly Federal Tax Return." Once a year, you also need to complete Form 940, "Employer's Annual Federal Unemployment (FUTA) Tax Return," for unemployment insurance payments to the feds.

TIP

If your business has a part-time or seasonal employee and the additional burden of filing Form 941 quarterly, the IRS has made the paperwork a tad easier. You may be able to file Form 944, "Employer's Annual Federal Tax Return," if your tax withholding on behalf of employees doesn't exceed $1,000 for the year (which translates to about $4,000 in wages). If you qualify, you need to file only once each year. To see whether you qualify, call the IRS at 800-829-0115 or visit its website at www.irs.gov. If you do qualify, the IRS will send you something in writing.

Also check to see whether your state has its own annual or quarterly unemployment insurance reporting requirements. Look for your state's department of labor or use the links on the U.S. Department of Labor website at www.dol.gov/whd/contacts/state_of.htm. And, unless you're lucky enough to live in one of those rare states with no state income taxes, don't forget to get your state's estimated income tax package.

TIP

Falling behind in paying taxes ruins some small businesses. When you hire employees, for example, you're particularly vulnerable to tax land mines. If you aren't going to keep current on taxes for yourself and your employees, hire a payroll company or tax advisor who can help you jump through the necessary tax hoops. Payroll companies and tax advisors are there for a reason, so use them selectively. They take care of all the tax filings for you, and if they mess up, they pay the penalties. Check with a tax advisor you trust for the names of reputable payroll companies in your area. Generally, using a payroll service for form preparation and tax deposits is money well spent. The cost is much less than the potential penalties (and time) if you prepare yourself.

Documenting expenses and income in the event of an audit

It doesn't matter whether you use file folders, software, apps, or a good old-fashioned shoe box to collate receipts and other important financial information. What does matter is that you keep complete and accurate records of both expenses and income.

WARNING

>> **Expenses:** You'll probably lose or misplace some of those little pieces of paper that you need to document your expenses. Thus, one advantage of charging expenses on a credit card or paying by check is that these transactions leave a trail, which makes it easier to total your expenses come tax time and prove your expenses if you're audited.

Just be careful when you use a credit card because you may buy more things than you can really afford. Then you're stuck with a lot of debt to pay off. I generally recommend only charging on a credit card what you can pay off in full by the time your statement payment due date rolls around.

On the other hand (as many small business owners know), finding lenders when you need money is difficult. Borrowing on a low-interest-rate credit card can be an easy and quick way for you to borrow money without groveling to bankers for a loan. (See the latest edition of my book *Personal Finance For Dummies* [Wiley] for details.)

>> **Income:** Likewise, leave a trail with your revenue. Depositing all your receipts in one account helps you when tax time comes or if you're ever audited. Be sure to use a dedicated account for your business; don't be tempted to deposit business income into a personal account. (See the next section for details.)

The later section "Keeping Good Tax Records for Your Small Business" provides full details on the process of stashing the right items.

Reducing your taxes by legally shifting income and expenses

Many small business owners elect to keep their business accounting on what's called a *cash basis*. This choice doesn't imply that all business customers literally pay in cash for goods and services or that the company owners pay for all expenses with cash. Cash-basis accounting simply means that, for tax purposes, you recognize and report income in the year you received it and expenses in the (tax) year you paid them.

By operating on a cash basis, you can exert more control over the amount of profit (revenue minus expenses) that your business reports for tax purposes from year to year. If your income fluctuates from year to year, you can lower your tax burden by doing some legal shifting of income and expenses.

Suppose that you recently started a business. Assume that you have little, but growing, revenue and somewhat high startup expenses. Looking ahead to the next tax year, you can already tell that you'll be making more money and will likely be in a much higher tax bracket. Thus you can likely reduce your tax bill by paying more of your expenses in the next year. Of course, you don't want to upset any of your company's suppliers. However, you can pay some of your bills after the start of the next tax year (January 1) rather than in late December of the preceding year (presuming that your business's tax year is on a regular January 1 through December 31 calendar-year basis). *Note:* Credit card expenses are recognized as of the date you charge them, not when you pay the bill.

Likewise, you can exert some control over when your customers pay you. If you expect to make less money next year, don't invoice customers in December of this year. Wait until January so that you receive more of your income next year.

WARNING

Be careful with this revenue-shifting game. You don't want to run short of cash and miss a payroll! Similarly, if a customer mails you a check in December, IRS laws don't allow you to hold the check until January and count the revenue then. For tax purposes, you're supposed to recognize the payment as revenue when you receive it.

Note: One final point about who can and who can't do this revenue and expense two-step. Sole proprietorships, partnerships (including limited liability companies, also known as LLCs), S corporations, and personal-service corporations generally can shift revenue and expenses. On the other hand, C corporations and partnerships that have C corporations as partners may not use the cash-accounting method if they have annual receipts of more than $5 million per year. Chapter 11 has details on all these business entities.

Keeping Good Tax Records for Your Small Business

Tax records pose a problem for many people because the IRS doesn't require any particular form of record keeping. In fact, the IRS recommends, in general terms, that you keep records only to file a "complete and accurate" return. This section explores what records you should keep, where you should maintain them, and for how long.

Ensuring a complete and accurate tax return

In case you don't feel like flipping through countless pages of government instructions on what constitutes a "complete and accurate" return, here are some common tax situations at a glance and the types of records normally required:

>> **Business expenses:** As I mention in the earlier section "Separating business from personal finances," the IRS is especially watchful in this area, so be sure to keep detailed proof of any expenses that you claim. This proof can consist of many items, such as receipts of income, expense account documentation and statements, and so on. Keep in mind that the IRS doesn't always accept canceled checks as the only method of substantiation, so make sure that you hang on to the bill or receipt for every expense you incur.

>> **Car expenses:** If, for the business use of your car, you choose to deduct the actual expenses rather than the standard mileage rate (which is 67 cents per mile for tax year 2024), you need to show the cost of the car and when you started using it for business. You also must record your business miles, your total miles, and your expenses, such as insurance, gas, and maintenance. You need a combination of a log and written receipts, of course! Stationery and office supply stores carry inexpensive logbooks that you can buy for your vehicle usage and expense tracking. You can also obtain smartphone apps to serve the same purpose.

>> **Home expenses:** If you own your home, you need to keep records of your mortgage and real estate tax payments, the purchase price and purchase expenses, and the cost of all the improvements and additions you make over time (save your receipts). Although you may not be selling your house this year, when you do, you'll be thankful you have all your receipts in a neat little file. If you rent a portion of your house or run a business from it, you also need your utility bills, general repair bills, and housecleaning and lawn-mowing costs to calculate your net rental income or your home office expense. (See the upcoming section "Checking out the New, Simplified Home Office Deduction.")

Setting up a record-keeping system

TIP

The tax year is a long time for keeping track of records that you need (and where you put them) when the filing season arrives. So here are some easy things you can do to make your tax-preparation burden a little lighter:

>> **Use an accordion file.** You can buy one with slots already labeled by month, by category, or by letters of the alphabet, or you can make your own filing system with the extra labels. All this can be yours for about $15.

>> **Set up a manila file folder system.** Decide on the organizational method that best fits your needs, and get

into the habit of saving all bills, receipts, and records that you think you may use someday for tax purposes or for things that affect your overall financial planning. This basic advice is good for any taxpayer, whether you file a simple tax return or a complicated one with far more supplemental schedules. Note that this plan, which should set you back about $5, is only minimal, but it's much better than the shoe-box approach to record-keeping. (A scanning program for documents may also be of interest here.)

>> **Track tax information on your computer and/or through smartphone apps.** A number of financial software packages and smartphone apps enable you to keep track of your spending for tax purposes. Just don't expect to reap the benefits without a fair amount of upfront and continuing work. You need to figure out how to use the software, and you must enter a great deal of data for the software to be useful to you. Don't forget, though, that you still need your receipts to back up your claims; in an audit, the IRS may not accept your computer records without verifying them against your receipts.

If you're interested in software, consider a business-oriented program, such as QuickBooks, for your small-business accounting. Check out their smartphone apps as well. For really simple businesses, consider Quicken. You can merge data into QuickBooks at a later date if you desire. Whichever software you choose, keep in mind that the package tabulates only what you enter or download into it. So if you use the software to write your monthly checks but neglect to enter data for things you pay for with cash, for example, you won't have the whole picture.

Deciding when to stash and when to trash

One of the most frequently asked questions is how long a taxpayer needs to keep tax records. The answer is easy — a minimum of three years. That's because the statute of limitations for tax audits and assessments is three years. If the IRS doesn't adjust or audit your 2024 tax return by April 15, 2028 (the three years start running on April 15, 2025), it missed its chance.

On April 15, 2028, feel free to celebrate another auditless year with a "Shredding the 2024 Tax Return" party. (If you filed after April 15 because you obtained an extension, you must wait until three years after the extension due date rather than the April 15 tax date. The same is true when you file late — the three-year period doesn't start until you actually file your return.)

TIP

However, I must add one point to the general three-year rule: Save all records for the assets that you continue to own. These records can include stocks and bonds, automobiles, your home (along with its improvements), and expensive personal property, such as jewelry, video cameras, or computers. Keep these records in a safe-deposit box in case you suffer a (deductible casualty) loss, such as a fire. You don't want these records going up in smoke!

Some taxpayers take the practical step of videotaping their home and its contents, but if you do, make sure that you keep that record outside your home. You can save money on safe-deposit box fees by leaving your video with relatives who may enjoy watching it because they don't see you often enough. (Of course, your relatives may also suffer a fire or an earthquake.)

WARNING

In situations where the IRS suspects that income wasn't reported, IRS agents can go back as far as six years. And if possible tax fraud is involved, forget all time limitations!

Watching out for state differences

Although the IRS requires that you keep your records for only three years, your state may have a longer statute of limitations with regard to state income tax audits. If you're curious what your state's rules are, check with your state's income tax collecting authority. Also, some of your tax-related records may be important to keep for other reasons. For example, suppose that you throw out your receipts after three years. Then the fellow who built your garage four years ago sues you, asserting that you didn't fully pay the bill. You may be out of luck in court if you don't have the canceled check showing that you paid.

The moral: Hang on to records that may be important (such as home improvement receipts) for longer than three years — especially if a dispute is possible. Check with a legal advisor whenever you have a concern because statutes of limitations vary from state to state.

Replacing lost business records

If your business records have been lost or destroyed, you can often obtain duplicate bills from major vendors. You shouldn't have a great deal of trouble getting copies of the original telephone, utility, rent, credit card, oil company, and other bills. Reconstructing a typical month of automobile use can help you make a reasonable determination of the business use of your car. If that month's use approximates an average month's business use of an auto, the IRS usually accepts such reconstructed records as adequate substantiation.

If you deposited all your business income in a checking or savings account, you can reconstruct that income from duplicate bank statements. Although banks usually don't charge for copies of bank statements, they do charge for copies of canceled checks if you can't obtain them online. These charges can be quite expensive, so do some legwork before ordering copies of all your checks. For example, obtain a copy of your lease and a statement from your landlord saying that all rent was paid on time before you request duplicate copies of rent checks.

By ordering copies of past returns with Form 4506, "Request for Copy of Transcript of Tax Form," you can have a point of reference for determining whether you accounted for typical business expenses. Past returns reveal not only gross profit percentages or margins of profit but also the amounts of recurring expenses. (You can find this form at www.irs.gov/pub/irs-pdf/f4506. pdf.) If you create an account on the www.irs.gov website, you can retrieve your past return information online and not bother with Form 4506.

Calculating Whether a Deduction Is Worth Itemizing

Deductions are just what they sound like: You subtract them from your income before you calculate the tax you owe. So the more deductions you take, the smaller your taxable income — and the smaller your tax bill. The IRS gives you two methods of determining your total deductions. You get to pick the method that leads to the largest total deductions — and thus a lower tax bill. But sometimes the choice isn't so clear, so be prepared to do some figuring.

Taking the standard deduction usually makes sense if you have a pretty simple financial life — a regular paycheck, a rented apartment, and no large expenses, such as medical bills, moving expenses, or loss due to theft or catastrophe. The standard deductions almost doubled in 2018 thanks to the Tax Cuts and Jobs Act. In 2024 single folks qualify for a $14,600 standard deduction, and married couples filing jointly get a $29,200 standard deduction.

The other method of determining your allowable deductions is to itemize them on your tax return. This painstaking procedure is definitely more of a hassle, but if you can tally up more than the standard deduction amount, itemizing saves you money. Schedule A of Form 1040 is the page for summing up your itemized deductions, but you won't know whether you have enough itemized deductions unless you give this schedule a good examination. You can obtain the latest version of Schedule A at: https://www.irs.gov/pub/irs-pdf/f1040sa.pdf.

If you currently don't itemize, you may be surprised to discover that your personal property and state income taxes are itemizable, subject to an annual cap of $10,000. If you pay a fee to the state to register and license your car, you can itemize the expenditure as a deduction ("Other Taxes" on Schedule A). The IRS allows you to deduct only the part of the fee that relates to the car's value, however. The state organization that collects the fee should be able to tell you what portion of the fee is deductible. If it's a user-friendly organization, it may even show this figure on your invoice.

When you total your itemized deductions on Schedule A and that amount is equal to or less than the standard deduction, take the standard deduction without fail (unless you're married filing separately and your spouse is itemizing — then you have to itemize). The total for your itemized deductions is worth checking every year, however, because you may have more deductions in some years than others, and you may occasionally be able to itemize.

TIP

Because you can control when you pay particular expenses for which you're eligible to itemize, you can shift or bunch more of them into selected years when you know that you'll have enough deductions to take full advantage of itemizing. For example, suppose that you're using the standard deduction this tax year because you just don't have many itemized deductions. Late in the tax year, though, you feel certain that you'll buy a home sometime during the next year. Thanks to the potential write-off of mortgage interest and property taxes, you also know that you'll be able to itemize next year. It makes sense, then, to shift as many deductible expenses as possible into the next year.

If you're near the threshold for itemizing, you could make several years' worth of charitable donations in one year. Also, in most cases, you can make an extra property tax payment near the year's end.

Checking Out the New, Simplified Home Office Deduction

To claim expenses for the business use of your home — or the so-called *home office deduction* — you have to complete a fairly complicated form: Form 8829, "Expenses for Business Use of Your Home," to be exact. Form 8829 weighs in at more than 40 lines (the most recent version is available at www.irs.gov/pub/irs-pdf/f8829.pdf).

The IRS may be slow, but it eventually finds ways to simplify the tax code. And it often chooses to simplify tax laws by making them more complicated! For example, rather than simplifying Form 8829, the IRS has created a new filing option for some tax filers.

Folks who qualify for claiming a home office deduction (which I explain in the next section) can now do so with the simplified home office deduction. Here are the details of this newer option:

>> Your deduction is limited to $1,500 per year, which is based on a deduction of $5 per square foot for up to a 300-square-foot home office.

>> No depreciation deduction is allowed.

>> You claim your mortgage interest and property tax deductions on Schedule A of Form 1040 (which you can access at www.irs.gov/pub/irs-pdf/f1040sa.pdf).

>> You can't deduct any other actual expenses related to your home.

>> You can't carry forward a loss.

>> You may use either the simplified method or the regular method for any taxable year.

>> You choose a method by using that method on your timely filed, original federal income tax return for the taxable year.

>> After you choose a method for a taxable year, you can't later change to the other method for that same year.

>> If you use the simplified method for one year and use the regular method for any subsequent year, you must calculate the depreciation deduction for the subsequent year using the appropriate optional depreciation table. This is true regardless of whether you used an optional depreciation table for the first year the property was used in business.

TIP

With the tax bill that took effect in 2018, know that you may only deduct up to $10,000 in state and local taxes including property taxes on Schedule A. And, you may only deduct mortgage interest on new mortgages of up $750,000 of debt. So, if you have more than these amounts, that would argue for you to consider using the "regular method."

Every now and then, the IRS actually produces a table or summary that's useful. Table 12-1 is its summary comparing the simplified and regular home office deduction.

TABLE 12-1   The Simplified Option versus the Regular Method

Simplified Option	Regular Method
Deduction for home office use of a portion of a residence allowed only if that portion is exclusively used on a regular basis for business purposes	Same
Allowable square footage of home used for business (not to exceed 300 square feet)	Percentage of home used for business
Standard $5 per square foot used to determine home business deduction	Actual expenses determined and records maintained
Home-related itemized deductions claimed in full on Schedule A	Home-related itemized deductions apportioned between Schedule A and business schedule (Schedule C or Schedule F)
No depreciation deduction	Depreciation deduction for portion of home used for business
No recapture of depreciation upon sale of home	Recapture of depreciation on gain upon sale of home
Deduction can't exceed gross income from business use of home less business expenses	Same
Amount in excess of gross income limitation may not be carried over	Amount in excess of gross income limitation may be carried over
Loss carryover from use of regular method in prior year may *not* be claimed	Loss carryover from use of regular method in prior year may be claimed if gross income test is met in current year

Internal Revenue Service / https://www.irs.gov/businesses/small-businesses-self-employed/simplified-option-for-home-office-deduction / Public domain

Qualifying for a home office deduction

REMEMBER

You're entitled to claim a home office deduction if you have a dedicated space in your house that you use for your business, even if you use it only to conduct administrative or management activities for your company, provided you have no other office or other place of business where you can perform the same tasks. To qualify as a "home office" for tax purposes, your home office doesn't have to be the place where you meet customers or the principal place where you conduct business.

So a person who simply brings work home is out of luck. So is the person who spreads out work over the dining room table. So long as you eat there, that table isn't dedicated solely to the pursuit of your business.

A carpenter who sets up their computer and desk in a corner of the dining room so they can price jobs and bill clients has a valid deduction. The reason: because that corner of their dining room is set aside solely for their company's administrative and management activities.

If you use a portion of your home to store inventory or samples, you're also entitled to deduct your home office expenses. Say that you sell cosmetics and use part of your study to store samples. You can deduct expenses related to the portion of your study that you use to store the cosmetics, even if you use the study for other purposes.

You can use Form 8829 whether you're a renter or a homeowner:

>> If you're a renter, filling out Form 8829 correctly means that you first determine your total rent — including insurance, cleaning, and utilities. Then you deduct the portion you use for business. For example, if you rent four rooms and use one room for business, you're entitled to deduct 25 percent of the total. (If the rooms are the same size, you can use this method. If not, you have to figure out the percentage on a square-footage basis.)

>> For homeowners, you compute the total cost of maintaining your home, including depreciation, mortgage interest, taxes, insurance, repairs, and so on. Don't forget to deduct the cost of your cleaning service if your office is cleaned in addition to the rest of the house. Then deduct the percentage you use for business.

Understanding the downsides to home office deductions

Because taking home office deductions can lower your tax bill, why would you not want to take them? Well, assuming that you may legally take home office deductions and that they actually lower your tax bill, by all means take them. But just be aware that taking these deductions can have some real drawbacks.

In this section, I discuss the increased audit risks for home-based businesses, especially those that regularly lose money, at least on paper for tax purposes. Also, I discuss the arcane-sounding topic of depreciation recapture, which can lead to a larger tax bill when you sell a home for which you've previously taken a home office deduction.

Audit risk and rejection of repeated business losses

According to the IRS, a sideline activity that generates a loss year in and year out isn't a business but a hobby. Specifically, an activity is considered a hobby if it shows a loss for at least three of the past five tax years. (Horse racing, breeding, and so on are considered hobbies if they show losses in at least six of the past seven tax years.)

Certainly, some businesses lose money. But a real business can't afford to do so year after year and still remain in business. Who likes losing money unless the losses are really just a tax deduction front for a hobby?

When the hobby loss rules indicate that you're engaging in a hobby, the IRS will disallow your claiming of the losses. To challenge this ruling, you must convince the IRS that you're seriously attempting to make a profit and run a legitimate business. The IRS will want to see that you're actively marketing your services, building your skills, and accounting for income and expenses. The IRS also will want to see that you aren't having too much fun! When you derive too much pleasure from an activity, in the eyes of the IRS, the activity must not be a real business.

The Tax Cuts and Jobs Act bill, which took effect in 2018, toughened the hobby loss rules further. Specifically, the IRS now requires you to report your revenue from a hobby, but you may not deduct any expenses from that hobby.

WARNING

Unfortunately, some self-anointed financial gurus claim that you can slash or even completely eliminate your tax bill by setting up a sideline business. They say that you can sell your services while doing something you enjoy. The problem, they argue, is that — as a regular wage earner who receives a paycheck from an employer — you can't write off many of your other (that is, personal) expenses. These hucksters usually promise to show you the secrets of tax reduction if you shell out far too many bucks for their audiotapes and notebooks of inside information.

"Start a small business for fun, profit, and huge tax deductions," one financial book trumpets, adding that, "The tax benefits alone are worth starting a small business." A seminar company that offers a course on "How to Write a Book on Anything in 2 Weeks . . . or Less!" also offers a tax course titled "How to Have Zero Taxes Deducted from Your Paycheck." This tax seminar tells you how to solve your tax problems: "If you have a sideline business or would like to start one, you're eligible to have little or no taxes taken from your pay."

Suppose that you're interested in photography. You like to take pictures when you go on vacation. These supposed tax experts tell you to set up a photography business and start deducting all your photography-related expenses: airfare, film, utility bills, rent for your "home darkroom," and restaurant meals with potential clients (that is, your friends). Before you know it, you've wiped out most of your taxes.

Sounds too good to be true, right? It is. Your business spending must be for the legitimate purpose of generating an income.

REMEMBER

What's the bottom line? You need to operate a legitimate business for the purpose of generating income and profits — not tax deductions. If you're thinking that it's worth the risk of taking tax losses for your hobby, year after year, because you won't get caught unless you're audited, better think again. The IRS audits an extraordinarily large number of small businesses that show regular losses.

Depreciation recapture when selling a home with previous home office deductions

If you've taken depreciation for your home office deduction after May 6, 1997, when you go to sell your home, you'll have to pay tax through *depreciation recapture*. Specifically, you'll owe tax at the rate of 25 percent on the amount of depreciation taken for your home office.

But if you qualify for the home office deduction, this shouldn't be a bad thing to have happen to you because the value of those deductions over the years should far exceed the cost of the depreciation recapture.

Deducting Health Insurance Costs

Self-employed people can deduct 100 percent of their health insurance costs for themselves and their covered family members.

Of course, a variety of insurance and related benefits are tax-deductible to corporations for all employees. These benefits include

>> Health insurance

>> Disability insurance

>> Term life insurance (up to $50,000 in benefits per employee)

- » Dependent care plans (up to $5,000 per employee may be put away on a tax-deductible basis for childcare and/or care for elderly parents)

- » Flexible spending or cafeteria plans, which allow employees to pick and choose the benefits on which to spend their benefit dollars

REMEMBER

For companies that aren't incorporated, the business owners can't deduct the cost of the preceding insurance plans for themselves, but they can deduct these costs for employees. Self-employed people can deduct all health insurance costs for themselves and their covered family members.

Finding Tax Breaks for Minority-Owned Businesses and Those in Low-Income Areas

There are actually no federal income tax breaks for minority owned businesses. There are, however, some tax incentives for working with other minority owned businesses or operating in qualifying low-income areas. So, this means that virtually every small business that is interested in these extra tax breaks can find a way to qualify.

Businesses that work with certified minority business enterprises (MBEs) may be eligible for certain tax benefits. MBEs are at least 51 percent owned and operated by one or more minority U.S. citizens, who also carry out management and the daily operations of the for-profit U.S.-based business.

The first credit to be aware of is called the New-Markets Tax Credit (NMTC), which was recently extended through 2025. The NMTC program provides federal income tax credits to investors who make investments through financial intermediaries called Community Development Entities (CDEs), which in turn make investments into qualifying low-income communities. The federal income tax credits are claimed over seven years and total 39 percent of the investor's investment in the CDE. For more information on this tax credit, visit the New Markets Tax Credit Coalition website at nmtccoalition.org.

The second batch of tax breaks encourage businesses to operate in economically distressed areas. The Department of Housing and Urban Development and the Department of Agriculture designate qualifying empowerment zones in urban and rural areas respectively for several tax credits including additional first year expensing write-offs, employment credits, and special capital gains exclusion. These credits have been extended through 2025. For more information, please visit: https://home.kpmg/us/en/home/insights/2021/03/tnf-rev-proc-2021-18-deemed-extension-empowerment-zones-through-2025.html.

5

Tax Breaks in Real Estate

Understand the tax benefits of home ownership.

Determine the tax benefits of investing in rental properties and other real estate.

Explore the tax angles and exit strategies for real estate investments.

Chapter **13**

Getting Tax Advantages from Your Home

Tax benefits are a significant reason why many people, especially people in the real estate business — such as real estate agents, bankers, mortgage brokers, and others in the lending business — advocate property ownership.

Buying a home or investing in real estate can provide financial and psychological rewards. And tax breaks can help reduce the cost of owning real estate. On the other hand, purchasing and maintaining property can be time-consuming, emotionally draining, and financially painful.

Surveying Real Estate Tax Breaks

Just as contributing money to retirement accounts (see Chapter 4) yields tax breaks, so does buying a home and investing in other real estate. The U.S. income tax system favors home and other real estate ownership because of the widely held belief that owners take better care of their property when they have a financial stake in its future value. Arguing with this logic is difficult if you have visited almost any government-subsidized tenement.

All the powerful real estate lobbies also contribute to the addition and retention of real estate tax benefits in our tax code. Builders, contractors, real estate agents, the banking industry, and many other real estate–related sectors have an enormous financial stake in the American hunger to own and improve properties.

You should understand the tax aspects of owning a home and investing in other real estate so that you can make the most of these tax-reduction opportunities. Making wise real estate decisions also requires that you know how to fit real estate into your overall financial picture. After all, you have limited income and other options on which to spend your money.

WARNING

Don't make the mistake of depending on those individuals involved in the typical real estate deal to help you see the bigger picture. Remember that these folks make their livings off your decision to buy real estate, and the more you spend, the more they generally make.

Before I get to detailing real estate tax breaks, I kindly ask you to remember two important caveats to gaining these property tax advantages:

>> You have to spend money on real estate — acquiring property, paying the mortgage and property taxes over the years, and improving the property while you own it — to even be eligible for the tax breaks. As I discuss in this chapter, if you purchase a high-priced home or make the wrong financial moves, you may not be able to claim some of the real estate tax benefits available (see the section

"Grasping that house losses aren't deductible," later in this chapter).

>> The price of real estate in the United States reflects the fact that buyers and sellers know about the tax deductions. This is a major reason why so many people are willing to pay sums with many zeroes for a piece of the American Dream. Other countries that don't offer tax breaks for home ownership, such as Canada, have comparatively lower prices because buyers can't afford to pay higher prices when they lack a tax deduction to help subsidize the cost.

The following sections offer an overview of the tax goodies available to U.S. homeowners. The benefits are similar to, but different from, the tax benefits for rental or income property owners, which I discuss later in this chapter (see the section "Converting a home into rental property").

Mortgage interest and property tax write-offs

When you buy a home, you can claim two big ongoing expenses of home ownership as tax deductions on Schedule A of Form 1040. These expenses are your property taxes and the interest on your mortgage.

You're allowed to claim mortgage-interest deductions on a primary residence (where you actually live) and on a second home for mortgage debt totaling $750,000. For mortgages taken out before December 16, 2017, you can take mortgage interest deductions on up to $1 million ($500,000 if married filing separately) of mortgage debt.

Property taxes on your home when combined with other deductible state income tax payments are deductible on Schedule A up to $10,000 per year. This deduction is typically referred to as the SALT (state and local tax) deduction. At the time this book goes to press in 2024, Congress has been considering raising this deduction limit to, say, $20,000 or $25,000 per year from the current $10,000.

Home ownership capital gains exclusion

Normally, when you make an investment in a stock or business, for example, and you later sell it for a profit (also known as a *capital gain*), you owe tax on the profit. Some real estate, however, receives special treatment in this regard.

The tax laws pertaining to the sale of a primary residence allow for a significant amount of profit to be excluded from taxation: up to $250,000 for single taxpayers and up to $500,000 for married couples filing jointly. Moreover, to take advantage of this tax break — unlike under the old house-sale rules — house sellers need not be over a particular age or buy a replacement residence of equal or greater value to the one just sold. In the five years leading up to the home sale, you would need to have lived in the home for at least two of those years.

When calculating your profit upon sale of your home, your "cost basis" for your home includes the price you originally paid to buy it plus improvements you've made over time. See the section "Tracking your home expenditures," later in this chapter.

So, if you're longing to move to a less-costly housing market, you're largely free of tax constraints to do so. This tax break also benefits empty nesters and others nearing or in retirement who want to buy a less-costly home and free up some of their home equity to use toward retirement.

Grasping that house losses aren't deductible

Some homeowners have discovered firsthand that real estate prices go down as well as up. If it's time for you to sell your house and move on, you may be disappointed to discover that you can't deduct the loss if your house sells for less than what you paid for it. If you lose money investing in the stock market, on the other hand, those losses are usually deductible (see Chapter 7). Although you may think it's unfair that home ownership losses aren't tax-deductible, remember that you're already getting many tax perks from your home — the mortgage interest and property tax deductions. And the substantial capital gains tax exclusion when you sell your home.

DEALING WITH "EXCESS" HOUSING PROFITS

Although the house-sale capital gains tax laws benefit many people, the rules do have a negative twist. If you live in an area with relatively inexpensive real estate, you may find this difficult to believe: Some longer-term homeowners, especially in the higher-cost sections of the country, may have profits in excess of the law's limits ($250,000 for singles and $500,000 for married couples filing jointly).

For those in that admittedly enviable position, the tax laws offer no escape hatch. At the time of sale, single homeowners with accumulated profits (which also include those profits rolled over, under the old tax laws, from previous sales) greater than $250,000 and couples with profits greater than $500,000 must pay capital gains tax on the excess.

When they start to bump up against the maximum amounts that can be shielded from capital gains taxation, long-term homeowners and those buying expensive homes may want to consider selling and moving, even if it's within the same neighborhood.

Those whose homes have appreciated well in excess of the limits may want to consider, if possible, holding their homes until their deaths, at which point, under current tax laws, the IRS wipes the capital gains slate clean (see Chapter 6). Please also be aware that increasing numbers of taxpayers are finding themselves subject to the dreaded Alternative Minimum Tax (AMT) for many reasons, including the realization of larger capital gains.

Also keep in mind that thanks to inflation, increasing numbers of house sellers over time will find their profits to be in excess of the $250K/$500K limits because those thresholds are fixed and aren't scheduled to increase with inflation. Thus, in the years ahead, increasing numbers of homeowners will be affected by the limits. That's why you should heed my advice to keep receipts for all of your home improvements, which allow you to increase your home's cost basis for tax purposes and thus reduce your potentially taxable capital gain. See the section "Tracking your home expenditures," later in this chapter.

Converting rental property to save on taxes

If you want to sell appreciated rental property, the house-sale rules may benefit you as well. How? By moving into a rental property that you own and making it your primary residence for at least two years, you can shield the profits from the sale of the property from taxation. (Obviously, this strategy is feasible only for certain types of properties that you would be willing or able to live in. Also, it doesn't apply to depreciation taken after May 7, 1997.)

WARNING

When you move from your house, rent it out for a period of time, and then sell it, the IRS may consider that you have converted your home from a primary residence to a rental property. Thus, you may lose the privilege of excluding tax on the profit from the sale. The only exception: You actively tried to sell the house after you moved and only rented it temporarily to help defray the costs of keeping it until you sold it.

Home office deductions

When you run your business out of your home, you may be able to take additional tax deductions beyond the mortgage interest and property taxes that you may claim as a homeowner. Check out Chapter 12 for a more in-depth discussion of this issue.

Purchasing Your Humble Home

Financially speaking, you really shouldn't buy your own place unless you anticipate being there for at least three years, and preferably five years or more. Many expenses accompany buying and selling a property, such as the cost of getting a mortgage (points, application and credit report fees, and appraisal fees), inspection expenses, moving costs, real estate agents' commissions, and title insurance. And remember, most of these expenses are not tax-deductible (at best, some of them can be added to your home's tax basis as I explain in the section "Tracking your home expenditures" later in this chapter). To cover these transaction costs plus the additional costs of ownership, a property needs to appreciate a fair amount before you can be as well off financially as if you had continued renting. A property needs to appreciate about 15 percent just to offset these expenses, even factoring in the tax benefits that homeowners enjoy.

If you need or want to move in a couple of years, counting on that kind of appreciation is risky. If you're lucky (that is, if you happen to buy before a significant rise in housing prices), you may get it. Otherwise, you'll probably lose money on the deal.

Some people are willing to buy a home even when they don't expect to live in it for long because they plan on turning it into a rental when it's time to move on. Holding rental property can be a good long-term investment, but don't underestimate the responsibilities that come with rental property.

Exploring the tax savings in home ownership

To quickly estimate your monthly tax savings from home ownership, try this simple shortcut: Multiply your marginal federal tax rate (refer to Chapter 1) by the total monthly amount of your property taxes and mortgage. (Technically, not all of your mortgage payment is tax-deductible; only the portion of the mortgage payment that goes to interest is tax-deductible. However, in the early years of your mortgage, the portion that goes toward interest is nearly all of the payment. On the other hand, your property taxes will probably rise over time, and you can also earn state tax benefits from your deductible mortgage interest and property taxes.)

To figure out more precisely how home ownership may affect your tax situation, try plugging some reasonable numbers into your tax return to guesstimate how your taxes may change. You can also speak with a tax advisor.

TIP

When you buy a home, make sure to refigure how much you're paying in income taxes, because your mortgage interest and property tax deductions should help lower your income tax bills (federal and state). Many homebuyers skip this step and end up getting a big tax refund when they file their tax returns. Although getting money back from the IRS and state may feel good, it means that, at a minimum, you made an interest-free loan to the government. In the worst case, the reduced cash flow during the year may cause you to accumulate debt or miss out on contributing to tax-deductible retirement accounts. If you work for an employer, ask your payroll/benefits department for Form W-4. If you're self-employed, you can complete a worksheet that comes with Form 1040-ES.

KEEP TRACK OF YOUR TAX BRACKET

When you first consider purchasing a home or purchasing a more expensive home, it usually pays to plan ahead and push as many so-called itemizable deductions as you can into the tax year in which you expect to buy your home.

For example, suppose that this year you're using the standard deduction because you don't have many itemized deductions. You decide late in the year that you expect to buy a home next year and therefore will have mortgage interest and property taxes to write off and you'll probably be able to itemize the next year. It makes sense, then, to collect as many deductible expenses as possible and shift them into next year. For example, if the solicitations surrounding the December holidays prompt you to contribute money to charities, you can wait until January to donate. Take a look at the deductible items on Schedule A to determine what else you may want to postpone paying.

Also, be aware that your income tax bracket may change from year to year. Thus, when possible, you can choose to pay more or less of some itemizable expenses in one year versus another. Suppose that you receive your monthly mortgage bill in the middle of the month and it's not due until early the following month. If for some reason you expect to be in a lower tax bracket next year — perhaps you're going to take a sabbatical and will earn less income — you may choose to pay your December mortgage bill before the current year ends. In this case, the mortgage interest deduction has greater value to you in the current year because you're in a higher tax bracket. (Conversely, if you expected to be in a higher tax bracket next year, you should wait to pay your December mortgage bill in early January, so you get more of your mortgage interest deduction next tax year.)

Be sure to read Chapter 1, which explains how to figure your tax bracket for planning purposes to minimize your taxes.

Should you make a small down payment (typically defined as less than 20 percent of the purchase price), many lenders insist on property tax and insurance *impound accounts*. These accounts require you to pay your property taxes and insurance to the lender each month along with your mortgage payment.

TIP

Property taxes are typically based on the value of a property. Although an average property tax rate is about 1.5 to 2.0 percent of the property's purchase price per year, you should understand what the exact rate is in your area. Call the tax collector's office (you can find the phone number in the government pages section of your local phone directory under such headings as "Tax Collector," "Treasurer," or "Assessor"; or enter one of those terms and the name of the municipality where you live into a search engine) in the town where you're contemplating buying a home and ask what the property tax rate is and what additional fees and assessments may apply.

Be careful to make sure that you're comparing apples with apples when comparing communities and their property taxes. For example, some communities may nickel-and-dime you for extra assessments for services that are included in the standard property tax bills of other communities.

WARNING

Real estate listings, which are typically prepared by real estate agents, may list what the current property owner is paying in taxes. But relying on such data to understand what your real estate taxes will be if you buy the property can be financially dangerous. The current owner's taxes may be based on an outdated and much lower property valuation. Just as it's dangerous to drive forward by looking in the rearview mirror of your car, you shouldn't buy a property and budget for property taxes based on the current owner's taxes. Your property taxes (if you buy the home) will be recalculated based on the price you pay for the property.

Deciding how much to spend on a home

When you fall in love with a home and buy it without looking at your monthly expenditures and long-term goals, you may end up with a home that dictates much of your future spending. Real estate agents and mortgage lenders are more than happy to tell you the maximum that you're qualified to borrow. They want your business, and the more money you spend, the more they make. But that doesn't mean that you should borrow the maximum.

Typical is the advice of this real estate broker who writes about real estate:

> The first step is to find out what price you can afford to buy. The easiest way to do this is to make an appointment with a loan agent or a mortgage broker.

Easy, yes. But doing so probably won't get you the right or best answer. Like real estate agents, mortgage brokers tell you the maximum loan you can qualify for. This amount isn't necessarily what you can "afford." Just ask one of the many folks who overextended and ended up with their home in foreclosure during the late 2000s real estate slump. Remember, mortgage and loan agents get a commission based on the size of your loan. Taking into consideration your other financial goals and needs, such as saving for retirement, isn't part of their job description (nor generally their expertise).

In addition to analyzing your retirement planning, questions you should ask yourself before buying a home may include how much you spend (and want to continue spending) on fun stuff, such as travel and entertainment. If you want to continue your current lifestyle (and the expenditures inherent in it), be honest with yourself about how much you can really afford to spend as a homeowner.

WARNING

Often, first-time homebuyers are apt to run into financial trouble because they don't know their spending needs and priorities and don't know how to budget for them. Buying a home can be a wise decision, but it can also be a huge burden. Some people don't decrease their spending as much as they should, based on the large amount of debt they incur in buying a home. In fact, some homeowners spend even more on all sorts of gadgets and furnishings for their homes. Many people prop up their spending habits with credit. For this reason, a surprisingly large percentage of people — some studies say about half — who borrow additional money against their home equity use the funds to pay other debts.

Don't let your home control your financial future. Before you buy property or agree to a particular mortgage, take stock of your overall financial health, especially in terms of retirement planning if you hope to retire by your mid-60s.

Tracking your home expenditures

TIP

Although it may be a bit of a hassle, documenting and tracking money spent improving your property is in your best financial interests. For tax purposes, you can add the cost of these improvements to your original purchase price for the home. So, when you sell the property someday, you get to reduce your profit, for tax purposes, accordingly.

Keep in mind that under the current tax laws, most people won't owe capital gains tax from the sale of a house. Single people can make a $250,000 profit, and married couples filing jointly can realize $500,000 in profit without paying tax on the proceeds of the sale. However, you still need to track your home improvement expenditures because it's impossible to know while you're living in your home if your future sale, which may be many years off, can trigger capital gains tax. Who knows how much real estate will appreciate in the interim or what changes can happen to the tax laws?

As I discuss later in this chapter, when you sell your house, you may need to report to the IRS, on Schedule D, Capital Gains and Losses, the selling price of the house, the original cost of the house, and how much you spent improving it. Therefore, I strongly advise setting up a simple file folder, perhaps labeled "Home Improvements," into which you deposit receipts for your expenditures.

The challenging part for most people is simply keeping the receipts organized in one place. Another task is correctly distinguishing between spending on *improvements*, which the IRS allows you to add to your cost of the home, and spending for *maintenance and repairs*, which you can't add to the original purchase price of the home.

REMEMBER

Improvements include expenses such as installing an alarm system, adding or remodeling a room, planting new trees and shrubs in your yard, installing a new fence, replacing your roof, and purchasing new appliances. These improvements increase the value of your home and lengthen its life. Maintenance and repairs include expenses such as hiring a plumber to fix a leaky pipe, repainting, repairing a door so that it closes properly, replacing a broken windowpane, and replacing missing roof shingles.

It's interesting to note that if you hire a contractor to do home improvements, the IRS allows you to effectively add the cost of the contractor's time (the labor charges) into the overall improvements that reduce your home's profit for tax purposes. On the other hand, if you elect to do the work yourself, you gain no tax benefit for your sweat. You can't add a cost for the value of your time — the IRS assumes that your time isn't worth anything. You work for free! Now you have another reason for hiring someone to do the work for you.

Also, don't forget to toss into your receipt folder the *settlement statement*, which you should have received in the blizzard of paperwork you signed when you bought your home. Don't lose this valuable piece of paper, which itemizes many of the expenses associated with the purchase of your home. You can add many of these expenses to the original cost of the home and reduce your taxable profit when it comes time to sell. You also want to keep proof of other expenditures that the settlement statement may not document, such as inspection fees that you paid when buying your home.

Per the IRS, the following are some of the settlement fees and closing costs that you can add to the original basis (purchase price) of your home:

>> Abstract fees (abstract of title fees)

>> Charges for installing utility services

>> Legal fees (including fees for the title search and preparation of the sales contract and deed)

>> Recording fees

>> Surveys

>> Transfer or stamp taxes

>> Owner's title insurance

- >> Any amount the seller owes that you agree to pay, such as back taxes or interest

- >> Recording or mortgage fees, cost for improvements or repairs, and sales commissions

Reporting revenue if you sometimes rent

The IRS allows you to rent your home or a room in your home for up to 14 days each year without having to declare the rental income and pay income taxes on it. Renting your home or a portion thereof for more than 14 days requires that you report the income when you file your annual tax return. You can declare real estate rental income by filing Schedule E.

Making Tax-Wise Mortgage Decisions

The largest expense of property ownership is almost always the monthly mortgage payment. In the earlier years of a mortgage, the bulk of the mortgage payment covers interest that generally is tax-deductible subject to IRS limits. In this section, I discuss how to factor taxes and your financial circumstances into making intelligent mortgage decisions.

15-year or 30-year mortgage?

Unfortunately, you have thousands of mortgage options to choose from. Fixed-rate and adjustable-rate mortgages come with all sorts of bells and whistles. The number of permutations is mind-numbing.

From a tax perspective, one of the most important mortgage selection issues is whether to take a 15-year or 30-year mortgage. To afford the monthly payments, most homebuyers need to spread the loan payments over a longer period of time, and a

30-year mortgage is the only option. A 15-year mortgage requires higher monthly payments because you pay it off more quickly.

Even if you can afford these higher payments, taking the 15-year option may not be wise. The money for making extra payments doesn't come out of thin air. You may have better uses for your excess funds. What you're really asking, if you're considering whether you should take a 30-year or a 15-year mortgage, is whether you should pay off your mortgage slowly or quickly. The answer isn't as simple as some people think.

First, think about alternative uses for the extra money you're throwing into the mortgage payments. What's best for you depends on your overall financial situation and what else you can do with the money. When you elect the slow, 30-year mortgage payoff approach and you end up blowing the extra money on a new car, for example, you're better off paying down the mortgage more quickly. In that case, take the 15-year version. (If you want to buy a car in the future, saving in a money market fund so that you don't need to take out a high-cost car loan makes sound financial sense.)

But suppose that you aren't so frivolous with your extra money, and instead, you take the extra $100 or $200 per month and contribute it to a retirement account. That step may make financial sense. Why? Because additions to 401(k)s, 403(b)s, SEP-IRAs, and other types of retirement accounts are typically tax-deductible (see Chapter 4).

REMEMBER

When you dump that $200 into a retirement account, you get to subtract it from the income on which you pay taxes. If you're paying 30 percent in federal and state income taxes, you shave $60 (that's $200 multiplied by 30 percent) off your tax bill. (You're going to pay taxes when you withdraw the money from the retirement account someday, but in the meantime, the money that would have gone to taxes is growing on your behalf.) You get no tax benefits from that $200 when added to your mortgage payment when you elect a faster payoff mortgage (15-year mortgage).

With kids, you have an even greater reason to fund your retirement accounts before you consider paying down your mortgage faster. Under current rules for determining financial aid for college expenses, money in your retirement accounts isn't counted as an asset that you must use toward college costs (see Chapter 5).

If you're uncomfortable investing and would otherwise leave the extra money sitting in a money market fund or savings account — or worse, if you would spend it — you're better off paying down the mortgage. Take the 15-year approach. If the investments in your retirement account plummet in value, the impact of the tax-deferred compounding of your capital may be negated. Paying off your mortgage quicker, on the other hand, is just like investing your money in a sure thing — but with a modest rate of return.

In most cases, you get to deduct your mortgage interest on your tax return. So if you're paying 5 percent interest, it really may cost you only around 3.5 percent after you factor in the tax benefits. If you think that you can do better by investing elsewhere, go for it. Remember, though, that you owe income tax from profits on your investments held outside retirement accounts. You aren't going to get decent investment returns unless you're willing to take risks. Investments such as stocks and real estate have generated better returns over the long haul. These investments carry risks, though, and aren't guaranteed to produce any return.

When you don't have a burning investment option, paying down your mortgage as your cash flow allows is usually wiser. If you have extra cash and have contributed the maximum allowed for retirement accounts, you may want to invest in real estate or perhaps a business. You have to decide if it's worth the extra risk in making a particular investment rather than paying down your mortgage.

WARNING

As I've stated for many years now, I was concerned with the increasing promotion and popularity in the past of interest-only and other low down payment mortgages. Not only do such loans carry higher interest rates and other costs (such as private mortgage insurance), but consumers may also be in for some rude surprises. For example, interest-only loans lure people with their relatively low initial payments. However, years into the mortgage, the payment leaps higher as you begin to finally work at paying down the principal. For more information regarding mortgage options and decisions, pick up a copy of *Mortgages For Dummies* by Eric Tyson and Robert Griswold (Wiley).

How large a down payment?

What if you're in the enviable and fortunate position of having so much money that you can afford to put down more than a 20 percent down payment (which generally is the amount needed to qualify for better mortgage terms, including not having to take out private mortgage insurance)? Perhaps you're one of those wise people who doesn't want to get stretched too thin financially, and you're buying a less expensive home than you can afford. How much should you put down?

Some people, particularly those in the real estate business (and even some tax and financial advisors), say that you should take as large a mortgage as you can for the tax deductions — that is, don't make a larger down payment than you have to. This is silly reasoning. Remember that you have to pay out money in interest charges to get the tax deductions.

Again, what makes sense for you depends on your alternative uses for the money. When you're considering other investment opportunities, determine whether you can reasonably expect to earn a higher rate of return than the interest rate you'll pay on the mortgage.

In the past century, stock market and real estate investors have enjoyed average annual returns of around 8 to 9 percent per year (just remember, the past doesn't guarantee the future). So if you borrow mortgage money at around 5 to 6 percent today, you may come out ahead by investing in these areas. Besides possibly generating a higher rate of return, other real estate and stock investing can help you diversify your investments.

Of course, you have no guarantee that you can earn 8 to 9 percent each year. And don't forget that all investments come with risks. The advantage of putting more money down for a home and borrowing less is that paying down a mortgage is essentially a risk-free investment (as long as you have emergency money you can tap).

If you prefer to limit the down payment to 20 percent and invest more elsewhere, that's fine. Just don't keep the extra money (beyond an emergency reserve) under the mattress, in a savings account, or in bonds that provide returns lower than the mortgage is costing you.

When to refinance?

When your mortgage has a higher rate of interest than loans currently available, you may save money by refinancing. Because refinancing requires money and time, you need to crunch a few numbers and factor in taxes to determine whether refinancing makes sense for you. Ask your mortgage lender or broker how soon you can recoup the refinancing costs, such as appraisal expenses, loan fees and points, title insurance, and so on.

For example, if completing the refinance costs you $2,000 and reduces your monthly payment by $100, the lender or broker typically says that you can save back the refinance costs in 20 months. This estimate isn't accurate, however, because you lose some tax write-offs when your mortgage interest rate and payments are reduced. You can't simply look at the reduced amount of your monthly payment (mortgage lenders like to look at that reduction, however, because lowering your payments makes refinancing more attractive).

To get a better estimate without spending hours crunching numbers, take your marginal tax rate as specified in Chapter 1 (for example, 24 percent) and reduce your monthly payment savings on the refinance by this amount. For example, if your monthly payment drops by $100, you really save only around $76 a month after factoring in the lost tax benefits. So you recoup the refinance costs in 26 months ($2,000 of refinance costs divided by $76) — not 20 months.

If you can recover the costs of the refinance within a few years or less, go for it. If it takes longer, refinancing may still make sense if you anticipate keeping the property and mortgage that long. If you estimate that you need more than five to seven years to break even, refinancing probably is too risky to justify the costs and hassles.

When you refinance, don't forget to adjust the amount of tax you pay during the year. See the section "Exploring the tax savings in home ownership," earlier in this chapter, for more information on how to change your tax withholding.

Besides getting a lower-interest-rate loan, another reason people refinance is to pull out cash from the house for some other purpose. This strategy can make good financial sense because, under most circumstances, mortgage interest is tax-deductible. If you're starting a business or buying other real estate, you can usually borrow against your home at a lower cost than on a business or rental property loan. (If you're a high-income earner and have a mortgage of more than $750,000 or considering one, you may lose some of the tax deductibility of your home mortgage interest deductions — read the explanation in the section earlier in this chapter, "Mortgage interest and property tax write-offs").

If you've run up high-interest consumer debt, you may be able to refinance your mortgage and pull out extra cash to pay off your credit cards, auto loans, or other costly credit lines, thus saving yourself money. You usually can borrow at a lower interest rate for a mortgage and get a tax deduction as a bonus, which lowers the effective borrowing cost further. Interest on consumer debt, such as auto loans and credit cards, isn't tax-deductible.

WARNING

Borrowing against the equity in your home can be addictive and may contribute to poor spending habits. An appreciating home creates the illusion that excess spending isn't really costing you. Remember that debt is debt, and you have to repay all borrowed money. In the long run, you wind up with greater mortgage debt, and paying it off takes a bigger bite out of your monthly income. Refinancing and establishing home-equity lines also costs you more in loan application fees and other charges (points, appraisals, credit reports, and so on).

Considering a reverse mortgage

Some homeowners find, particularly in their later years of retirement, that they lack cash. The home in which they live is usually their largest asset. Unlike other investments, such as bank accounts, bonds, or stocks, a home does not provide any income to owners unless they decide to rent out a room or two.

A *reverse mortgage* allows a homeowner who is 62 years of age or older and low on cash to tap home equity. For an elderly homeowner, using home equity can be a difficult thing to do psychologically. Most people work hard to pay a mortgage month after month, year after year, until it's finally all paid off. What a feat and what a relief after all those years!

Taking out a reverse mortgage reverses this process. Each month, the reverse mortgage lender sends you a check that you can spend on food, clothing, travel, or whatever you want. The money you receive each month is really a loan from the bank against the value of your home, which makes the monthly check free from taxation. (There are other payment options such as a lump sum or line of credit.) A reverse mortgage also allows you to stay in your home and use its equity to supplement your monthly income.

The main drawback of a reverse mortgage is that it can diminish the estate that you may want to pass on to your heirs or use for some other purpose. Also, some loans require repayment within a certain number of years. The fees and the effective interest rate you're charged to borrow the money can be quite high.

Because some loans require the lender to make monthly payments to you as long as you live in the home, lenders assume that you'll live many years in your home so they won't lose money when making these loans. If you end up keeping the loan for only a few years because you move, for example, the cost of the loan is extremely high.

TIP

You may be able to create a reverse mortgage with your relatives. This technique can work if you have family members who are financially able to provide you with monthly income in exchange for ownership of the home when you pass away.

You have other alternatives to tapping the equity in your home. Simply selling your home and buying a less expensive property (or renting) is one option. Under current tax laws, qualifying house sellers can exclude a sizable portion of their profits from capital gains tax: up to $250,000 for single taxpayers and $500,000 for married couples.

Selling Your House

As I discuss earlier in this chapter (see "Home ownership capital gains exclusion"), homeowners can realize large profits (capital gains) when selling their house. Schedule D, Capital Gains and Losses, is filed only when gains exceed the $250,000/$500,000 threshold. You file Schedule D with Form 1040 from the same tax year in which you sell your house.

Form 1099-S must be filed to report the sale or exchange of real estate unless the sale price is $250,000 or less ($500,000 or less for married couples) and all the sellers provide written certification that the full gain on the sale is excludable from the sellers' gross income. Neither you nor the IRS receives Form 1099-S from the firm handling the sale of your house unless the gross sale price exceeds $500,000 for married couples or $250,000 for an unmarried seller.

The following sections discuss the tax issues affecting house sales.

Not wanting to sell at a loss

Many homeowners are tempted to hold on to their properties when they need to move if the real estate market is soft or the property has a lower value than when they bought it, especially because the loss isn't tax-deductible. I don't recommend this strategy.

You may reason that in a few years, the real estate storm clouds will clear and you'll be able to sell your property at a higher price. Here are three risks associated with this way of thinking:

>> You can't know what's going to happen to property prices in the next few years. They may rebound, but they may also stay the same or drop even further. A property generally needs to appreciate at least a few percentage points each year just to make up for all the costs of holding and maintaining it. So you're losing more money each year that you hold the property and it doesn't appreciate at least a few percentage points in value.

>> If you haven't been a landlord, don't underestimate the hassle and headaches associated with the job. Being a long-distance landlord is even more of a challenge. You can always hire someone to manage your property, but that approach creates costs, too — usually about 6 to 10 percent of the monthly rental income.

>> After you convert your home into a rental property, you need to pay capital gains tax on your profit when you sell (the only exception is if you temporarily rent your home while you're still actively trying to sell it). This tax wipes out much of the advantage of having held on to the property until prices recovered. If your desire is to become a long-term rental property owner, you can, under current tax laws, do a tax-free exchange into another rental property after you sell.

I understand that selling a house that hasn't made you any money isn't much fun. But too many homeowners make a bad situation worse by holding on to their homes for the wrong reasons after they move. No one wants to believe that they're losing money. But remember, the money is already lost. Many people who hold on rub salt into their real estate wounds. If and when the value of the property you're waiting to sell finally increases, odds are that other properties you'd next buy also will have increased. Unless you have sufficient money for the down payment to buy your next home, or you want to keep such a property as a long-term investment, holding on to a home you move from usually isn't wise.

Converting a home into rental property

One advantage to keeping your current home as an investment property after you move is that you already own it. Locating and buying a property takes time and money. Also, you know what you have with your current home. When you go out and purchase a different property to rent, you're starting from scratch.

One of the tax benefits of rental real estate is the depreciation deduction. As your property ages, the IRS allows you to write off or deduct from your rental income the "wearing out" of the building. Although this deduction helps reduce your income taxes, be aware that you may not be able to deduct as much for depreciation expenses when you convert your home to rental property as you can on a rental bought separately. If your home has appreciated since you bought it, the IRS forces you to use your original (lower) purchase price for purposes of calculating depreciation. To make tax matters worse, if your home has declined in value since you originally purchased it, you must use this lower value, at the time you convert the property, for purposes of depreciation.

Don't consider converting your home into a rental when you move unless this decision really is a long-term proposition. As I discuss in Chapter 15, selling rental property has tax consequences.

If the idea of keeping the home you move from as a long-term investment appeals to you, take stock of your overall financial situation before you make the final call. Can you afford to purchase your next home given the money that's still tied up in the home you're considering keeping as a rental? Can you afford to contribute to tax-deductible retirement plans, or will the burden of carrying two properties use up too much of your cash flow? Will your overall investments be well-diversified, or will you have too much of your money tied up in real estate (perhaps in one area of the country)?

Looking at house sales, taxes, and divorce

A divorce complicates many personal and financial issues. Real estate is no different. In the past, if ownership of a home that had appreciated in value were transferred between spouses because of a divorce, capital gains tax was owed. This is no longer one of the additional costs of divorce. Transfers of property between spouses aren't taxed if the transfers are made within one year of divorce (and both spouses are U.S. residents or citizens).

If you're selling your house because of a divorce, when you sell the house can have significant tax ramifications. If you agree to sell the house in the divorce settlement, each of you can make up to $250,000 in profit before any tax is levied.

Chapter **14**

Evaluating Real Estate as an Investment

The challenge involved with real estate investing is that it takes some real planning to get started. Contacting an investment company and purchasing some shares of your favorite mutual fund or stock is a lot easier than acquiring your first rental property. Buying property need not be too difficult, though. With a financial and real estate investment plan, a lot of patience, and the willingness to do some hard work, you can be on your way to building your own real estate empire!

In this chapter, I give you information that can help you decide whether you have what it takes to make money *and* be comfortable with investing in real estate. I compare real estate investments to other investments. And finally, I offer guidance on how real estate investments can fit into your overall personal financial plans.

Understanding Real Estate's Income- and Wealth-Producing Potential

Compared with most other investments, good real estate can excel at producing periodic or monthly cash flow for property owners. So in addition to the longer-term appreciation potential, you can also earn investment income year in and year out. Real estate is a true growth *and* income investment.

REMEMBER

The vast majority of people who don't make money in real estate make easily avoidable mistakes, which I help you avoid.

The following list highlights the major benefits of investing in real estate:

>> **Tax-deferred compounding of value:** In real estate investing, the appreciation of your properties compounds *tax-deferred* during your years of ownership. You don't pay tax on this profit until you sell your property — and even then, you can roll over your gain into another investment property and avoid paying taxes. (See the "Being aware of the tax advantages" section later in this chapter.)

>> **Regular cash flow:** If you have property that you rent out, you have money coming in every month in the form of rents. Some properties, particularly larger multi-unit complexes, may have some additional sources, such as from parking, storage, or washers and dryers.

REMEMBER

When you own investment real estate, you should also expect to incur expenses that include your mortgage payment, property taxes, insurance, and maintenance. The interaction of the revenues coming in and the expenses going out is what tells you whether you realize a positive operating profit each month.

>> **Reduced income tax bills:** For income tax purposes, you also get to claim an expense that isn't really an out-of-pocket cost — depreciation. Depreciation enables

you to reduce your current income tax bill and hence increase your cash flow from a property. (I explain this tax advantage and others later in the "Being aware of the tax advantages" section.)

>> **Rate of increase of rental income versus overall expenses:** Over time, your operating profit, which is subject to ordinary income tax, should rise as you increase your rental prices faster than the rate of increase for your property's overall expenses. What follows is a simple example to show why even modest rental increases are magnified into larger operating profits and healthy returns on investment over time.

Suppose that you're in the market to purchase a single-family home that you want to rent out and that such properties are selling for about $200,000 in the area you've deemed to be a good investment. (*Note:* Housing prices vary widely across different areas, but the following example should give you a relative sense of how a rental property's expenses and revenue change over time.) You expect to make a 20 percent down payment and take out a 30-year fixed rate mortgage at 6 percent for the remainder of the purchase price — $160,000. Here are the details:

Monthly mortgage payment	$960
Monthly property tax	$200
Other monthly expenses (maintenance, insurance)	$200
Monthly rent	$1,400

In Table 14-1, I show you what happens with your investment over time. I assume that your rent and expenses (except for your mortgage payment, which is fixed) increase 3 percent annually and that your property appreciates a conservative 4 percent per year. (For simplification purposes, I ignore depreciation in this example. If I had included the benefit of depreciation, it would further enhance the calculated investment returns.)

TABLE 14-1 How a Rental Property's Income and Wealth Build Over Time

Year	Monthly Rent	Monthly Expenses	Property Value	Mortgage Balance
0	$1,400	$1,360	$200,000	$160,000
5	$1,623	$1,424	$243,330	$148,960
10	$1,881	$1,498	$296,050	$133,920
20	$2,529	$1,682	$438,225	$86,400
30	$3,398	$1,931	$648,680	$0
31	$3,500	$1,000	$674,625	$0

Now, notice what happens over time. When you first buy the property, the monthly rent and the monthly expenses are about equal. By year five, the monthly income exceeds the expenses by about $200 per month. Consider why this happens — your largest monthly expense, the mortgage payment, doesn't increase. So, even though I assume that the rent increases just 3 percent per year, which is the same rate of increase assumed for your nonmortgage expenses, the compounding of rental inflation begins to produce larger and larger cash flows to you, the property owner. Cash flow of $200 per month may not sound like much, but consider that this $2,400 annual income is from an original $40,000 investment. Thus, by year five, your rental property is producing a 6 percent return on your down payment investment. (And remember, if you factor in the tax deduction for depreciation, your cash flow and return are even higher.)

In addition to the monthly cash flow from the amount that the rent exceeds the property's expenses, also look at the last two columns in Table 14-1 to see what has happened by year five to your *equity* (the difference between market value and mortgage balance owed) in the property. With just a 4 percent annual increase in market value, your $40,000 in equity (the down payment) has more than doubled to $94,370 ($243,330 – 148,960).

By years 10 and 20, you can see the further increases in your monthly cash flow and significant expansion in your property's equity. By year 30, the property is producing more than $1,400 per month cash flow and you're now the proud owner of a mortgage-free property worth more than triple what you paid for it!

After you get the mortgage paid off in year 30, take a look at what happens in year 31 and beyond to your monthly expenses (big drop as your monthly mortgage payment disappears!) and therefore your cash flow (big increase).

Recognizing the Caveats of Real Estate Investing

Despite all its potential, real estate investing isn't lucrative at all times and for all people — here's a quick outline of the biggest caveats that accompany investing in real estate:

>> **Few home runs:** Your likely returns from real estate won't approach the biggest home runs that the most accomplished entrepreneurs achieve in the business world. That said, by doing your homework, improving properties, and practicing good management (and sometimes enjoying a bit of luck), you can do extremely well!

WARNING

>> **Upfront operating profit challenges:** Unless you make a large down payment, your monthly operating profit may be small, nonexistent, or negative in the early years of rental property ownership. During soft periods in the local economy, rents may rise more slowly than your expenses or they may even fall. That's why you must ensure that you can weather financially tough times. In the worst cases, I've seen rental property owners lose both their investment property and their homes.

>> **Ups and downs:** You're not going to earn an 8 to 10 percent return every year. Although you have the potential for significant profits, owning real estate isn't like owning a printing press at the U.S. Treasury. Like stocks and other types of ownership investments, real estate goes through down periods as well as up periods. Most people who make money investing in real estate do so because they invest and hold property over many years.

>> **Relatively high transaction costs:** If you buy a property and then want out a year or two later, you may find that even though it has appreciated in value, much (if not all) of

your profit has been wiped away by the high transaction costs. Typically, the costs of buying and selling — which include real estate agent commissions, loan fees, title insurance, and other closing costs — amount to about 8 to 12 percent of the purchase price of a property. So, although you may be elated if your property appreciates 10 percent in value in short order, you may not be so thrilled to realize that if you sell the property, you may not have any greater return than if you had stashed your money in a lowly bank account.

>> **Tax implications:** Last, but not least, when you make a positive net return or profit on your real estate investment, the federal and state governments are waiting with open hands for their share. Throughout this book, I highlight ways to improve your after-tax returns. As I stress more than once, the profit you have left after government entities take their bites (not your pretax income) is what really matters.

These drawbacks shouldn't keep you from exploring real estate investing as an option; rather, they simply reinforce the need to really know what you're getting into with this type of investing and whether it's a good match for you. The rest of this chapter takes you deeper into an assessment of real estate as an investment as well as introspection about your goals, interests, and abilities.

Comparing Real Estate to Other Investments

Surely, you've considered or heard about many different investments over the years. To help you grasp and understand the unique characteristics of real estate, I compare and contrast real estate's attributes with those of other wealth-building investments like stocks and small business.

Returns

Clearly, a major reason that many people invest in real estate is for the healthy total *returns* (which include ongoing cash flow and the appreciation of the property). Real estate often generates robust long-term returns because, like stocks and small business, it's an *ownership investment*. By that, I mean that real estate is an asset that has the ability to produce periodic income *and* gains or profits upon refinancing or sale.

My research and experience suggest that total real estate investment returns are comparable to those from stocks — about 8 to 9 percent on average, annually. Over recent decades, the average annual return on real estate investment trusts (REITs), publicly traded companies that invest in income-producing real estate such as apartment buildings, office complexes, and shopping centers, has appreciated at about this pace as well.

And you can earn long-term returns that average much better than 10 percent per year if you select excellent properties in the best areas, hold them for several years, and manage them well.

Risk

Real estate doesn't always rise in value — witness the decline occurring in most parts of the U.S. during the late 2000s and early 2010s. That said, market values for real estate generally don't suffer from as much volatility as stock prices do. You may recall how the excitement surrounding the rapid sustained increase of technology and internet stock prices in the late 1990s turned into the dismay and agony of those same sectors' stock prices crashing in the early 2000s. Many stocks in this industry, including those of leaders in their niches, saw their stock prices plummet by 80 percent, 90 percent, or more. Generally, you don't see those kinds of dramatic roller-coaster shifts in values over the short run with the residential income property real estate market.

However, keep in mind (especially if you tend to be concerned about shorter-term risks) that real estate can suffer from declines of 10 percent, 20 percent, or more. If you make a down payment of, say, 20 percent and want to sell your property after a 10 to 15 percent price decline, you may find that all (as in 100 percent) of your invested dollars (down payment) are wiped out after you factor in transaction costs. So you can lose everything.

You can greatly reduce and minimize your risk investing in real estate through buying and holding property for many years (seven to ten or more). Remember that many of these fantastic success stories about amazing profits on "flipping" single-family homes and small rental properties are just like gamblers who only tell you about their biggest winnings or forget to tell you that they turned around and lost much of what they won. While there is a lot of hype on cable television and the internet about "flipping properties" for crazy short-term profits, always think of real estate as a long-term investment.

Liquidity

Liquidity — the ease and cost with which you can sell and get your money out of an investment — is one of real estate's short-comings. Real estate is relatively *illiquid:* You can't sell a piece of property with the same speed with which you can whip out your ATM card and withdraw money from your bank account or sell a stock or an exchange-traded fund with a click of your computer's mouse or by tapping on your cellphone.

I actually view real estate's relative illiquidity as a strength, certainly compared with stocks that people often trade in and out of because doing so is so easy and seemingly cheap. As a result, some stock market investors tend to lose sight of the long term and miss out on the bigger gains that accrue to patient buy-and-stick-with-it investors. Because you can't track the value of investment real estate daily on your computer and because real estate takes considerable time, energy, and money to sell, you're far more likely to buy and hold onto your properties for the longer term.

Although real estate investments are generally less liquid than stocks, they're generally more liquid than investments made in your own or someone else's small business. People need a place to live and businesses need a place to operate, so there's always demand for real estate (although the supply of such available properties can greatly exceed the demand in some areas during certain time periods).

Capital requirements

Although you can easily get started with traditional investments such as stocks and mutual funds with a few hundred or thousand dollars, the vast majority of quality real estate investments require far greater investments — usually on the order of tens of thousands of dollars.

TIP

If you're one of the many people who don't have that kind of money, don't despair. I present you with lower-cost real estate investment options. Among the simplest low-cost real estate investment options are real estate investment trusts (REITs). You can buy these as exchange-traded stocks or invest in a portfolio of REITs through a REIT mutual fund.

Diversification value

An advantage of holding investment real estate is that its value doesn't necessarily move in tandem with other investments, such as stocks or small-business investments that you hold. You may recall, for example, the massive stock market decline in the early 2000s. In most communities around America, real estate values were either steady or actually rising during this horrendous period for stock prices.

However, real estate prices and stock prices, for example, *can* move down together in value (witness the severe recession and stock market drop that took hold in 2008). Sluggish business conditions and lower corporate profits can depress stock *and* real estate prices.

Opportunities to add value

Although you may not know much about investing in the stock market, you may have some good ideas about how to improve a property and make it more valuable. You can fix up a property or develop it further and raise the rental income accordingly. Perhaps through legwork, persistence, and good negotiating skills, you can purchase a property below its fair market value.

Relative to investing in the stock market, tenacious and savvy real estate investors can more easily buy property in the private real estate market at below fair market value because the real estate market is somewhat less efficient and some owners don't realize the value of their income property or they need to sell quickly. Theoretically, you can do the same in the stock market, but the scores of professional, full-time money managers who analyze the public market for stocks make finding bargains more difficult.

Being aware of the tax advantages

Real estate investment offers numerous tax advantages. In this section, I compare and contrast investment property tax issues with those of other investments.

Deductible expenses (including depreciation)

Owning a property has much in common with owning your own small business. Every year, you account for your income and expenses on a tax return. For now, I want to remind you to keep good records of your expenses in purchasing and operating rental real estate. One expense that you get to deduct for rental real estate on your tax return — depreciation — doesn't actually involve spending or outlaying money. *Depreciation* is an allowable tax deduction for buildings because structures wear out over time. Under current tax laws, residential real estate is depreciated over 27½ years (commercial buildings are less favored in the tax code and can be depreciated over 39 years). Residential real estate is depreciated over shorter time periods because it has traditionally been a favored investment in our nation's tax laws.

Tax-free rollovers of rental property profits

When you sell a stock, mutual fund, or exchange-traded investment that you hold outside a retirement account, you must pay tax on your profits. By contrast, you can avoid paying tax on your profit when you sell a rental property if you roll over your gain into another like-kind investment real estate property.

The rules for properly making one of these 1031 exchanges are complex and involve third parties. Make sure that you find an attorney and/or tax advisor who is an expert at these transactions to ensure that you meet the technical and strict timing requirements so everything goes smoothly (and legally).

If you don't roll over your gain, you may owe significant taxes because of how the IRS defines your gain. For example, if you buy a property for $200,000 and sell it for $550,000, you not only owe tax on the gain from the increased property value, but you also owe tax on an additional amount, the property's depreciation you used during your ownership. The amount of depreciation that you deduct on your tax returns reduces the original $200,000 purchase price, making the taxable difference that much larger. For example, if you deducted $125,000 for depreciation over the years that you owned the property, you owe tax on the difference between the sale price of $550,000 and $75,000 ($200,000 purchase price − $125,000 depreciation).

Deferred taxes with installment sales

Installment sales are a complex method that can be used to defer your tax bill when you sell an investment property at a profit and you don't buy another rental property. With such a sale, you play the role of banker and provide financing to the buyer. In addition to often collecting a competitive interest rate from the buyer, you only have to pay capital gains tax as you receive proceeds over time from the sale that are applied toward the principal or price the buyer agreed to pay for the property.

Special tax credits for low-income housing and old buildings

If you invest in and upgrade low-income housing or certified historic buildings, you can gain special tax credits. The credits represent a direct reduction in your tax bill from expenditures to rehabilitate and improve such properties. These tax credits exist to encourage investors to invest in and fix up old or run-down buildings that likely would continue to deteriorate otherwise. The IRS has strict rules governing what types of properties qualify. See IRS Form 3468 to discover more about these credits.

The 2017 Tax Cuts and Jobs Act bill created "qualified opportunity zones" to provide tax incentives to invest in "low-income communities," which are defined by each state's governor and may comprise up to 25 percent of designated "low-income communities" in each state. (States can also designate census tracts contiguous with "low-income communities" so long as the median family income in those tracts doesn't exceed 125 percent of the qualifying contiguous "low-income community.")

The new qualified opportunity zone tax incentive allows real estate investors the following potential benefits:

>> The capital gains tax due upon a sale of the property is deferred if the capital gain from the sale is reinvested within 180 days in a qualified opportunity fund.

>> For investments in the qualified opportunity fund of at least five years, investors will receive a step-up in tax basis of 10 percent of the original gain.

>> For investments in the qualified opportunity fund of at least seven years, investors will receive an additional 5 percent step-up in tax basis.

>> For investments of ten or more years or earlier than December 31, 2026, investors can exclude all capital gains of the investment.

20% Qualified Business Income (QBI) deduction for "pass-through entities"

The Tax Cuts and Jobs Act includes lower across-the-board federal income tax rates, which benefit all wage earners and investors, including real estate investors. If you spend at least 250 hours per year on certain activities (defined in a moment) related to your real estate investments, you may also be able to utilize an additional tax break targeted to certain small business entities.

In redesigning the tax code, Congress realized that the many small businesses that operate as so-called pass-through entities would be subjected to higher federal income tax rates compared with the 21 percent corporate income tax rate (reduced from 35 percent). Pass-through entities are small businesses such as sole proprietorships, LLCs, partnerships, and S corporations and are so named because the profits of the business *pass through* to the owners and their personal income tax returns.

To address the concern that individual business owners who operated their business as a pass-through entity could end up paying a higher tax rate than the 21 percent rate levied on C corporations, Congress provided a 20 percent Qualified Business Income (QBI) deduction for those businesses. Please see Chapter 15 for more details.

Retirement account funding

If you're not taking advantage of your retirement accounts (such as 401(k)s, 403(b)s, SEP-IRAs, and so on), you may be missing out on some terrific tax benefits. Funding retirement accounts gives you an immediate tax deduction when you contribute to them. And some employer accounts offer "free" matching money — but you've got to contribute to earn the matching money.

In comparison, you derive no tax benefits while you accumulate your down payment for an investment real estate purchase (or other investments such as for a small business). Furthermore, the operating positive cash flow or income from your real estate investment is subject to ordinary income taxes as you earn it. To be fair and balanced, I must mention here that investment real estate offers numerous tax benefits, which I detail in the "Being aware of the tax advantages" section earlier in this chapter.

Thinking about Asset Allocation

With money that you invest for the longer term, you should have an overall game plan in mind. Fancy-talking financial advisors like to use buzzwords such as *asset allocation*, a term that indicates what portion of your money you have invested in different types of investment vehicles, such as stocks and real estate (for appreciation or growth), versus lending vehicles, such as bonds and certificates of deposit, also known as CDs (which produce current income).

TIP

Here's a simple way to calculate asset allocation for long-term investments: Subtract your age from 110. The result is the percentage of your long-term money that you should invest in ownership investments for appreciation. So, for example, a 40-year-old would take 110 minus 40 equals 70 percent in growth investments such as stocks and real estate. If you want to be more aggressive, subtract your age from 120; a 40-year-old would then have 80 percent in growth investments.

As you gain more knowledge, assets, and diversification of growth assets, you're in a better position to take on more risk. Just be sure you're properly covered with insurance.

REMEMBER

These are simply guidelines, not hard-and-fast rules or mandates. If you want to be more aggressive and are comfortable taking on greater risk, you can invest higher portions in ownership investments.

As you consider asset allocation, when classifying your investments, determine and use your *equity* in your real estate holdings, which is the market value of property less outstanding mortgages. For example, suppose that prior to buying an investment property, your long-term investments consist of the following:

Stocks	$150,000
Bonds	$50,000
CDs	$50,000
Total	$250,000

So, you have 60 percent in ownership investments ($150,000) and 40 percent in lending investments ($50,000 ± $50,000). Now, suppose you plan to purchase a $300,000 income property making a $75,000 down payment. Because you've decided to bump up your ownership investment portion to make your money grow more over the years, you plan to use your maturing CD balance and sell some of your bonds for the down payment. After your real estate purchase, here's how your investment portfolio looks:

Stocks	$150,000
Real estate	$75,000 ($300,000 property – $225,000 mortgage)
Bonds	$25,000
Total	$250,000

Thus, after the real estate purchase, you've got 90 percent in ownership investments ($150,000 ± $75,000) and just 10 percent in lending investments ($25,000). Such a mix may be appropriate for someone under the age of 50 who desires an aggressive investment portfolio positioned for long-term growth potential.

HOW LEVERAGE AFFECTS YOUR REAL ESTATE RETURNS

Real estate is different from most other investments in that you can typically borrow (finance) up to 70 to 80 percent or more of the value of the property. Thus, you can use your small down payment of 20 to 30 percent of the purchase price to buy, own, and control a much larger investment. (During market downturns, lenders tighten requirements and may require larger down payments than they do during good times.) So when your real estate increases in value (which is what you hope and expect), you make money on your investment as well as on the money that you borrowed. That's what I mean when I say that the investment returns from real estate are enhanced due to *leverage.*

Take a look at this simple example. Suppose you purchase a property for $150,000 and make a $30,000 down payment. Over the next three years, imagine that the property appreciates 10 percent to $165,000. Thus, you have a profit (on paper) of $15,000 ($165,000 – $150,000) on an investment of just $30,000. In other words, you've made a 50 percent return on your investment. (***Note:*** I ignore *cash flow* — whether your rental income that you collect from the property exceeds the expenses that you pay or vice versa, and the tax benefits associated with rental real estate.)

Remember, leverage magnifies all of your returns, and those returns aren't always positive! If your $150,000 property decreases in value to $135,000, even though it has only dropped 10 percent in value, you actually lose (on paper) 50 percent of your original $30,000 investment. (In case you care, and it's okay if you don't, some wonks apply the terms *positive leverage* and *negative leverage*.) Please see the "Understanding Real Estate's Income- and Wealth-Producing Potential" section earlier in this chapter for a more detailed example of investment property profit and return.

Chapter **15**

Looking at Tax Considerations and Exit Strategies

R eal estate is a great investment that offers you the opportunity to leverage a small cash investment to own and control large holdings that generate cash flow and can appreciate significantly over time. But cash flow, leverage, and appreciation aren't the only advantages of real estate. Utilizing current real estate tax laws has always been a key benefit for real estate investors.

Applying tax strategies properly allows rental real estate investors the ability to shelter income and even to eliminate — or at least defer — capital gains. Success in real estate, like all investments, is generally determined by how much money you keep on an *after*-tax basis. Real estate offers the potential to minimize taxation, so real estate investors need a thorough understanding of the best techniques to optimize their financial positions.

REMEMBER

I discuss tax advantages in this chapter, but don't let tax considerations drive your decisions. Purchasing real estate should always be an economic decision. Only when a deal makes economic sense (both at the time of purchase and after the sale) should you consider the tax aspects. Also, real estate taxation is a constantly changing, complicated area. Although this chapter covers the key concepts, it isn't a substitute for professional tax advice. Every real estate investor needs a competent accountant or tax advisor (who specializes in real estate) on their investment team. I recommend that you meet with your tax advisors regularly throughout the year, rather than only just before the tax filing due date.

Because the subject is so entwined in tax considerations, I also cover real estate sales — also known as *exit strategies*. The tax implications of various exit strategies are important to understand so that the real estate investor can select the best one for each sale and minimize the tax consequences of selling real estate holdings.

Understanding the Tax Angles

The tax laws regarding investment real estate are unique and far more complex than those regarding homeownership. For example, a homeowner can't deduct their costs of operating and the repairs and maintenance of their home — but as the owner of a rental property, you can deduct such costs. Also, the benefits of depreciation apply only to rental real estate and aren't available for property held as a personal residence.

TIP

Tax laws change frequently, so check with your tax advisor before taking any action. Use a tax attorney, a certified public accountant (CPA), an enrolled agent (EA), or a tax specialist to prepare your tax returns if you have investment real estate. In the sections that follow, I discuss some important rental real estate tax concepts that you should understand if you want to make the most of your property investments.

Sheltering income with depreciation

Depreciation is an accounting concept that allows you to claim a deduction for a certain portion of the acquisition value of a rental property because the building wears out over time. Depreciation is an expense, but it doesn't actually take cash out of your bank account. Instead, you treat the depreciation amount as an expense or deduction when tallying your income on your tax return, which decreases your taxable income and allows you to shelter positive cash flow from taxation. Depreciation lowers your income taxes in the current year by essentially providing a government, interest-free loan until the property is sold.

WARNING

The use of depreciation by real estate investors can be used to defer, but not permanently eliminate, income taxes. The annual deduction for depreciation is a reduction in the *basis* (calculated as your original cost in the property plus capital improvements) of the rental property, which is *recaptured* (added to your taxable profit) in full and taxed upon sale. Currently, all deductions taken for cost recovery are recaptured and taxed at 25 percent when you sell the property.

TIP

Depreciation is only allowed for the acquisition value of the buildings and other improvements because the underlying land isn't depreciable. The theory is that the buildings and other improvements ultimately wear out over time, but the land will always be there. Because the amount of your depreciation deduction depends on the highest portion of the overall property value being attributable to the buildings, it's advantageous to allocate the highest fair market value of your rental property value to the improvements to increase your potential deduction for depreciation.

To determine the appropriate basis for calculating depreciation, many real estate investors have traditionally used the property tax assessor's allocation between the value of the buildings and land. But the IRS doesn't allow the assessor's allocation. It does accept an appraisal, which can be quite expensive unless you have a recent one available. But a more cost-effective method that the IRS accepts is the Comparative Market Analysis (CMA) that most brokers offer at a nominal charge or even for free.

Under current tax laws, recently acquired rental properties can only use straight-line depreciation. *Straight-line depreciation* reduces the value of the rental property by set equal amounts each year over its established depreciable life. The period of time during which depreciation is taken is called the *recovery period*. For properties placed in service or purchased on or after May 13, 1993, the IRS requires straight-line depreciation with the following recovery periods:

>> **Residential rental property:** The recovery period is 27.5 years (or a cost recovery factor of 3.636 percent each year). A property qualifies as residential if the tenants stay a minimum of 30 days or more and no substantial services are provided, such as medical or health care.

>> **Commercial properties:** The recovery period is 39 years (or an annual cost recovery of 2.564 percent). Mixed-use properties are classified as commercial unless the income from the residential portion is 80 percent or more of the gross rental income.

The cost recovery deductions for both the year of acquisition and the year of sale must use the midmonth convention requirement, which means that regardless of the actual day of sale, the transaction is presumed to have been completed on the 15th of the month. Thus, the depreciation deduction is prorated based on the number of full months of ownership plus ½ month for the month of purchase or sale.

WARNING

Commercial property owners typically modify vacant spaces to get potential tenants to sign a lease. The IRS requires that the cost of those improvements be depreciated over 39 years even though the lease and the actual useful life of the improvements are much shorter. This topic is a constant source of lobbying by commercial real estate interests seeking depreciation schedules that more closely coincide with the actual length of lease. The tax laws were changed temporarily to a 15-year cost recovery from 2004 through 2013. You can take a deduction in the current year for the full remaining undepreciated portion of the tenant improvements that were torn out as a result of one tenant vacating and new tenant improvements being installed for the next tenant. For example, if you replace carpet that hasn't been fully depreciated, you can deduct the remaining unamortized value in that tax year.

Minimizing income taxes

Taxpayers generally have two types of income:

>> **Ordinary income:** This category includes wages, bonuses and commissions, rents, and interest and is taxed at the federal level at various rates up to 37 percent. The taxable income you receive from your rental property is subject to taxation as ordinary income.

>> **Capital gains:** These are generated when investments (such as real estate and stock) are sold for a profit. The income you realize upon the sale of your investment property is subject to taxation as a capital gain. Capital gains are classified as short-term and long-term:

- **Short-term:** For property held for 12 months or less, capital gains are taxed at the same rate as ordinary income.

- **Long-term:** For property held for longer than 12 months, gains are taxed at lower rates than ordinary income with a current rate of 0, 15, or 20 percent, depending on your overall tax bracket.

But you can't pay taxes until you figure out exactly what part of your income will be taxed. To do that, you need to perform a cash-flow analysis. The cash flow from a property — positive or negative — is determined by deducting all operating expenses, debt service interest, capital improvement expenses, damages, theft, and depreciation from rental income.

Calculating the cash flow of a property follows the format shown in Table 15-1. Following, I provide a quick summary and then factor in the taxman.

1. **Start with the *Gross Potential Income* (GPI) for the property.**

   This figure is the hypothetical maximum rent collections if the property were 100 percent occupied at market rents and all rents were collected.

2. Subtract the *loss to lease* (which is the amount the contract rent is less than the market rent) and the rent that isn't collected due to vacancy and collection loss (the failure of tenants to pay) to arrive at the Net Rent Revenue (NRR).

3. Add the other income (laundry, parking, money collected from former tenants, income from the rental of a cellphone tower on the roof, and so on) to the NRR to establish the Effective Gross Income (EGI).

4. Subtract the operating expenses from the EGI to calculate the Net Operating Income (NOI).

   The NOI is the essential number used in the income capitalization method of determining the value of the property.

5. Subtract the capital improvements and interest paid on the debt service from the NOI to arrive at the before-tax cash flow (BTCF).

6. Subtract the *straight-line depreciation* (which is merely a noncash accounting deduction that reduces your tax liability without requiring an actual cash expenditure) from the before-tax cash flow.

   The result is the *taxable income.*

7. Multiply this year's taxable income or reportable loss by your ordinary marginal income rate to determine your tax liability or savings.

8. Deduct the tax liability (or savings, if the taxable income is negative and the loss can be used in the current tax year) and the annual debt service principal payments from the net taxable income, and then add the noncash deduction for the straight-line cost recovery.

   You now have the after-tax cash flow (ATCF).

TABLE 15-1   Calculating After-Tax Cash Flow

Gross Potential Income	$100,000
Minus loss to lease	(2,000)
Minus vacancy and collection losses	(2,500)
Net Rent Revenue (NRR)	95,500
Plus other income	2,500
Plus common area maintenance (CAM) reimbursement (if any)	2,000
Effective Gross Income (EGI)	100,000
Minus operating expenses	(40,000)
Net Operating Income (NOI)	60,000
Minus capital improvements	(5,000)
Minus annual debt service interest	(35,000)
Before-tax cash flow (BTCF) without principal payments	20,000
Minus the straight-line cost recovery	(12,000)
Net taxable income	8,000
Minus tax liability (or savings)*	(3,120)
Minus annual debt service principal payments	(4,000)
Plus the cost recovery	12,000
After-tax cash flow (ATCF)	$12,880

*Calculation of tax liability

Net Operating Income	**$60,000**
Minus annual debt service interest	(35,000)
Minus the straight-line cost recovery	(12,000)
Net taxable income	13,000
Times investor's tax rate	24%
Tax liability	**$3,120**

New tax breaks for pass-through entities

The Tax Cut and Jobs Act, which took effect in tax year 2018, includes lower across-the-board federal income tax rates that benefit all wage earners and investors, including real estate investors. If you spend at least 250 hours per year on certain activities (defined in a moment) related to your real estate investments, you may also be able to utilize an additional tax break targeted to certain small business entities.

In redesigning the tax code, Congress realized that the many small businesses that operate as so-called pass-through entities would be subjected to higher federal income tax rates compared with the new 21 percent corporate income tax rate (reduced from 35 percent). Pass-through entities are small businesses such as sole proprietorships, LLCs, partnerships, and S-corporations and are so named because the profits of the business pass through to the owners and their personal income tax returns.

To address the concern that individual business owners who operated their business as a pass-through entity could end up paying a higher tax rate than the 21 percent rate levied on C-corporations, Congress provided a 20 percent deduction for those businesses.

REMEMBER

Another way to look at this is that the business would only pay taxes on 80 percent of its profits and would be in the 22 percent federal income tax bracket. This deduction effectively reduces the 22 percent tax bracket to 17.6 percent.

This 20 percent pass-through deduction gets phased out for service business owners (for example, lawyers, doctors, real estate agents, consultants, and so on) at single taxpayer incomes above $191,950 (up to $241,950) and for married couples filing jointly incomes over $383,900 (up to $483,900). For other types of businesses above these income thresholds, this deduction may be limited, so consult with your tax advisor.

The Internal Revenue Service has clarified that certain rental real estate investor entities are eligible for the 20 percent Qualified Business Income (QBI) pass-through deduction in a given tax year if the following conditions are met:

>> Separate books and records are maintained to reflect income and expenses for each rental real estate enterprise.

>> For tax years 2023 and beyond, in any three of the five consecutive taxable years that end with the taxable year (or in each year for an enterprise held for less than five years), 250 or more hours of rental services are performed (as described in this revenue procedure) per year with respect to the rental real estate enterprise.

>> The taxpayer maintains contemporaneous records, including time reports, logs, or similar documents, regarding the following:

- Hours of all services performed

- Description of all services performed

- Dates on which such services were performed

- Who performed the services

Such records are to be made available for inspection at the request of the IRS.

Per the Internal Revenue Service, rental services include:

>> Advertising to rent or lease the real estate

>> Negotiating and executing leases

>> Verifying information contained in prospective tenant applications; collection of rent

>> Daily operation, maintenance, and repair of the property

>> Management of the real estate

>> Purchase of materials

>> Supervision of employees and independent contractors

REMEMBER

Rental services may be performed by owners or by employees, agents, and/or independent contractors of the owners. The term "rental services" does not include financial or investment management activities, such as arranging financing; procuring property; studying and reviewing financial statements or reports on operations; planning, managing, or constructing long-term capital improvements; or time spent traveling to and from the real estate.

Also keep in mind, real estate used by the taxpayer (including an owner or beneficiary of a relevant pass-through entity) as a residence for any part of the year is not eligible for this tax break. Real estate rented or leased under a triple net lease is also not eligible.

The taxation of investment real estate can get complicated and is constantly changing, so I have covered the most important and topics here. Please consult the latest edition of *Real Estate Investing For Dummies* which I co-authored with Robert Griswold for the latest details.

TIP

Considering Exit Strategies

A successful investment strategy doesn't simply involve buying and operating properties. The *disposition* or *exit strategy* has a significant impact on overall success.

Begin your exit-strategy planning while you're acquiring property. That is, develop a game plan to work toward before you buy the asset. You can always change or modify your plans, but knowing your exit strategy prior to acquisition is good practice.

You do your homework, buy the right property at the right price, and add value by maintaining and improving the property and obtaining good tenants. So, why undo your good work by selling the property for less than it's worth or paying too much in taxes because you failed to explore ways to defer your capital gains (which can keep more of your money working to keep your portfolio growing)?

When you're looking to buy rental real estate with appreciation potential, seek those properties that have deferred maintenance and cosmetic problems that allow you to buy them at a good price. When you go to sell your property, you want to get full value, so before you begin to list or show your available property, scrutinize the curb appeal and physical condition, looking for those items that need attention. Don't rely on your own eye; ask a trained, professional real estate agent or property manager who isn't familiar with the property to give you some feedback.

TIP

Some individuals and companies offer services called staging (placing temporary furniture and other items in the dwelling to make it more appealing) to reduce the required marketing time and maximize the value of the property being sold.

Robert Griswold and I thoroughly cover the purchase agreement and other issues involved in a real estate transaction in *Real Estate Investing For Dummies*. Because I firmly believe that the proper and ethical way to conduct business in real estate is to use standardized forms and practices, there's no need to present new forms or tactics that are slanted to favor your position as the seller. In the long run, you benefit by treating people fairly in your real estate transactions. If you build a reputation for being ethical, you receive many more opportunities than if you use one-sided methods designed to take advantage of others.

When it's time to sell the property, you have several options, but not all of them have the same tax consequences.

Selling outright

One exit strategy is to simply sell the property and report the sale to the IRS. As long as capital gains tax rates are low, this strategy may work for taxpayers who are nearing the end of their prime real estate investing years and are looking to slow down and simplify their lives.

In an outright or all-cash sale, you simply sell the property, report the sale to the IRS, and determine whether you have a taxable gain or loss. If it's a gain, taxes are due; if you've held the property for at least 12 months, the low capital gains tax rates of 0 percent or 15 or 20 percent apply. (Seller financing isn't considered an all-cash sale, nor is an installment sale, which I cover later in this chapter, in the section "Selling now, reaping profits later: Installment sale.") Don't forget the 25 percent tax rate on cost recovery deduction that's triggered on the sale.

Although an outright or all-cash sale is fairly straightforward, real estate investors are often interested in postponing the recognition of their gain on sale so that they can postpone the payment of taxes due. This situation is where an installment sale or an exchange (discussed later) can be useful.

Although the sale of a property can make sense, remember that refinancing an investment property with substantial equity is another great way to free up additional cash for real estate acquisitions, or other investments or purposes.

Calculating gain or loss on a sale

Preparing and retaining accurate records from the initial purchase of your rental property and throughout the ownership is extremely important because the sale of a real estate investment property must be reported to the IRS.

Several factors go into the required calculation to determine whether there's a gain or loss on the sale that can either increase or reduce the overall income:

>> The sales price is a major factor.

>> Any capital improvements made to the property should be included.

>> Accumulated depreciation taken during the holding period increases your taxes when it's recaptured.

>> Also, if the property had operating losses that couldn't be taken in prior tax years, those suspended losses increase the adjusted basis and lower the potential taxable gain (or increase the loss available to shelter other income).

Table 15-2 outlines the following gain (or loss) on sale calculation.

TABLE 15-2 ## Calculating Total Gain or Loss on Sale

Gross Sales Price	$1,500,000
Minus selling expenses	(50,000)
Net sales proceeds	1,450,000
Minus adjusted basis (see Table 15-3)	(700,000)
Total gain (or loss) on sale	**$750,000**

Step 1: Determine the net sales proceeds

The *net sales proceeds* are the gross sales price minus the selling expenses. The *selling expenses* are all costs incurred to complete the sales transaction such as real estate commissions, attorney and accountant fees, settlement and escrow fees, title insurance, and other closing costs.

Step 2: Determine the adjusted basis for the property

When the property is just acquired, the *basis* is simply the original cost of the property (the equity down payment plus the total debt incurred to finance the property plus closing costs, appraisal, and environmental reports). If the owner didn't purchase the property, the basis is one of the following:

>> The fair market value at the time of transfer for property received as an inheritance

>> The carry-over basis if the property is received as a gift

>> The substituted basis if the property was acquired in a tax-deferred exchange

However, the basis isn't static — it changes during the ownership period. To adjust the original basis, take three factors into account (see Table 15-3 for the sample calculations):

>> **Capital improvements:** During the holding period, owners often make some capital improvements or additions to the property. Capital improvements are money spent to improve the existing property or construct new property. These capital improvements are added to the original acquisition cost to determine the adjusted basis.

Routine and normal repairs required to keep the property in good working order over its useful life are deductible expenses during the tax year in which they're incurred. They're not capital improvements for the purpose of the adjusted basis calculation. For example, replacing a few shingles or even re-roofing a portion of the property is a repair, but completely replacing the roof is a capital improvement. A newly constructed addition that increases the rentable square footage of the rental property is a capital improvement. The capital improvement includes all costs incurred, such as contractor payments, architect fees, building permits, construction materials, and labor costs.

>> **Depreciation:** At the same time, the straight-line depreciation taken each tax year is accumulated and reduces the adjusted basis of the property. Note that the total accumulated depreciation is included in the overall calculation of the gain or loss upon sale as part of the adjusted basis but is reported separately and is taxed at a different rate on the taxpayer's tax return.

>> **Casualty losses taken by the taxpayer:** Casualty losses can result from the destruction of or damage to your property from any sort of sudden, unexpected, or unusual event such as a flood, hurricane, tornado, fire, earthquake, or even volcanic eruption.

TABLE 15-3 **Adjusted Basis Calculation**

Original acquisition cost or basis	$750,000
Plus capital improvements	50,000
Minus accumulated cost recovery	(100,000)
Minus any casualty losses taken	0
Adjusted basis	**$700,000**

Step 3: Determine the total gain or loss on the sale

The total gain or loss is determined by taking the net sales price and subtracting the adjusted basis (see Table 15-2).

Step 4: Factoring in accumulated cost recovery and suspended losses

If you have suspended losses reported on the taxpayer's tax returns during the ownership period, deduct them from the net sales proceeds (see Table 15-4). The suspended losses are those losses that the taxpayer couldn't use in prior tax years because they didn't meet the strict IRS requirements. That figure is the capital gain from appreciation.

TABLE 15-4

Capital Gain from Appreciation

Total Gain on Sale (from Table 15-2)	$750,000
Minus straight-line cost recovery	(100,000)
Minus suspended losses	(75,000)
Capital gain from appreciation	**$575,000**

Step 5: Determine total tax liability

The net gain on sale is taxed as ordinary income unless the property was held for more than 12 months. Fortunately, most real estate investors do hold the property for more than 12 months and can qualify for the lower long-term capital gains tax rates. In fact, if the property has been held less than 12 months, all depreciation that has been taken is recaptured as ordinary income.

For tax purposes, the net gain on sale must be allocated between the capital gain from appreciation and the recapture of the accumulated depreciation. The seller doesn't automatically get the benefits of the lower flat 0 or 15 percent maximum capital gains tax and may even have to pay the maximum depreciation recapture tax rate of 25 percent if they're in a higher income tax bracket, as is the investor in our example. (The depreciation recapture rate is based on your ordinary income tax bracket but won't exceed 25 percent.)

In Table 15-4, the total gain on a sale of $750,000 is reduced by $100,000 in accumulated depreciation and suspended losses of $75,000 for a gain from appreciation of $575,000. In Table 15-5, I break the taxation of the capital gain down between capital gain from appreciation and depreciation recapture. The accumulated depreciation is recaptured at 25 percent, resulting in a tax liability of $25,000. The gain from appreciation was taxed at the maximum capital gains flat rate of 20 percent, resulting in a tax liability of $115,000. So, the total tax liability is $140,000.

TABLE 15-5	Total Tax Liability Calculation	
Straight-line cost recovery	$100,000
Times tax rate on recapture	25%
Total tax due for recapture	**$25,000**
Capital gain from appreciation	$575,000
Times tax rate on capital gain	20%
Total tax due on capital gain	**$115,000**
Total tax liability	**$140,000**

If the sale of the property results in a net loss, the loss must first be applied to offset net passive-activity income or gains. If there are none, or after they're exhausted, the net loss can be applied to reduce the income or gains from nonpassive activities such as earned income or wages.

Selling now, reaping profits later: Installment sale

An *installment sale* is the disposition of a property in which the seller receives any portion of the sale proceeds in a tax year following the tax year in which they sell the property. The time value of money indicates that it's generally better to have the use of money today than in the future. Knowledgeable real estate investors seek ways to minimize or defer the taxes that they need to pay. One way to accomplish this goal is by using the *installment sale method* — within specified IRS limits, the sellers of real estate can report their receipt of funds as actually received over time rather than as a lump sum at the time of the sale.

REMEMBER

A taxpayer who sells their property on the installment method is able to report only the *pro rata* (proportionate) part of the proceeds actually received in that tax year. The advantage is that the taxable gain is spread over several years and can be reported in years in which the taxpayer may have a lower tax bracket. This technique is ideal for property sellers who don't need to take their equity at the time of sale because they have other sources of income or want to minimize taxes, or both.

This scenario includes transactions in which the seller provides the financing and received payments over time. When financing is difficult for buyers to obtain, sellers may offer to take a mortgage note from the buyer for some (or even all) of their equity in the property. Having the seller take a note for equity is a common no-money-down strategy.

TIP

An installment sale can be an effective way for a seller to assist the buyer in making the purchase as well as to defer the recognition of income and thereby reduce the capital gains tax.

Here's how it works: A real estate investor sells a property for $1.5 million that has an adjusted basis of $700,000. The buyer makes a down payment of $250,000, assumes the current loan balance of $500,000, and accepts seller financing of $750,000. The terms of the installment sale require the buyer to pay the principal balance of $750,000 owed to the seller at $250,000 each year over the following three years, plus interest. The buyer reports the gain according to the timing of the principal payments.

The amount of the gain that must be reported in a given tax year is equal to the total principal payment multiplied by the profit ratio. The profit ratio is calculated as follows:

Profit Ratio = Gross Profit ÷ Contract Price

The *gross profit* is the sale price minus the selling costs and adjusted basis.

Sale price	$1.5 million
Minus costs	$50,000
Minus adjusted basis	$700,000
Gross profit	$750,000

The *contract price* is the sale price minus the current loan balance.

Sale price	$1.5 million
Minus loan balance	$500,000
Contract price	$1 million

Therefore, in this example, you figure the profit ratio as follows:

Profit Ratio = Gross Profit ÷ Contract Price

Profit Ratio = $750,000 ÷ $1 million

Profit Ratio = 75 percent

With the profit ratio, you can compute the gain that must be reported each year.

Year of sale: $250,000 × 75% =	Year of sale: $250,000 x 75% = $187,500
Year two: $250,000 × 75% =	Year two: $250,000 x 75% = $187,500
Year three: $250,000 × 75% =	Year three: $250,000 x 75% = $187,500
Year four: $250,000 × 75% =	Year four: $250,000 x 75% = $187,500

Thus, the seller reports $187,500 as the gain in the year of sale, plus $187,500 for each of the next three years. The seller reports the interest paid by the buyer to the seller on the deferred principal payments as ordinary interest income.

If this example were an outright sale, the seller would report the entire $750,000 gain in the year of sale, but the installment sale allows them to report the gain as the principal payments of $187,500 are received each year for four consecutive years. There's no difference in the total gain, simply the timing of the reporting of the gain.

WARNING

Although there are many proponents of the buying-and-flipping real estate investment strategy, they often overlook the fact that flipping properties for a quick profit can have significant and expensive tax implications. If the IRS sees that you routinely buy and flip properties, it classifies you as a dealer — a taxpayer who buys property (called inventory in this case) with the intention of selling it in the short run — as opposed to an investor, a person who purchases properties seeking appreciation and income from long-term ownership. It's possible for real estate investors to simultaneously hold some properties for long-term investment and other properties the IRS classifies as inventory, making the owner a dealer. The dealer label comes with two drawbacks:

>> Dealers aren't allowed to use the installment sales method to spread the recognition of their gain over multiple tax years. The entire profit must be reported and fully taxed in the year of the property sale.

>> Profit from the sale of a property is considered earned income and is taxed as ordinary income at your personal income tax rate — even if you hold the property for longer than 12 months. (If you hold a property for longer than 12 months, it's typically eligible for the long-term capital gains tax rate, and a dealer would thus lose this benefit.)

Transferring equity to defer taxes

The concept behind a tax-deferred exchange is that an investor can transfer the built-up equity in one property to a new property and maintain, essentially, the same investment except that the physical asset is different. The IRS considers a qualified tax-deferred exchange to be one continuous investment, and thus no tax is due on the profit from the sale of the relinquished asset as long as the investor invests all proceeds into the replacement property.

Tax-deferred exchanges are often referred to as 1031 exchanges — the name comes from Section 1031 of the IRS Code that covers them. And there are actually three different types of tax-deferred exchanges:

>> A straight exchange in which two parties trade properties of approximate or equal value.

>> A three-party or multiparty exchange, which involves three or more parties buying, selling, or exchanging properties. This situation happens when one party in an exchange doesn't want a property owned by the other party but prefers the property currently owned by a third party. These transactions can actually involve any number of owners and can be quite complex. They should only be done with the ongoing advice and consultation of an experienced tax professional.

>> A delayed exchange — sometimes also referred to as a Starker exchange — which allows the sale of the relinquished property and the purchase of the replacement property to occur at different times as long as strict rules are followed. This exchange is by far the most used 1031 exchange. (Reverse Starker exchanges can also be completed when an accommodator, on behalf of the taxpayer, acquires a replacement property first and then sells the relinquished property at a later date.)

REMEMBER

The capital gains tax is deferred, not eliminated. If you sell your property during your lifetime and don't qualify for a tax-deferred exchange, you pay tax on both the capital gain and the recapture of the total depreciation taken since the original investment.

Meeting your goals

A tax-deferred exchange is an important tool if you're looking to increase the size of your real estate holdings. Tax-deferred exchanges can be effective tools to postpone the recognition of a gain on real estate investments. They allow the investor to transfer equity to a larger property without paying taxes. Plus, there's no limit to how often or how many times a taxpayer can use an exchange. Therefore, you can keep exchanging upward in value, adding to your assets over your lifetime without ever having to pay any capital gains tax.

TIP

The tax-deferred exchange is particularly useful for real estate investors who specialize in buying and renovating properties and want to reinvest their profits into a larger property rather than sell the property and run the risk of being classified by the IRS as a dealer. A tax-deferred exchange can also help you achieve other goals such as

>> Trading for a property in a better location.

>> Acquiring a property with better cash flow.

>> Making better use of the significant equity that can exist in properties held for many years. Plus, those properties have typically exhausted their depreciable basis, and an exchange can enhance that.

Following the rules

As with any transaction that involves those three letters — IRS — you must play by the rules for the 1031 exchange:

>> **The relinquished property and the replacement property must both be investment real estate properties located in the United States.** Actually, the majority of all tax-deferred exchanges involve properties domestically, but the IRS does allow a tax-deferred exchange of a foreign property for another foreign property. The key is that both properties must be domestic or foreign — no mixing and matching is allowed!

>> **You must trade only like kind real estate.** *Like kind real estate* means property held for business, trade, or investment purposes. The broad definition of *like kind* doesn't mean *same kind*. It allows real estate investors to use a 1031 exchange, for example, to defer taxes when they sell an apartment building and buy raw land, or vice versa; exchange a single-family rental home for a small office building; and so on. But neither your personal primary residence nor property held as inventory where the investor is defined as a dealer (see the "Selling now, reaping profits later: Installment sale" section earlier in the chapter) qualifies.

>> **An exchange must be equal to or greater in both value and equity.** Any cash or debt relief received is considered to be boot (any receipt of money, property, or reduction in liability owed) and is taxable. For example, if you want to complete a tax-deferred exchange and the property you relinquish is valued at $1 million with a loan balance of $500,000, you must purchase the replacement property for more than $1 million, and its equity has to be equal to or greater than $500,000.

>> **A neutral third party should be involved.** This neutral third party, called a facilitator, exchanger, or accommodator, should be appointed prior to the closing of any escrow. An exchange agreement must be signed, and the neutral third party must hold the proceeds unless the properties close simultaneously.

>> **The potential replacement property must be clearly and unambiguously identified in writing within 45 days from the close of the relinquished property.** The IRS has limitations on how many replacement properties may be designated, or taxpayers would simply identify a long list of potential replacement properties. There are three specific tests to meet this requirement; they can get quite technical, but the most commonly used is the three property rule. Under this rule, you can designate a maximum of three replacement properties of any fair market value, and you must purchase one or more of those properties.

>> **The closing of the replacement property must occur within 180 days of the close of the relinquished property.** Meeting this requirement isn't as easy as it may sound, as I detail in the next section.

Counting (and countering) complications and risks

The tax-deferred exchange has some complications and risks. My experience is that the identification of the replacement property within 45 days can be a real challenge, especially because only a limited number (usually three) properties can be identified. In a tight or competitive real estate market, the real estate investor can quickly find himself unable to actually complete the purchase of the replacement property within the 180-day limit, in which case the sale becomes a taxable event.

WARNING

Real estate owners looking for a replacement property (commonly called an *upleg*) are often tempted to chase a property and overpay. They rationalize that the capital gains deferral is so valuable that they can justify overpaying for the property because they'd otherwise have to pay taxes on the recognized gain. But such investors should realize that this isn't a tax-*free* exchange, only a deferral of a gain that may be taxable in the future.

TIP

In 2000, the IRS issued new guidelines that clarify the proper use of the reverse 1031 exchange. A reverse 1031 exchange can be complicated and should only be done with the guidance of an experienced tax advisor. Essentially, it allows real estate investors to have an accommodator purchase and hold their new investment properties while they then follow the 1031 guidelines to sell the relinquished property. The advantage is that the real estate investor is sure to have the replacement property in hand; one of the major challenges to a 1031 exchange is the risk involved in having to identify the replacement property within 45 days and complete the acquisition within the 180-day limitation. You should have a written exchange agreement, and title to the replacement property must be taken in the name of the accommodator until your relinquished property is sold.

Calculating the substituted basis

The calculation of the basis of the new property can be quite complicated if anything other than the property is exchanged. In an exchange, the tax is deferred and the potential gain is carried forward by calculating the substitute basis for the new replacement property. An example of a substitute basis calculation without any boot is shown in Table 15-6. This substitute basis would be used in the event you sell the property during your lifetime without doing a tax-deferred exchange and have a taxable transaction. See your tax specialist to deal with any additional variables in the transaction.

TABLE 15-6 Substituted Basis Calculation in an Exchange

Value of property exchanged	$1,500,000
Minus basis of property exchanged	700,000
Gain on property exchanged	800,000
Value of property acquired	3,000,000
Minus gain on property exchanged	800,000
Substituted basis on property acquired	**$2,200,000**

Using the capital gains exclusion to earn a tax-free gain

Another great tax benefit available for homeowners and real estate investors alike is the capital gains exclusion under Internal Revenue Code 121. Many investors have found that the principal residence capital gains exclusion can be the core of a profitable (and tax-free) investment strategy known as *serial home selling.* Simply buy and move into a property that can be renovated and sell it after a minimum of two years, and you can earn a tax-free gain of up to $500,000.

The gain on the sale of a principal residence is tax free up to $250,000 for individual taxpayers and up to $500,000 for married taxpayers who file jointly if they meet some simple requirements:

» You must own and have occupied or used the home as your principal residence for a total of 730 days (24 months) in the last 60 months — ending on the date of sale or exchange. The occupancy doesn't have to be continuous, and the home doesn't need to be your principal residence at the time of the sale or exchange. Only one spouse needs to legally hold title, but both must meet the use test.

   The factors considered by the IRS to determine whether a property meets the principal residence use test include

   • Is the residence used as the address of record for driver's license, tax returns, utilities, credit card bills and other billed items, and employment purposes?

   • Is this residence where you actually reside and where you keep your furniture, furnishings, and clothes?

» Generally, the seller can only use the exclusion once every two years. Vacations and short absences count as usage for the two-year use test.

The IRS provides partial principal residence exemptions for sellers who don't qualify for the full exemption. The partial exemption is based on the number of actual months the seller qualified divided by 24 months. A partial exemption is allowed for

>> **Work reasons:** For instance, a change in employment where the home seller's new job location is at least 50 miles farther away from the old principal residence than the former job location.

>> **Health reasons:** For instance, the need to move to care for a family member or a broad range of health-related reasons. Consult with your tax advisor, because you can meet this requirement in many ways — particularly if a physician recommended the move.

>> **Unforeseen circumstances:** Examples run the gamut and include a divorce or legal separation, engagement break-up, death, incarceration, multiple births, large increase in assessment dues, lost job or demotion, becoming ineligible for unemployment compensation, and so on. Many circumstances can qualify as unforeseen circumstances, so see your tax advisor for more information about your specific situation.

Selling as a lease-to-own purchase

The typical lease option combines a standard lease with a separate contract giving the tenant a unilateral option to purchase the rental property during a limited period of time for a mutually agreed upon purchase price. The tenant isn't required to exercise the option.

REMEMBER

Investors can use the lease option to increase cash flow and also sell their properties without paying the usual brokerage commissions. A lease option is really a real estate rental transaction combined with a potential sales transaction and financing technique. The seller can generate additional cash flow because a lease option generally consists of a monthly rental payment that's higher than the market rent, with a portion of the additional payment being applied to the option purchase price. Both parties can realize a savings on the brokerage commission because the transaction is usually completed without the full services of real estate brokers. But it's a good idea to have either an experienced broker or real estate attorney review the transaction documents, which is a minor (but worthwhile) expense.

Working through an example

Each lease option is unique, but here's an example of how a deal may be structured: An investor owns a rental home with a current market rent of $1,000 per month and a current market value of $120,000. Real estate forecasts indicate that appreciation will be 4 percent, or approximately $5,000, in the next 12 months.

The tenant signs a 12-month standard lease and agrees to pay $1,200 per month with $1,000 in rent and $200 as a nonrefundable option fee that applies to the down payment. The investor and tenant also enter into an option-to-purchase agreement that offers the tenant the right to buy the property within 12 months of the lease for $125,000 (the agreed upon estimated fair market value of the property by the end of the option period).

The investor receives an additional cash flow of $200 per month. If the tenant exercises the option, the tenant receives a credit toward the down payment of $200 per month for each month that they paid the option fee. If the investor has used their standard lease form and the lease option documents are drafted properly, they still has the right to evict the tenant for nonpayment of rent or any other material lease default.

REMEMBER

In most cases, tenants don't exercise the purchase option because they haven't accumulated the money required for the down payment and their share of the closing costs. In the meantime, you've increased your monthly rental income by $200 and had a good tenant. At the end of the option, the tenant is aware that they have paid an additional $2,400 in rent that would've been applied to the down payment or purchase price if they'd exercised their option. You can either renegotiate an extension of the purchase option with the tenant or you can negotiate a new lease without the purchase option.

Proceeding with caution

Avoid long-term lease options. Real estate appreciation can be unpredictable. Don't provide a set option purchase price for any longer than one or two years, or include a clause that the purchase price will increase by an amount equal to the increase in the average median home price in your local area.

If you're interested in using a lease option, have a real estate attorney with extensive experience in lease options review the lease and option contract in advance. Lease options can have serious business and even ethical problems if not properly drafted. If poorly structured, your lease option may be considered a sale with the following negative consequences:

>> A lease option may trigger the due-on-sale clause with your lender, who may force you to pay off the entire outstanding loan balance.

>> If the property is deemed a sale by the IRS, you can no longer use your tax benefits of depreciation and deductible expenses.

>> Your property may be reassessed for property taxes. In many parts of the country, reassessment is based on a change in ownership. An aggressive tax assessor can use the lease option to increase the assessed value. Investigate local reassessment policies in advance.

>> You may be liable for failure to comply with seller disclosure laws. There are severe penalties if you don't make the legally required disclosures, including those found on the transfer disclosure statement (TDS).

>> You may not be able to evict the tenant even if they default on the lease. The courts may consider that the tenant is really a buyer and that a traditional eviction action doesn't apply because the lease option is essentially a contract to purchase real estate. This situation may require expensive and lengthy court proceedings.

TIP

Ethically, keep the nonrefundable option fee reasonable, so if the value of the property declines or your tenant doesn't exercise their option for any reason, you can feel comfortable that the tenant has been treated fairly. Or you may want to renegotiate or consider offering an extension.

Gaining tax savings by investing in "opportunity zones"

The Tax Cuts and Jobs Acts bill created "qualified opportunity zones" to provide tax incentives to invest in low-income communities, which are defined by each state's governor and may comprise up to 25 percent of designated low-income communities in each state. States can also designate census tracts contiguous with low-income communities so long as the median family income in those tracts doesn't exceed 125 percent of the qualifying contiguous low-income community.

The new qualified opportunity zone tax incentive allows real estate investors the following potential benefits:

>> To defer the capital gains tax due upon a sale of the property if the capital gain from the sale is reinvested within 180 days in a qualified opportunity fund.

>> For investments in the qualified opportunity fund of at least five years, investors will receive a step-up in tax basis of 10 percent of the original gain.

>> For investments in the qualified opportunity fund of at least seven years, investors will receive an additional 5 percent step-up in tax basis.

>> For investments of the earlier of ten or more years or December 31, 2026, investors can exclude all capital gains of the investment.

Transferring your property through a gift or bequest

A property given as a gift carries the same tax basis from the seller to the new owner. For example, if the tax basis of the property is $100,000, even though the fair market value at the time of the gift is $500,000, the recipient's tax basis remains $100,000. If the recipient were to immediately sell the property, they would have a taxable gain of $400,000. Thus, gifting property to heirs during your lifetime may not be the best strategy.

Taking in a Final Note on Taxes on Your Profits

Holding an appreciated asset like investment real estate (or stocks or mutual funds) until your passing provides a tax-free transfer of real estate. Some investors are determined to avoid paying tax completely and have adopted a strategy of buy and hold for life. They use the tax-deferred exchange for years to roll over their gains into larger and larger properties and then completely avoid paying tax by never selling. Under current tax law, real estate transferred to your heirs upon death receives a full step-up in basis. So, in the preceding example, the party inheriting the real estate with a fair market value of $500,000 now has a tax basis of $500,000 and will only owe taxes on any future gain as the property appreciates further in the future after the death of the original owner.

Think of this as a family investment strategy. As discussed earlier, installment sales and tax-deferred exchanges are great for delaying the imposition of taxes, but the goal should be eliminating depreciation recapture, income, capital gain, and/or estate taxes completely.

Some real estate investors seek to buy and hold properties for their lifetime. Yes, as rents increase and your cash flow improves, so does the value of your property. You now have more equity in your property and with the improved cash flows, your property can handle more debt which means you can pay off the old loan and have cash that you can use tax-free. Remember that you haven't sold the property, so there are no taxes to be paid nor the recapture of depreciation (currently at a rate of 25 percent). Over time, your equity has increased, and you are just tapping that equity by refinancing and pulling out tax-free cash to invest in additional properties.

This is the key to long-term success in real estate investing and is known as "hypothecating your real estate portfolio" where you are leveraging and borrowing against your current equity in seasoned and stable properties to use the tax-free cash as the down payment to buy additional real estate assets.

Of course, the key is to be conservative and not overleverage or you may end up in bankruptcy court. Many real estate investing books will share this idea with you, but they fail to mention that you must always be very patient and only refinance when the timing is optimal such as when interest rates and loan terms for borrowing against real estate are reasonable. Also, you need to reinvest those cash proceeds into new real estate deals when the market prices are lower and better returns are available. Sometimes these two separate and distinct time frames will overlap, but often you will need to refinance and then wait for the market prices to come down before you purchase additional properties.

TIP

Another good strategy to use so that you ultimately have just larger properties, and not a scattered portfolio of small properties all over town (or worse, all over the country), is to use the tax-deferred exchange. You want to consolidate your individual or smaller properties which are very inefficient to own and manage into larger properties in the best locations. I suggest you achieve this through utilizing the tax-deferred exchange to trade smaller properties and get into a larger property that offers more upside as well as economies of scale and management efficiencies. That may take many transactions over the years but recall that the key to success in real estate is a long-term plan.

6

The Part of Tens

Take advantage of often overlooked tax reduction opportunities.

Know the tax benefits available to members of the military.

Chapter **16**

Ten Overlooked Opportunities to Trim Your Taxes

This chapter presents the more commonly overlooked opportunities to reduce individual income taxes. The income tax you pay is based on your taxable income minus your deductions. I start first with overlooked ways to minimize your taxable income. Then I move on to often-ignored deductions. I don't want you to be like all those people who miss out on perfectly legal tax-reduction strategies simply because they don't know what they don't know.

Make Your Savings Work for You

Out of apathy or lack of knowledge of better options, far too many people keep extra cash dozing away in their bank accounts. Yes, the bank has a vault and sometimes-friendly tellers who may greet you by name if you bank locally, but banks also characteristically pay relatively low rates of interest. Keeping your household checking account at a bank is fine, but even with such transaction accounts you've got other options today with investment firms' cash management accounts. You're generally throwing away some interest if you keep your extra savings money in most banks.

During periods of normal interest rates, the better money market mutual funds often pay substantially greater interest than bank savings accounts and offer equivalent safety. And if you're in a high tax bracket, money market funds come in tax-free flavors. Please see Part 3 to find out more about tax-friendly investments.

Getting a slightly higher interest rate on your cash balances is a step in the right direction but hardly the golden ticket you're looking for! In my experience, oftentimes folks accumulating excess cash don't know where else they can and should invest for better returns. They sense correctly that higher-return investments fluctuate far more in value, especially over the short-term, but they may be overlooking the risk of their cash balances not keeping them up with inflation and taxes. So, be sure to read the rest of the tips in this chapter and make an investment of time to find out more about sound investment options.

Invest in Wealth-Building Assets

During your working years, while you're earning employment income, you probably don't need or want taxable income from your investments because it increases your income tax bill. Real estate, stocks, and small-business investments offer the best long-term growth potential, although you need to be able to withstand downturns in these markets.

Most of the return that you can earn with these wealth-building investments comes from appreciation in their value, making them tax-friendly because you're in control and can decide when to sell and realize your profit. Also, as long as you hold onto these investments for more than one year, your profit is taxed at the lower, long-term capital gains tax rate. (Stock dividends are also subject to these lower tax rates — see Chapter 7.)

Fund "Tax-Reduction" Accounts

When you funnel your savings dollars into retirement accounts, such as a 401(k), 403(b), SEP-IRA, self-employed/i401(k), or IRA, you can earn substantial upfront tax breaks on your contributions. If you think that saving for retirement is boring, consider the tens of thousands of tax dollars these accounts can save you during your working years. Roth accounts — both IRA and employer-based — don't offer upfront tax breaks but present opportunities to grow your money without taxation over time and withdraw investment returns in retirement without taxation.

If you don't use these accounts to save and invest, you may well have to work many more years to accumulate the reserves necessary to retire. Refer to Chapter 4 to find out more, including how recent tax law changes significantly increased the benefits of these accounts.

Make Use of a "Back-Door" Roth IRA

If you're a higher-income earner, you may not be able to contribute to a Roth IRA. In that case, you can make a nondeductible contribution to a traditional IRA and then immediately convert that money into your Roth IRA. This is called a "back-door" Roth IRA.

This strategy makes sense to consider when your new contribution to the regular IRA is the only money you would have in regular IRA accounts. Otherwise, if you have additional money in a regular IRA and those investments have generated returns, converting to a Roth IRA will trigger tax on the investment earnings that are transferred. That may still make sense to do for the longer-term tax benefits that a Roth account offers, but you should run some numbers to decide. See Chapter 4 for information on all your retirement plan options.

Work Overseas

When you go to work in some foreign countries, you may be able to save some money on income taxes. For tax year 2024, you can exclude $126,500 of foreign-earned income (whether working for a company or on a self-employed basis) from U.S. income taxes. To qualify for this income tax exclusion, you must work at least 330 days (about 11 months) of the year overseas or be a foreign resident. You claim this income tax exclusion on Form 2555, Foreign Earned Income Exclusion.

If you earn more than $126,500, don't worry about being double-taxed on the income above this amount. You get to claim credits for foreign taxes paid on your U.S. tax return on Form 1116, Foreign Tax Credit. Perhaps to give you more time to fill out this form and others, the IRS gives Americans working abroad two extra months (until June 15) to file their tax returns.

As with many things in life that sound too good to be true, this pot of overseas gold has some catches. First, many of the places you've romanticized about traveling to and perhaps living in — such as England, France, Italy, Sweden, Germany, and Spain — have higher income tax rates than the ones in the United States. Also, this tax break isn't available to U.S. government workers overseas.

TIP

Look at the whole package when deciding whether to work overseas. Some employers throw in a housing allowance and other benefits. And be careful of the allure of supposedly low-cost countries. Be sure to consider all costs and benefits of living overseas, both financial and emotional. And also explore the safety of living in specific countries that you're considering.

Check Whether You Can Itemize

The IRS gives you two methods of determining your total deductions. *Deductions* are just what they sound like: You subtract them from your income before you calculate the tax you owe. So the more deductions you take, the smaller your taxable income — and the smaller your tax bill. You get to pick the method that leads to the largest total deductions — and thus a lower tax bill. But sometimes the choice isn't so clear, so be prepared to do some figuring.

Taking the *standard deduction* usually makes sense if you have a pretty simple financial life — a regular paycheck, a rented apartment, and no large expenses, such as medical bills, or loss due to theft or catastrophe. Single folks qualify for a $14,600 standard deduction, and married couples filing jointly get a $29,200 standard deduction for tax year 2024.

The other method of determining your allowable deductions is to *itemize* them on your tax return. This painstaking procedure is definitely more of a hassle, but if you can tally up more than the standard deduction amounts, itemizing saves you money. Schedule A of your 1040 is the page for summing up your itemized deductions, but you won't know whether you have enough itemized deductions unless you give this schedule a good examination.

If you currently don't itemize, you may be surprised to discover that your personal property and state income taxes are itemizable. So too are state sales taxes that you pay, especially if your state doesn't have an income tax or your state income tax payments are relatively low.

If you pay a fee to the state to register and license your car, you can itemize the expenditure as a deduction ("Other Taxes" on Schedule A). The IRS allows you to deduct only the part of the fee that relates to the value of your car, however. The state organization that collects the fee should tell you what portion of the fee is deductible on your invoice.

When you total your itemized deductions on Schedule A and that amount is equal to or less than the standard deduction, take the standard deduction without fail (unless you're married filing separately, and your spouse is itemizing — then you have to itemize). The total for your itemized deductions is worth checking every year, however, because you may have more deductions in some years than others, and you may occasionally be able to itemize.

TIP

Because you can control when you pay particular expenses for which you're eligible to itemize, you can shift or bunch more of them into selected years when you know that you'll have enough deductions to take full advantage of itemizing. For example, suppose that you're using the standard deduction this year because you just don't have many itemized deductions. Late in the tax year, though, you feel certain that you'll buy a home sometime during the next year. Thanks to the potential write-off of mortgage interest and property taxes, you also know that you'll be able to itemize next year. It makes sense, then, to shift as many deductible expenses as possible into the next year.

Trade Consumer Debt for Mortgage Debt

Suppose that you own real estate and haven't borrowed as much money as a mortgage lender currently allows (given the current market value of the property and your financial situation). And further suppose that you've run up high-interest consumer debt. Well, you may be able to trade one debt for another. You probably can refinance your mortgage and pull out extra cash to pay off your credit card, auto loan, or other expensive consumer credit lines.

You usually can borrow at a lower interest rate for a mortgage, thus lowering your monthly interest bill. Plus, you may get a tax-deduction bonus, because consumer debt — auto loans, credit cards, credit lines — isn't tax-deductible, but mortgage debt generally is. Therefore, the effective borrowing rate on a mortgage is even lower than the quoted rate suggests.

Don't forget, however, that refinancing your mortgage and establishing *home equity lines* involve application fees and other charges (points, appraisals, credit reports, and so on). You must include these fees in the equation to see whether it makes sense to exchange consumer debt for more mortgage debt.

WARNING

Swapping consumer debt for mortgage debt involves one big danger: Borrowing against the equity in your home can be an addictive habit. I've seen cases in which people run up significant consumer debt three or four distinct times and then refinance their homes the same number of times over the years so they can bail themselves out. At a minimum, continued expansion of your mortgage debt handicaps your ability to work toward other financial goals. In the worst case, easy access to borrowing encourages bad spending habits that can lead to bankruptcy or foreclosure on your debt-ridden home.

Consider Charitable Contributions and Expenses

When you itemize your deductions on Schedule A, you can deduct contributions made to charities. For example, most people already know that when they donate money to their favorite church or college, they can deduct it. Yet many taxpayers overlook the fact that they can also deduct expenses on work done for charitable organizations. For example, when you go to a soup kitchen to help prepare and serve meals, you can deduct your transportation costs to get there. You just need to keep track of your bus fares or driving mileage.

You can also deduct the fair market value of donations of clothing, household appliances, furniture, and other goods to charities — many of these charities will even drive to your home to pick up the stuff. Just make sure to keep some documentation: Write a detailed list and get it signed by the charity. Please see Chapter 2 for more on writing off charitable contributions and expenses.

Scour for Self-Employment Expenses

If you're self-employed, you already deduct a variety of expenses from your income before calculating the tax that you owe. When you buy a computer or office furniture, you can deduct those expenses (sometimes they need to be gradually deducted or depreciated over time). Salaries for your employees, office supplies, rent or mortgage interest for your office space, and phone expenses are also generally deductible.

Although more than a few business owners inflate their expenses, some self-employed folks don't take all the deductions they should. In some cases, people simply aren't aware of the wonderful world of deductions. For others, large deductions raise the concern of an audit. Taking advantage of deductions for which you're eligible makes sense and saves you money.

Read This Book, Use Tax Software, Hire a Tax Advisor

Informing yourself better about taxes and possibly hiring tax help is worth the money. You've got this book — read it and use the information in it. Also consider using tax software to help ensure you're leaving no stone unturned. And, you may benefit by hiring a tax preparer/advisor to review your return (even if just for one year).

Chapter **17**

Ten (Plus One) Tax Tips for Military Families

Members of the military and their families have always received special consideration from all branches of the U.S. government, and tax relief is no exception. This chapter highlights important elements of tax relief available to military families together with some other factors you may want to consider if you or your spouse is a member of the armed forces (including the reserves).

This chapter only provides some of the basics. If you or your spouse is in the military, you need to explore further. You can find additional information regarding paying income tax while you're in the military in IRS Publication 3 (*Armed Forces Tax Guide*), which is available online at www.irs.gov or by phone by calling 800-829-3676.

Some Military Wages May Be Tax-Exempt

In fact, if you're serving in a combat zone or a qualified hazardous duty area, all your compensation from active duty while you're stationed there is exempt from taxation unless you're a commissioned officer. Commissioned officers' pay earned while in a combat zone or a qualified hazardous duty area may be partially taxed. In addition, if you're hospitalized due to an injury in a combat zone, or because of disease that you caught there, your pay continues to be tax-exempt.

Even if you're not stationed in a combat zone, much of your military compensation is tax-exempt. For example, living allowances, including the Basic Allowance for Housing and the Basic Allowance for Subsistence, the Overseas Housing Allowance, and other housing costs, whether paid by the U.S. government or a foreign government, are exempt. So are moving allowances and travel allowances, including an annual round-trip for dependent students and leave between consecutive overseas tours of duty.

REMEMBER

Even though you can exclude some or all of the income you've earned while serving in a combat zone or qualified hazardous duty area, you may still use these nontaxable amounts when calculating your Earned Income Credit (EIC), child tax credit, additional child tax credit, or the recovery rebate credit in order to give yourself a bigger credit. Remember, making the election to include nontaxable combat pay when calculating these credits doesn't mean you have to include this income when calculating your tax. This income remains nontaxable!

Rule Adjustments to Home Sales

Chapter 13 covers in great detail the sale of your principal residence and the exclusion of $250,000 of capital gain if single and $500,000 if married filing jointly. One of the requirements to obtain this capital gains break is that you must be living in that house for at least two of the previous five years. This created a hardship for members of the military, and the Military Family Tax Relief Act has addressed this rule.

Now, if you or your spouse serve on qualified official extended duty as a member of the armed forces during any part of the five-year qualifying period, you may choose to exclude your period of service from the five years. The five-year qualifying period can be extended for up to another ten years. Therefore, a military member need only live in the home for two of the previous 15 years to qualify for the capital gains' tax exclusion.

The provisions here are quite extensive, but they're clearly laid out in Publication 3. Check it out if you think this rule may apply to you.

Tax Benefits for Your Family if You're Killed in Action

The Military Family Relief Act increased from $6,000 to $12,000 the amount of benefits paid to the family of any member of the armed forces in the case of that member's death. The full death benefit paid isn't taxed to anyone.

In addition to the $12,000 tax-free payment a family receives when a member of the military is killed in combat, any income tax liability due to that person's income for the year of death and for any earlier tax years that the member served in a combat zone is forgiven. This means that any unpaid tax liability no longer needs to be paid, and any liability for these periods that was already paid will be refunded.

In addition, if the decedent, whether a military or civilian U.S. employee, is killed or later dies from wounds received in a military or terrorist attack, even if it does not happen in a designated combat zone, income tax is forgiven for the year of the attack and the year immediately prior for that person's income tax liability. Refunds will be given for taxes already paid that are later forgiven.

WARNING

For couples filing jointly and surviving spouses, even though the military decedent's tax liability is forgiven, the nonmilitary spouse's isn't. For any income-producing assets that you held jointly with your spouse, only one-half of the income will be excluded, and only one-half of the deductions will be allowed.

TIP

IRS Publication 3920 (*Tax Relief for Victims of Terrorist Attacks*) gives you clear examples of how to calculate the amount of tax forgiveness. It also tells you which income is included in the forgiveness and which isn't. However, the rules are complex; you may want to consult a professional tax preparer before filing the necessary documents to obtain your refunds.

Deadlines Extended During Combat and Qualifying Service

If you're currently stationed in a combat zone or you have qualifying service outside a combat zone, the deadlines for filing your tax returns, paying your taxes, filing claims for refunds, or taking any other actions with the IRS are automatically extended. The deadline for the IRS to take action against you in an audit or in collections is also extended.

WARNING

Extensions are extensions only, not a forgiveness of any tax owed. After you're no longer on active duty in a qualifying area (or no longer hospitalized continuously because of an injury or illness that resulted from duty in one of those areas), the clock begins to run again. You have 180 days after you're no longer stationed in a combat zone or a qualifying hazardous duty area plus the number of days that were left for you to take action with the IRS before you were sent to that combat zone or other qualifying area.

Income Tax Payment Deferment Due to Military Service

Even if you're not serving in a combat zone or other qualifying area, you may elect to delay the payment of your income tax that is due either before or during your period of military service. In order to defer payments, though, you must be performing active military service (part-time reserve service doesn't qualify), and you must notify the IRS, in writing, that you can't pay because you're in the military.

This provision is clearly intended for reservists and National Guard members with higher-paying jobs who have been called up for a period of active duty. In order to qualify for this deferral, your period of active service must be longer than 30 consecutive days and must be mandated by either the president or the secretary of defense.

After you're no longer on active duty, you have 180 days to pay the amount of tax you deferred. After that point, the IRS will begin to charge you interest and penalties on any unpaid balance you have.

Travel Expense Deductions for National Guard and Reserves Members

If you fall into this category and you had to travel more than 100 miles from home for a meeting or a drill, you can deduct unreimbursed expenses for transportation, meals, and lodging as a deduction on your Form 1040. You'll need to complete Form 2106 to calculate this deduction, but you'll take it on Schedule 1 of your Form 1040.

No Early Retirement Distribution Penalty for Called Reservists

Qualified military reservists may take retirement account distributions (for example, from their IRA, 401(k), 403(b) plan, and so on) without paying the 10 percent penalty for early distributions. While your distributions are still subject to income tax, you won't be charged the additional 10 percent tax for taking an early distribution from your IRA (whether traditional, nondeductible, or Roth), your 401(k) plan, or your 403(b) plan.

If, after you've completed your military service, you want to recontribute to an IRA all or part of any distribution you took back, you can. Just make that recontribution within two years of the end of your active service.

No Education Account Distribution Penalty for Military Academy Students

If you've been fortunate enough to obtain one of the coveted spots at West Point, the U.S. Naval Academy, the U.S. Air Force Academy, the U.S. Coast Guard Academy, or the Merchant Marine Academy, you're in luck. The taxpayer is paying for all of your tuition, room, board, books, and so on.

But what happens to the money your parents or other friends and relatives scrimped and saved and put into either an ESA or a Section 529 plan? Are you, or they, now going to be penalized because you don't need that money for your education?

In a word, no. Although the investment returns portion of distributions will still be taxed to you, there will be no 10 percent penalty on top of the ordinary income tax, provided that you don't take more in distributions each year than the amount that your qualified educational expenses would cost if you had to pay for them. These amounts should be readily available from the financial offices of the military academy.

Military Base Realignment and Closure Benefits Are Excludable from Income

If you receive payment for moving and storage services due to a permanent change of station, you're entitled to exclude these amounts from your income to the extent that your expenses involved in that move don't exceed the amount of the payment. In addition, don't include in income any amounts you receive as a dislocation allowance, a temporary lodging expense, temporary lodging allowance, or a move-in housing allowance.

Obviously, allowances are never as accurate as reimbursements (but are much easier for the government to administer), so the amounts that you spend on your move may be more or less than the amounts you actually receive. If you receive more than you spent, you must report the excess on your Form 1040. If you received less than the actual costs of your move, you are, of course, entitled to deduct the nonreimbursed portion of your moving costs. Complete Form 3903, Moving Expenses, to determine the total amount of your deduction. This form may only be used by members of the Armed Forces.

State Income Tax Flexibility for Spouses

The Military Spouses Residency Relief Act provided the same state income tax choices for spouses of military members as the military members themselves have had. Thus, military spouses can choose among their original home state of record, their current location where their military spouse is serving, or a prior location. Given the variation in state income rates and terms around the country, having these options can save military families tax dollars.

Deductibility of Some Expenses When Returning to Civilian Life

If the day comes when you elect to leave the military and return to civilian life, your job search, travel, and related moving expenses may be deductible. Please see the latest edition of *Taxes For Dummies* for details.

Index

capital improvements, 275–276

capital requirements, in real estate investing, 255

capitalization, 156

car expenses, 181–182, 208

cash flow from rental properties, 248–251, 267–269

cash-basis accounting, 206–207

cash-value life insurance, 91, 101–103, 123–124

casualty losses, 276

CDEs (Community Development Entities), 221

certified public accountants (CPAs), 30

charitable contributions, 23–24, 301

charitable lead trust, 105

charitable remainder trust, 105

child tax credit, 14, 78

childcare assistance, 76–77

children. *See also* college expenses
  adoption, 66, 78
  child tax credit, 78
  dependent-care spending accounts, 77–78
  dependent-care tax credit, 76–77
  overview, 75
  penalty-free IRA withdrawals for birth or adoption, 66
  second income, costs and benefits of, 78–79
  Social Security numbers for, 76
  taxes on investments of, 88–91

collectibles, 146

college expenses
  American Opportunity tax credit, 85–86
  distribution penalty waived for military, 308–309
  Education Savings Accounts, 83–85
  financial aid system, 41–42, 80
  Lifetime Learning Credit, 85–86
  overview, 79
  paying for, 86–88
  penalty-free IRA withdrawals, 66
  Section 529 plans, 81–83
  tax deductions for, 25–26, 81
  tax-wise investments for, 90–91

commercial properties, 266

commodity futures, 147–148

Community Development Entities (CDEs), 221

consumer debt
  paying off, 115–116, 242
  trading for mortgage debt, 22–23, 300–301

continuity of life, 194

contract price, 280

Cornfeld, Bernie, 158

corporate commercial paper, 154

corporations
  cash-accounting method and, 207
  corporate taxes, 178–183, 192–194
  corporate-friendly states, 195
  costs of, 189
  liability insurance, 191–192
  liability protection, 190–191
  other considerations, 194
  overview, 189–190
  professional advice for, 195–196
  S corporations, 192–193, 196–198

cost basis, 132

coupon, 134

Coverdell ESA, 83–85

CPAs (certified public accountants), 30

Crummey Trust, 98

cryptocurrencies, 143–145, 149

D

day trading, 148

deadline extensions for military families, 306–307

dealers, 281

death benefits for military families, 305–306

debt, paying off, 115–116, 242

deductions. *See also* home office deduction
  allowable, 17
  bunching or shifting, 42–43
  car expenses, 24, 181–182
  charity contributions, 23–24, 301
  college costs, 81

income taxes
  on children, 88–90
  payment deferment for military families, 307
  in real estate investing, 267–269
  reducing
    "back-door" Roth IRAs, 297–298
    charitable contributions, 301
    consumer debt, trading for mortgage debt, 300–301
    health savings accounts, 20
    income shifting, 20
    investing in wealth-building assets, 296–297
    itemized deductions, 299–300
    money market mutual funds, 295–296
    overview, 18, 295
    retirement accounts, funding, 297
    retirement investment plans, 18–20
    self-employment expenses, 302
    staying informed, 302
    working overseas, 298
  refunds, 8
  for small businesses, 203–205
index funds, 112, 121, 159–160
individual retirement account (IRA)
  income taxes, reducing, 18–19, 297
  nondeductible contributions, 64
  overview, 61
  penalty-free withdrawals, 66–67
  regular, 61–63
  rollovers, 68–70
  Roth IRAs, 63, 64–66, 297–298
  SECURE ACTs of 2019 & 2022, 16
  SEP-IRA plans, 18–19, 60, 297
individual stocks, investing in, 139
inheritance taxes, 95–96
inherited retirement accounts, 16
installment sales, 257, 278–281
insurance
  cash-value life insurance, 91, 101–103, 123–124
  health insurance deductions, 219–220

health insurance mandate, elimination of, 24
  liability, 188, 191–192
  state, deducting, 24
  term life insurance, 101
interest, taxes on, 113
interest deductions, 182
interest-only loans, 239
intermediate-term fund, 155
international funds, 157–159
international stocks, 139–141
investments. See also selling investments
  annuities, 124–125, 145–146
  asset allocation, 260–261
  to avoid, 122–124
  bonds, 134–135
  of children, taxes on, 88–91
  collectibles, 146
  cryptocurrencies, 143–145
  day trading, 148
  derivatives, 147–148
  for educational funds, 90–91
  "get rich quick" schemes, 149
  ignoring tax considerations in, 39–40
  income taxes, reducing, 25
  overview, 109–110, 133
  ownership investments
    international stocks, 139–141
    overview, 135–136
    real estate, 141
    small business, 141
    stocks, selecting, 136–139
  precious metals, 142
  retirement accounts, 51–52
  taxes on, 110–111, 113–114
  tax-reduction strategies
    funding retirement accounts, 116
    longer-term capital gains, 114–115
    overview, 111–112
    paying off high-interest debt, 115–116
    tax-free money market and bond funds, 117–118
    tax-friendly stock funds, 118–122

About the Author

Eric Tyson, MBA, has been a personal financial writer, lecturer, and counselor for the past 25+ years. As his own boss, Eric has worked with and taught people from a myriad of income levels and backgrounds, so he knows the small-business ownership concerns and questions of real folks just like you.

After toiling away for too many years as a management consultant to behemoth financial-service firms, Eric decided to take his knowledge of the industry and commit himself to making personal financial management accessible to everyone. Despite being handicapped by a joint BS in Economics and Biology from Yale and an MBA from Stanford, Eric remains a master at "keeping it simple."

An accomplished freelance personal-finance writer, Eric is the author or coauthor of numerous other For Dummies national bestsellers on personal finance, investing, for seniors, and home buying and is a syndicated columnist. His *Personal Finance For Dummies* won the Benjamin Franklin Award for Best Business Book.

Eric's work has been critically acclaimed in hundreds of publications and programs, including *Newsweek, The Los Angeles Times, The Chicago Tribune, Kiplinger's Personal Finance Magazine, The Wall Street Journal, Bottom Line Personal,* as well as NBC's Today show, ABC, CNBC, PBS's Nightly Business Report, CNN, FOX-TV, CBS national radio, Bloomberg Business Radio, and Business Radio Network. His website is www.erictyson.com.

Publisher's Acknowledgments

Executive Editor: Steve Hayes

Compilation Editor: Colleen Diamond

Project Editor: Colleen Diamond

Copy Editor: Jennifer Connolly

Proofreader: Debbye Butler

Production Editor: Tamilmani Varadharaj

Senior Managing Editor: Kristie Pyles

Cover Image: © Thanasis/Getty Images